AUGSBURG SERMONS 2

*New Sermons
on
Gospel Texts*

AUGSBURG
SERMONS 2

Gospels Series C

AUGSBURG Publishing House • Minneapolis

AUGSBURG SERMONS 2 — Gospels — Series C

Copyright © 1982 Augsburg Publishing House

Library of Congress Catalog Card No. 82-70955

International Standard Book No. 0-8066-1930-9

Scripture quotations unless otherwise noted are from the Revised Standard Version of the Bible, copyright 1946, 1952, and 1971 by the Division of Christian Education of the National Council of Churches.

Biblical passages marked TEV are from Good News for Modern Man: Today's English Version, © American Bible Society, 1966, 1971.

NEB refers to The New English Bible, © The Delegates of the Oxford University Press and the Syndics of the Cambridge University Press, 1961, 1970.

Manufactured in the United States of America

CONTENTS

8

12

Introduction

The first volume in the original *Augsburg Sermons* series was published in 1973 to help pastors become familiar with the new Lectionary and Calendar prepared by the Inter-Lutheran Commission on Worship (ILCW). Ten volumes in all comprised that first *Augsburg Sermons* series—three volumes on the Gospels, three volumes on the Epistles, three volumes on the Old Testament Lessons, and one volume on texts for the Lesser Festivals. The widespread acceptance of these volumes is an indication both of the quality of the sermons and of the favorable reception of the Lectionary and Calendar.

One outstanding feature of the Lectionary is its use of a Gospel of the Year. Each year, one of the Synoptic Gospels is featured, providing continuity to the reading and telling of the Gospel story throughout the entire church year. This approach makes the uniqueness of each Gospel stand out in all its clarity and richness. It also enables pastors to study the Gospel of the Year with greater thoroughness and to share their insights with their congregations in preaching.

Augsburg Sermons 2 builds on the momentum of the original volumes. It provides a fresh look at the Gospel of Luke, the basis for Series C. And it is offered with the confidence that the message of Luke the Evangelist will speak as clearly and powerfully to Christians in the 1980s as it has to all previous generations.

The Irresistible Praise of God
Luke 19:28-40

From the second chapter of Luke:

And suddenly there was with the angel a multitude of the heavenly host praising God and saying,

"Glory to God in the highest
and on earth peace among men
    with whom he is pleased!"

From the nineteenth chapter of Luke:

As he was now drawing near . . . the whole multitude of the disciples began to rejoice and praise God with a loud voice . . . saying "Blessed is the King who comes in the name of the Lord! Peace in heaven and glory in the highest!"

The Noise of Christmas

Christmas has always been noisy. Census-time in Judea, with crowds of people travelling to their tribal cities, must have been wearing on everybody. Fathers worried about accommodations, mothers fussed about their children's behavior on the way, and the national mood was darkly suspicious. What was Caesar up to? Why this sudden interest in getting everyone registered? It certainly was not the best time for religion to capture the headlines. People had their minds on other things.

We know how that feels. Here we are, starting the inexorable countdown of shopping days until Christmas, already behind, feeling vaguely uneasy about getting everything done, and a little resentful that the so-called "holiday season" gets longer and longer.

That's why the phrase about "putting Christ back in Christmas" arouses such a "yes" inside us. We'd really like to call time out and "stop the music." Christmas seems to deserve more time, more earnest, thoughtful consideration, than we're able to give it. It would be so nice if we could just drop everything and go to some quiet, star-lit place where we could think about God—and somebody else would cook the food and wash the dishes.

The Gospel for today says, "Don't worry. God is able to manage quite well in crowds." It puts us right down in the middle of a noisy disturbance in Jerusalem at the absolutely busiest time of year—Passover. Bethlehem with its crowded inn was peaceful compared to this! We are so familiar with the account of Jesus' triumphal entry into Jerusalem that some of its detail slips right past us. But remember that the authorities, who certainly were used to flocks of pilgrims at Passover, became so concerned about the uproar made by Jesus' followers that they asked him to tone it down. "Rebuke your disciples," they said. It was the Christians who were making all the noise.

More than that, Luke purposely makes his account of the entry into Jerusalem echo his earlier description of the angels at Bethlehem. The "multitude of the heavenly host" has become the "whole multitude of the disciples;" both groups break out in praise of God for what he has done, and they even use the same words: "Glory in the highest!" The angels sing about "peace on earth" and the crowds respond with "peace in heaven." It's as though Luke envisions two great choirs, separated by years of time and the vastness of heaven and earth, yet united in praise of God's astounding incarnation.

Remember that old favorite,

> "The Lord is in his holy temple
> Let all the world keep silence before him."?

Not any more! The Lord has come out of his holy temple and is claiming this clamoring world. So let it make all the noise it wants to—the power, the glory, and the last word still belong to God.

Maybe that's why we enjoy the *Messiah* so much at Christmas. Handel's music lifts us and carries us to match that mood of triumph in God's mighty works. Religion becomes more than thinking about our own faith or our doubts. It becomes a celebration with the whole world. It sings of events beyond our understanding—events that have consequences for Caesars and innkeepers, merchants and musicians. It does not try to put Christ back in Christmas but to proclaim that Christ *is* Christmas. We can find him and celebrate him precisely in our busyness and through our added holiday duties.

What Are We Looking For?

Let's begin by remembering that we are not looking for a baby. We are not searching desperately for a wandering toddler in a department store crowd. Today's Gospel paints a different picture. The crowd is there indeed, but the Christ comes pushing through relentlessly. He is the center of attention, the focus of shouts of praise. Yet even this image of Christ's entry into Jerusalem is too tame. After all, he was still subject to the whim of the crowd and to the plotting of his enemies. Within a week they would send him out of town walking, bearing a cross toward Golgotha. But Easter freed our liberator from those who tried to silence him. He has been exalted above all other powers. He is the center of creation; all things hold together in him. The book of Revelation tries to convey this overwhelming presence: "And I saw one like a son of man . . . his voice was like the sound of many waters . . . and his face was like the sun shining in full strength" (Rev. 1:13, 15, 16).

But it's hard to hold on to that vision. The same Easter victory that freed Christ from a particular time and place also removed him from our daily sight. We want something more tangible! A cartoon strip shows a young child waking in the middle of the night and calling out, "Daddy!" His sleepy parent opens one eye and calls back, "It's okay, I'm right here." But the child isn't convinced. "Come here," he calls. "I want somebody in here with skin and bones on."

If we fail to find Christ at Christmastime, it's not because he is so tiny a baby, but because he is so great a God. He is hidden by his immensity. We just can't step back far enough to take him all in. Our vision is like those photographs in puzzle magazines, taken so close to a familiar object that it becomes unrecognizable. But he's still there, and this Lord of the Universe still acts in our lives. He took on skin and bones to enter our lonely and frightened hours, but his actions are so vast and his purposes so sweeping that we each catch only a bit of it, and sometimes we don't even realize that he has touched our lives. You may have had a moment of discovery in which the meaning of an illness or the reality of an idea suddenly became clear. You may remember an incident or the words of a friend that could only have been the answer to prayer. At that point your life touched the work Christ is doing in the world.

The Irresistible Praise

These personal experiences seem few and far between. Sometimes, taken by themselves, they can be interpreted as accidental. But when you hear others tell of similar experiences, a pattern begins to emerge. It is said that the retina of the human eye is made up of one hundred million receptor cells. What we see as a single scene is actually composed of the combined reactions of these individual cells. In the same way, our vision of Christ's rule among humanity requires the combined reactions of countless believers. Only in that way can the big picture be put together.

Perhaps you do not live in a situation where your vision can be shared with others. Your family may be indifferent, or even hostile. Perhaps you do not have a family. Even fellow-Christians can sometimes be hesitant to talk about their experiences of Christ's presence. Where do you turn when there are no supportive voices around you?

Remember what Jesus said to those who wanted him to silence his disciples? He said if his disciples were to become silent, the stones would cry out. So it is today. The praise of God's work in Christ cannot be muted. Even the stones have taken up the chorus first sung by the angels.

There is a famous echo in Norway. It is supposed to be so long and persistent that one can sing three notes in a row and the echo will respond in harmony. Climbers who shouted "Onward!" when they began their climb would hear "Onward!" reechoed back to them after they had dropped by the trail in exhaustion. I can't vouch for the reliability of that tale, but it does describe the way in which one generation of Christians has been able to commit its praise to rock and stone so that later generations can benefit. Look at stained glass, into which men and women of faith melted their praise of God so that it could brighten our lives. Marvel at the great cathedrals whose stones seem to summon our hearts to soaring. Listen to simple epitaphs carved in marble or granite, distilling the life experience of individuals into a single phrase like "Hope in the Lord." Read lines set by lead type and printed so that thousands can share the insights of one author. Let your soul reverberate with great organ pipes as they sound forth harmonies that move us profoundly.

There is a whole chorus of testimony to the living, present Christ all around us. It far exceeds the tinkle of cash registers, the rattling of swords, and the babble of holiday crowds. The song of praise to God-with-us cannot be stilled, because it does not depend merely on us or on any other generation. We live with the echoes of earlier believers still sounding in our ears. And even before men and women took up the chorus, angels announced the good news over Bethlehem. So if one day our human voices should fall silent, the rocks and hills would take up the song. We have Jesus' assurance of that.

In fact, it has already happened. After Good Friday, when the disciples had nothing to say and every other human voice was stilled, it was a stone that first testified to the resurrection.

H. George Anderson
Luther College
Decorah, Iowa

SECOND SUNDAY IN ADVENT

Proper Preparation
Luke 3:1-6

The Tonight Show starring Johnny Carson has an opening that is always predictable. Ed McMahon bursts forward with the phrase that never varies, "Here's Johnny!" With that preparatory remark Johnny Carson comes forth through the curtain to entertain his audience and TV viewers. As the herald of the show, Ed McMahon plays an important role in getting the show off the ground with gusto.

Jesus was coming to the stage to unveil the greatest drama the world would ever witness. It would unfold the mighty act of redemption. While he was in the wings there was a man out front preparing the people for his entrance. His name was John. He was a big man. He had gusto. As Jesus was stepping forward to assume his major role on the stage of history, John cried out, "Here comes Jesus!" The words are recorded in this way: "Behold the Lamb of God, who takes away the sin of the world" (John 1:29).

Big John was born into a family which had prayed for years to have a child. In fact, this husband and wife had given up hope of producing a baby since they were well advanced in age. But one day an angel appeared to Zechariah and told him that in due time his wife, Elizabeth, would bear a baby boy and his name would be called John. So it happened.

John developed into a rugged man who loved the outdoor life. His dress was comprised of a garment of camel hair with a leather girdle around his waist. His manner of speech was direct and convincing, filled with the wisdom of the soil. He was on the side of the poor and oppressed, the distressed and the needy.

John the Baptist's life could be summed up in a word called preparation. His ministry was molded by preparation in the wilderness and his preaching was preparation for the Savior.

Prayer Preparation

"The word of God came to John the son of Zechariah in the wilderness" (Luke 3:2). Here was the secret of this man's power. John was convinced that he had been called, not merely to reflect the moods and opinions of his time, but to speak the truth given him by God. He lived for years in the solitude of the stretches of desert. He was alone, and yet not alone, for God was whispering to him about eternal things. At night he would lie and watch the stars blaze in the untroubled sky. There were no crowds clamoring for his attention. In prayer and meditation the word of God was being forged in this forceful personality, making him ready for preaching at the riverbank.

Before every sports event there is a warm-up session to loosen up the limbs and sharpen the skills of the participants. Before every concert there is the vocalizing of voices and the tuning up of instruments. Even before a space shot there is the final countdown of exacting last-minute preparations.

For the Christian, prayer paves the way for decision making and should be the preliminary event to all the great contests of life in which the people of God are involved. Before Jesus broke the bondage of death that gripped Lazarus, he lifted his voice in prayer. Before Jesus entered the conflict at Calvary he strengthened and steadied his soul in the silence of Gethsemane. Prayer becomes the process by which our lives are placed parallel to the purposes of God so that God's power may flow through them. Prayer is not the manipulation of a mighty God, but rather letting the Master move us in mission.

A long time ago, when the broadcasting industry was still in its infancy, a letter was sent to the National Broadcasting Company from a prospector in the hills of Montana. Written on a piece of a brown paper bag was an unusual request: "I am a regular listener to your programs, and as a friend I want to ask you for a favor. It gets lonely up here, and besides my radio and my dog, I have not much else for company. I do have a violin that I used to play, but now it is badly out of tune. Would you be kind enough to strike me an "A" at seven o'clock next Sunday night so that I can put my fiddle back in tune?"

At first the officials smiled at that request. But then the manager of NBC thought about it, and the request took on a bit more perspective. So the following Sunday night the network interrupted its scheduled programming to sound an "A" and give their friend the proper pitch.

All of us get out of tune. We need the pitch again. And God wants to give it. There will be notes of repentance, love, forgiveness, hope, patience, and many more. Each situation may have its special tuning note. In prayer God strikes the tuning fork. Jenny Lind, the late opera superstar, used to ask for a few moments in the quietness of her dressing room before every performance. This Swedish nightingale would strike one clear vibrant note and hold it as long as she could. Then she would pray, "Master, let me ring true tonight. Let me ring true as thou art true."

John the Baptist's ministry was not out of tune, because the man had been properly prepared in prayer and meditation. Dr. Alexis Carrell, a great physician and Nobel prize winner, said, "Prayer is the most powerful form of energy that man can generate. The influence of prayer on the mind and body is as demonstrable as secreting glands. Its results can be measured in terms of increased buoyancy, greater intellectual vigor, moral stamina, and a deeper understanding of human relationships. Prayer is absolutely indispensable to the development of the human personality." This was certainly evident in the life of John the Baptist.

Preaching Preparation

John's ministry was wrapped up in the power of the spoken word. There is no record of anything else that he did. "And he went into all the region about the Jordan, preaching . . ." (Luke 3:3). Preaching was bridge-building, proclaiming a message enabling God and his people to meet. John took aim in his preaching which was the transformation of a person and not merely the elucidation of a subject. He knew that repentance was required and forgiveness was God's gift. His emphasis was not on explaining something, but rather persuading them to see the salvation of God. We see this same procedure in Christ's ministry to the woman at the well in Samaria. With love and skill he turned what might have been an academic discussion of history and worship into a personal appeal and the conviction of sin. It went beyond exposition to persuasion.

Have you ever made candles from a Christmas kit? First you must melt the wax and then you mold it into the desired shape before you place it in a cold liquid to make it hard. It would do no good to try to mold the wax before it is pliable and soft. We often attempt to shape people in church and family before they are melted, and we fail. Perhaps the melting process takes the longest time in dealing with relationships. Trust and credibility must be established before you will even secure a listening ear. Awareness of where people are, where they have need and are hurting, what their dreams are—these are necessary in the art of persuasion.

There is no question about the fact that John the Baptist believed that awareness of sin was preparatory to seeing the need of a Savior. Therefore in his ministry he did not smother the people with motherly solicitude. His words were full of life, stern, demanding, yet leading to salvation. He moved the exhortations of God into close location with the hearers. He called for fruits that befit repentance. He thundered words of condemnation upon Herod for taking his brother's wife—words that reached right into the palace. If John were alive today he would not leave the Bible stories in Palestine, for then the congregation could sleep through it. He would move the story of the Good Samaritan from the Jericho Road to Main Street. He would move the rich fool from Judea to our own neighborhood in Minnesota or Alabama. He would move Judas into our own congregation. Then ears would perk up and people would sit up and listen.

John's sermons were tailored to fit the customers. Truth unlocked closed doors. George Buttrick once said that people are not driven from church by stern truths that make them uncomfortable, but rather by weak nothings that make them contemptuous. The Lutheran bishops of Norway during the Nazi occupation declared: "Harmlessly edifying preaching would be a denial of God."

23

So John was out with his plow and disc working up the soil of the human soul so that the seed of the Savior would come and find fertile furrows in which it could quickly germinate and grow.

Participation Preparation

From prayer to preaching and then to participation. That is the road that John built. It was a highway that he was building for Christ along which the Lord's holiness and truth could find their access to all areas of human life. Perhaps John knew intuitively that Jesus wasn't going to build a seminary of classrooms to start kingdom expansion. Rather Jesus would be addressing men and women with the action-filled words, "Follow me!" Salvation must be out on the road for people to see it. The game was not to end on the coach's blackboard. The same is true in every generation. Kierkegaard wrote in one of his parables the danger of becoming a specialist in the mere hearing of religion. It could become an occupation in itself. He imagined that near the cross of Christ stood a man who beheld the terrible scene and then became a professor of what he saw. Later he witnessed the persecution of the early church as the martyr's blood was spilled, and he became a professor of what he witnessed. So this man studied the drama of the cross, but was never crucified with Christ. He studied apostolic history, but he never lived apostolically.

The late Dr. Tom Dooley, who worked in Laos, said, "Today demands deeds, human deeds; principles enunciated and hopes expressed are not enough." Dag Hammarskjold was quoted saying, "The road to holiness necessarily passes through action."

John the Baptist prepared the people for action. In the picturesque language of Scripture the mountains shall be brought low, the crooked made straight, and the rough ways were to be made smooth. People came to John and asked him, "Teacher, what shall we do?" And he told them. And they did it. I doubt that very many of us preachers today have that kind of response after our preaching!

I remember an athletic coach telling one of his athletes practicing the long jump in track, "You go so far back for your run that you are all tired out when you come to the place to jump." The run means nothing if the jump doesn't happen. Now the preacher must jump and his effectiveness can honestly be measured by whether the congregation jumps. The old saying is still true that when the worship ends the real service begins. John the Baptist got the people of his day ready to follow Jesus in word and deed. We salute the faithfulness of big John who got himself prepared, as well as the people to whom he preached, to meet Jesus. That is the calling that comes to all of us.

JAMES BJORGE
First Lutheran Church
Fargo, North Dakota

Preparing the Way of the Lord
Luke 3:7-18

I stood with a friend at the top of a high ridge. In the valley before us, construction workers were preparing the way for a new interstate highway. Off in the distance almost for as far as we could see, earthmovers, scrapers, and trucks were leveling the ground and preparing the earth for a new road. Especially at the site where a cloverleaf was taking shape, we were aware of the intense planning as surveyors checked the angles for the on and off ramps where two highways would cross.

This is the kind of imagery which Luke sets before us in the third chapter of his gospel. Quoting from the ancient prophetic book of Isaiah with words that we heard in the Gospel for last Sunday, Luke sets the theme:

> Prepare the way of the Lord,
> make his paths straight.
> Every valley shall be filled,
> and every mountain and hill shall
>   be brought low,
> and the crooked shall be made straight,
> and the rough ways shall be made smooth;
> and all flesh shall see the salvation of God.
>   (Luke 3:4-6)

To be sure, highway construction methods have changed rather dramatically from the time of Isaiah or Luke. I doubt that those ancient writers could even begin to envision the extensive preparation studies, design and layout and actual construction procedures now used to build freeways. And yet the imagery of preparing a highway is still challenging and meaningful for us today. For we see in the gospel today that Luke is really most concerned about the ways in which we prepare our hearts and our minds for the coming of Christ. The frightening aspect of our

25

gospel today is that we are asked to look at rough places, crooked places and low spots in our own lives which make it difficult for us to welcome God into our lives in this Advent and Christmas season. Our gospel suggests that we probably have some construction work to do.

A Memory of John the Baptist

Luke recalls that before Jesus began his public ministry, a man we remember as John the Baptist was calling people to turn from selfishness if they wanted to discover newness in life and peace with God. Like the prophets of old, John warned the people not to seek security in the fact that they were descendants of Abraham. The Lord God, declares John, does not take note of pedigree. If God wishes, he can raise up children from stones! If people come seeking renewal in life while harboring secret plots or malicious thoughts, they are then nothing more than a swarm of snakes! It is by their actions, their "good fruit," that God will see and declare people to be upright.

Then Luke becomes very specific in this memory of John. He recalls that the people asked John what they could do to repent before God. The answers John gave are frightening! They must have been frightening for those who first heard him; they certainly are frightening words for us today.

• To the people John said: He who has two coats, let him share with him who has none; and he who has food, let him do likewise.

• To tax collectors who sought to be baptized, he said: Collect no more than is appointed you.

• To soldiers, he said: Rob no one by violence or by false accusation, and be content with your wages.

Hard Words

These are certainly hard words. They are particularly hard for us who live in relative abundance. Most of us have been richly blessed with food and clothing. The temptation arises to soften this text, to explain it away by one means or another, to find some ways to justify our abundance. And yet we know that we cannot do that!

Our God is Lord over the entire world. God sees the glaring differences between people of great wealth and people in extreme poverty. We who stand in the heritage of faith of John and Luke need to listen carfully to these words. We need to ponder these words as we purchase Christmas presents and plan our celebrations in honor of the birth of the Christ child. For we are well aware that we do not procure God's presence in our midst

26

through the accumulation of consumer goods. Rather, we prepare a way for God's coming in our lives as we root out selfishness and seek renewal individually and as a community in our servant ministry to people in need.

Pointing the Way

Luke remembers John the Baptist as more than another prophet of Israel. Luke sees John as the messenger anticipated by the prophet Malachi as the forerunner of the Messiah. In a grand interpretation of history, Luke declares that John was part of God's plan that all people, Gentiles as well as Jews, might be blessed with responsible, compassionate and hopeful life before their God through the coming of Christ.

John the Baptist lived and was at work before Jesus began his public ministry. We live and work in a time two centuries after the appearance of the one whom we also point to as the Christ. John pointed the way by calling people to repentance and directing their attention to one who was coming. We are called to do the same. To be sure, we also look back and study with great care the heritage that is ours in the scriptures. We look back to Bethlehem and Nazareth and Capernaum and Jerusalem, retelling the stories of Christ. But like John, we are called primarily to help each other discover repentance and what it means to repent today as responsible people of faith. And we are called to point the way to the One who will come anew in our midst today and at Christmas!

A Strange Suggestion

Not long ago I visited a very poor village in Mexico. Only a few houses had electricity; one pump provided water for the entire village and there were no sewers or waste treatment facilities. The greatest problem was that there was no employment; the few men who did work traveled fifteen miles by bus to the nearest city where they worked for very poor pay.

I cannot do much about the actual poverty of that village. But I am very aware of how that visit has altered my life-style and my understanding of our country. My suggestion is that Christian people should take every opportunity that is available to travel. We ought to travel with our eyes wide open and our minds tuned to discover both the pain and the misery of so many people in our world. As we travel and as we return home, we will find ourselves challenged in all sorts of new ways to ask about the causes of poverty and the possible directions for alleviating world hunger.

Good News for People

On the morning when I stood watching the construction of an interstate highway, I was with a man who had extensive experience in road preparation. He spoke of the massive boulders and tree root systems which often created massive problems. Even more difficult were the underground springs and strange contours of the earth. Often it was necessary to excavate far down into the earth in order to rebuild a solid base for a highway.

I have thought about earthmoving as I have reflected on the difficulties that we have in changing habits or patterns in life. Sometimes we need to delve deep within ourselves and within our culture to uncover the fears and insecurities that keep us from being what our Lord calls us to be.

And yet, we know that change is possible. We can be renewed in integrity with each other; we can be renewed with compassion for others in our world. Luke tells us that John shared his strong words to the tax collectors, soldiers, and the crowd to help them. In fact, Luke says that with these and other exhortations, John preached good news to the people. The good news is that Christ is coming. We are called to help prepare the way! Let us do so with joy as we overcome our fears, renew our commitment to integrity and our calling to be the servant church that lives to love and to care for a needy world.

A. JOSEPH EVERSON
Hope Lutheran Church
St. Paul, Minnesota

FOURTH SUNDAY IN ADVENT

Sing Faith's Song
LUKE 1:39-45 (46-55)

The carols of Christmas are in the air all around us. Even the secular world joins in singing the songs of Christmas, if only to promote the sale of this world's goods. In the Christian calendar the Fourth Sunday in Advent is C minus one and counting. Christmas is only six days off. That is the real reason for singing. In today's Gospel, Elizabeth and Mary tell us why and invite us to join them in singing faith's song.

Without a Song

Is there a song in your heart? The only song many people sing is one of dirge or lament. A tyranny of evil holds them in bondage and oppression.

Take ancient Israel, for example, the people to whom Elizabeth and Mary belonged. They suffered under the yoke of Roman conquerors and yearned for the day of deliverance long promised by the prophets. One of those prophets, Micah, whose words we heard in the First Lesson, told of a ruler to come out of Bethlehem who would "feed his flock in the strength of the LORD, in the majesty of the name of the LORD his God. And they shall dwell secure, for now he shall be great to the ends of the earth" (Micah 5:4-5). Strength! Security! Century after century Israelites yearned for the coming of that great day.

African slaves transported to America identified with ancient Israel in bondage. In a song of lament they sang to old Pharaoh, "Let my people go." Ancient Israel is an illustration of what is true in the world today. The heel of the oppressor tramps on people everywhere—behind the Iron Curtain, in Southeast Asia, in Southwest Africa, in Black America. For many people the only song to sing is in a mournful minor key. In Central America, in South Korea, in the Soviet Union people sing sad songs for loved ones behind prison walls.

Sin is loose in the world. Those who have, want more—at the expense of those who have not. We cannot escape sin's effect, whether we are sinned against or sinner. Love of self pervades us all. It makes us live for self and hurt others in the process.

The Sound of Silence

In a short story John Cheever tells about the Hartleys, a young couple with a seven-year-old daughter, who are at a ski resort. Their marriage is on the rocks; they have been separated once and are trying to make another go at life together. That is why they are at the ski resort. They are visiting old haunts that meant so much to them in the earlier, happy days of their marriage. Their daughter doesn't want her father to leave her, even to go up the ski slope without her. One day when he does, she starts after him, gets caught in the ski-tow machinery, and is crushed to death. Behind her hearse the Hartleys ride back to the city in silence.

Evil comes crashing in when you least expect it. It brings heartache, causes disease, and destroys life. The tyranny of evil silences our songs.

The Spirit Speaks

But God gives us reason to sing. The reason is a promise. In today's Gospel, Mary hurries to visit her relative Elizabeth. She did that because of a promise she received. The angel Gabriel had come to her to tell her that of all possible people, she was to be the one to give birth to the long-awaited ruler whose kingdom would never end. According to Gabriel, the sign of the promise was that her relative Elizabeth was pregnant—she who was too old to have children. Mary could see for herself. So she did.

29

No sooner had she arrived, when Elizabeth's baby stirred within her. Filled with the Holy Spirit, Elizabeth greeted Mary as the most blessed of all women. For she was to be the mother of the Lord. And Mary responds in song—that exultant song which we have come to know from the Latin translation of its first word as the Magnificat:

> My soul magnifies the Lord,
> and my spirit rejoices in God my Savior,
> for he has regarded the low estate of his handmaiden.

We too have reason to sing. The promise to Mary is meant for us. The Christ to whom she gave birth came to free us from the tyranny of sin and evil in our world. In today's Second Lesson the writer of the Letter to the Hebrews told us that because Jesus Christ did what God wanted him to do, we are all purified from sin by the offering that he made of his own body once and for all (Heb. 10:10). Through Jesus' death and resurrection God has broken the power of sin and evil. Though we continue to experience the effects of sin and evil in our world, they don't have the last word. God does! In baptism God has claimed us as his children and put his life within us. We can therefore escape the prison of our own selfishness. We can help people instead of hurt them. God sees to it that all things—even the evil we experience—work out for good.

The Ultimate Promise

For us even death is but the road to everlasting life. In *Context,* Martin Marty has shared a true story about a Sunday school class. To teach the class the meaning of new life the teacher had given each of her eight students an empty L'Eggs container and asked them to bring it back the next week with something in it that was a sign of new life. The following week the teacher was concerned that one of the students, a sickly, retarded boy named Steven, might not have done the assignment. In the first container was a flower, and a girl claimed it as her symbol. In the second container was a stone; the teacher thought it must be Steven's, but another boy claimed it as his: "There's moss on the stone," he said, "and that's a sign of new life." A butterfly was in the third container, claimed by another student. The next container was empty. Knowing this one was surely Steven's, the teacher started to set it aside. "Don't put it aside," Steven said. "That's mine." "But it's empty," the teacher responded. "So was Jesus' tomb," said Steven, "and that's a sign of new life."

Several months later Steven became very ill and died. On his coffin, amid the flowers, were eight L'Eggs containers—open and empty!

God's promise of deliverance from evil is meant not just for us but for the whole world. God has chosen not just Mary but us as well to bear the ruling and freeing Christ into the world for others. Through the power of the Spirit Christ has been born in us. As we tell about Christ to others, we unleash a power by which Christ can be born in them and they can experience freedom from the tyranny of evil. We can be a liberating force that frees people from oppression. We have the power to love them into the kingdom of God. Think of it: instead of adding to the world's problems we can be part of solving them. That is reason for song.

The Song of Faith

You either believe a promise, or you don't. Elizabeth's husband, Zechariah, laughed at the promise the angel made that his wife would bear him a son, and he no longer had voice to speak. Mary believed the angel's promise to her. In the Gospel, speaking by the power of the Spirit, Elizabeth tells Mary that she is fortunate to believe, for now she will see the promise come true. Far from losing her voice, Mary breaks forth into a song so full of faith that its words proclaim the promise already fulfilled: "He has shown strength with his arm, he has scattered the proud in the imagination of their hearts." Faith is like that. We like to say, "Seeing is believing." God turns it around, "Believing is seeing." Jesus said it again and again: "Your faith has made you well."

Like Mary, we will be fortunate if we take God at his word. That means, first, that we trust that it is true that there is nothing God cannot do. When every evidence around us tells us otherwise, we need to keep on trusting in God's power to save. As we look death in the face, like Mary's Son we need to place our spirit into God's all-powerful hands. In the second place, to take God at his word means that we act on his promise. Like Mary, we become God's servants. We do God's liberating work in the world. We proclaim the greatness of the Lord to the people around us. Through our love we become the means by which God frees those in bondage from the tyranny of evil.

As we believe, we will see God's promise come true. Christians down through the ages attest that it is so. Believing *is* seeing. Hasn't it been so for you? God will deliver us from evil. And through us he will do so for others. We will see it happen:

> He has put down the mighty from their thrones,
>   and exalted those of low degree.
> He has filled the hungry with good things,
>   and the rich he has sent empty away.

The Christ born of Mary comes to us hungry people today in bread and wine to fill us with good things—his body and blood—himself! Believe! Approach the Lord's Table with Mary's song on your lips. God will put a song in your heart, the song of Christmas, faith's song.

JOHN H. TIETJEN
Christ Seminary-Seminex
St. Louis, Missouri

THE NATIVITY OF OUR LORD — CHRISTMAS DAY

Is There Any Hope?
Luke 2:1-20

One of the popular maxims that has come down from generation to generation affirms that "where there is life there is hope." Up to a point, that maxim describes the human spirit; hope does die hard in the human breast. But it *does* die. The Christian, perceiving this dimension of life, turns that maxim to read, "Where there is Christian hope there is authentic life." This morning, I want to speak about that kind of hope. I can do that with confidence because a Savior, Christ the Lord, is born to us this day.

Sometime in the late 1940s, a newly-commissioned submarine in the United States fleet, the last of its type manufactured to run on turbines, sank in the North Atlantic not far from the coast of New England. With ample rescue-salvage equipment at hand, everyone expected the crew to be saved. That judgment was wrong. As the hours dragged on, the power for the internal equipment of the submarine was exhausted. The last recorded message from the doomed men on the submarine was this forlorn question, "Is there any hope?"

Everywhere—from the mass of poor along the Ganges to the dispossessed in Appalachia, from the oppressed in South Africa to the oppressed on American Indian reservations—people are asking, "Is there any hope?" When human beings come to the end of their rope, are pushed into a corner from which there is no escape, lose all hope, they give up or drift or, in some desperate hour, commit suicide. When hope is gone, really gone, life is over.

The mighty Nazi army that attacked and then laid siege to Stalingrad was General Von Paulus' Sixth Army of 300,000 troops. Successful in the early months of that campaign, the Sixth Army soon came on hard days.

The harsh winter of 1942-43, the dogged spirit of the Russian army, and the fury of Stalingrad's inhabitants chewed up and then encircled Von Paulus' army. The General pled with Hitler for reinforcements. None came. Hilter, consumed by one of his psychotic furies, left the Sixth Army to die. When all hope for reinforcements and supplies was gone, General Von Paulus surrendered the remnants of his once mighty army to the Russians. When hope is gone, the human fight is over.

Hope does not spring eternal in the human breast. A time comes in the experience of all human beings when they reach the end of their rope, are backed into a corner from which they see no escape and hope evaporates. That grim reality is a common human experience. We visit our loved one after serious surgery and, looking lovingly and anxiously at him or her through a welter of technological equipment, we tremulously ask the doctor when we are alone, "Is there any hope?" You, a high school senior who has fiddled away the year in this or that class and now face a final exam, ask the teacher, "Is there any hope for me to pass?" Again, you and your friend are swimming a mile off shore in the Gulf of Mexico. Suddenly your friend is seized by cramps; he disappears from view. You search for him wildly, but you cannot find him. He does not surface. After an hour of frantic searching and calling his name, you whisper sorrowfully to yourself as you swim to shore, "There is no hope for him anymore."

In every human life and in every human situation there are seasons and hours when human hope dies. Then, we have no place to turn except to God. And God's answer to this common human plight is his gift of that little child at Bethlehem, that gracious healer of broken bodies and wounded spirits, that dying Man on Calvary, that victorious Lord on Easter morn—the Friend we know as Jesus Christ. In him we have hope. Indeed, for centuries, Christians have been proclaiming Christ as "the hope of the world." In what sense, then, is Jesus Christ the hope of the world?

To Improve Our Moral and Spiritual Nature

Jesus is the hope of the world because he is the only person who can improve our moral and spiritual nature. Across the centuries, because of God's providential gifts, man has been able to enlarge his knowledge of his world, universe, physical being, mental perceptions, and emotional resources. Man, richly endowed by his Creator, has produced the sciences of astronomy, archaeology, geology, biology, engineering—and more. Over the centuries, human beings have gained a larger and larger mastery over their natural world, their physical body, and their psychological being. But from the dawn of civilization to this hour, no human being has ever been able to improve his or her own moral or spiritual nature. And no

33

human being has been able to improve another person's moral or spiritual nature.

Psychiatric, marriage, family, and vocational counselors can help some people to understand themselves and other selves better. They can free some people from inhibitions, dated emotions, and neurotic compulsions. They can help some people to accept and face reality. But neither they nor any other human specialist can alter any person's basic nature. Medical science can give us a face lift, cut away cancer, replace a diseased organ, and change the sex of some people. But there is no science that can free us from our innate selfishness, envy, greed, pride, and lust.

Throughout the nineteenth century and into the twentieth century until World War I erupted among the most civilized nations on earth, human beings in Western society were convinced that human reason could solve all personal and social problems; they believed that human nature could be changed by reason. The popular form of this superficial hope was expressed in the early 1920s by the French psychologist Henri Coué: "Every day, we are getting better in every way." That sounds hollow today. We live in an overarmed nuclear world where European and North American civilization could be wiped out in thirty minutes. Is that rational? One billion people will spend this Christmas Day in hunger, squalor, and degradation. Is that rational? Almost two billion people will spend this Christmas Day in an authoritarian or totalitarian state where God-given human rights are denied. Is that rational? And here at home thirty million Americans—whites, blacks, Indians, and Hispanics—will spend this Christmas Day without adequate food, shelter, or clothing. Is that rational? And millions of middle-class homes in America—rent asunder by jealousy and strife and bitterness—will not, in spite of their overabundance of material gifts, experience Christ's peace and joy this Christmas Day. Is that rational? As the leopard cannot change its spots, human beings cannot change their own nature or the nature of any other person. Unless God takes a hand in the human mess, there is no hope for any of us.

Jesus Christ is not only our best hope; he is also our last hope. That is so because he enables us to recognize this irradicable flaw in human nature —our own and others'. No one has described this reality better than Paul: "I do not do the good I want, but the evil I do not want is what I do." As the leopard cannot change its spots, none of us can change his or her nature. Christ is our hope because in his true humanity we recognize that we are rebellious against God, entrapped in self-interest, and are rushing toward a death that none of us can stave off.

That is one side of the coin. It is covered with grime. But there is another side of the coin that shines like the star of Bethlehem. It not only shows us what happens to us when we trust ourselves and other selves; it also shows us what we can become when we rely on Christ. Sigmund Freud, the father of psychoanalysis, was never able to free himself from his own neurotic inhibitions. But he did show us the dark and frightening depths of human nature. He called that abyss the subconscious—a place of envy, crass selfishness, hatred, perversion, murder, and stygean darkness. Jesus called the subconscious a rotting, stinking tomb. Either description strips us of our pride. Left to its own devices, human nature leads us into darkness, destruction, and death. But Jesus, demonstrating our true humanity, can change our basic moral and spiritual nature and enable us to grow in his likeness every day.

That is our imperishable hope. Because God has come in Christ to do for us what we cannot do for ourselves, we can change. We can put on the garments of righteousness. We can let Christ's mind grow in us. We are no longer doomed to live with our unredeemed selves and other unredeemed selves here or in eternity. That is the best news human beings ever received. Jesus Christ, the hope of all humanity, has come to us at Bethlehem.

To Change the World

The other reason why we Christians call Jesus Christ the hope of the world is that he is able, using our radically changed and maturing persons, to change the world itself. Since Christ has the power to remake our moral nature, we can expect that people in the process of becoming new creatures in him will be motivated and empowered to reshape society to be more just, reflecting something of God's kingdom.

Specifically, living as we do in a natural world that is being exploited and polluted to death and in an insane human society where nuclear weaponry is proliferating wildly and hunger and oppression are rampant, we Christ-followers are enabled to become responsible environmentalists, active peacemakers, and indefatigable workers for social justice. In a world groaning under political oppression from Korea to Iran, from Poland to Pakistan, from South Africa to Chile; and in a world where a billion people have a life expectancy under forty years, Christians are sensitized to the human dignity of others and enabled to care for these hard-pressed and oppressed people.

To be sure, we have to work out the details of how best to help people in each human situation, but when our attitudes, expectations, and daily concerns are shaped to Christ's mind, we are motivated and equipped to take active steps personally and collectively to protect this earth and its people so that both have viable futures.

Do not underestimate the influence of a single dedicated Christian or play down the power of a dedicated minority to improve communities, churches, nations, and the world. Do not concentrate on the complexity of planned, humane social, political, and economic change. Do not lose sight of these two truths: Christ, who makes willing human beings over in his likeness, uses them to reshape society.

There was a time in the life of William Grenfell when he was a fashionable London physician. When Christ got hold of Grenfell, the fashionable doctor gave the remainder of his life as a medical missionary in poverty-stricken Labrador. There was a time when John Wesley carried on a perfunctory ministry in the Anglican church. When his "heart was strangely warmed" by Christ, Wesley poured out his life in the service of London's poor and oppressed people. In the early 1950s, Martin Luther King Jr. was a successful pastor in Montgomery, Alabama, waiting patiently to co-pastor with his father the leading black Baptist church in Atlanta. Then in 1955, a middle-aged black woman refused to go to the back of a bus in Montgomery. Through her deed and subsequent events, Christ took hold of Martin Luther King Jr. and made him one of the brightest beacons of freedom and sanity in America from 1955-1968. Thirty years ago, critical-minded Christians in Lutheran church circles held little hope for dying Trinity Church. But a hundred or so lay people and two clergymen, turning penitently and expectantly to Christ, were motivated and enabled to turn Trinity around and set it on the course to become the strong, vital congregation that it is today. That brings this business of miraculous change down to your experience and mine.

But we can be more intimate. Hundreds of you know how—when you gave up on your marriage, gave up on your parenting a rebellious child, gave up on your profession or job, gave up on being a responsible citizen—you turned one last time to Christ, pleading for help, and he turned you around, made you over, and, in his strength, enabled you to make something good from those once failing human ventures.

Jesus Christ, the hope of the world, is the Savior born to us at Bethlehem. Everywhere in this unjust and warring society, men and women—feeling that they are trapped on a huge submarine sunk deep in a dark ocean of hopelessness—are tapping out this message: "Is there any hope?" We Christians can answer that in a thousand caring ways. We know that Christ is the hope of the world because he saves us from self-destruction, changes our moral and spiritual nature, and through our new persons, changes and saves the world. History gives substance to this interpretation of the human situation. So does your firsthand experience of Christ and mine. He *is* the hope of the world because he is the Savior, Christ the Lord, born to us at Bethlehem.

One final word. The Christian gospel requires it. If a Broadway play has a good script and a good director yet fails to turn out well, you and I do not blame the author or the director or the scenery. We blame the actors. Jesus Christ is the author and finisher of our faith. In him each of us can find our own proper script for life. If things turn out badly for you and me, we cannot blame the author or the script. We must, in all honesty and fairness, blame ourselves.

For unto you is born this day in the city of David, a Savior who is Christ the Lord. He is the best, the brightest, and the only hope any of us really has.

WALLACE E. FISHER
The Lutheran Church of the Holy Trinity
Lancaster, Pennsylvania

FIRST SUNDAY AFTER CHRISTMAS

They Did Not Understand
Luke 2:41-52

Pretend that words have calories—calories you need to grow mentally, emotionally, and spiritually. Some words are rich in calories. Others are empty and contribute nothing to your well-being. Others pass through our minds without being assimilated. Words are in abundance today. Everywhere you turn words are spoken and written before your eyes and ears. It would seem that we should be fat in mind, emotion, and spirit.

But not so. Our problem is not to restrict our intake of word calories. Rather we need to seek and to receive words with high calorie counts to give us strength. We need to plan a word diet that will help us grow mentally, emotionally, and spiritually. The concern of this sermon will be for your spiritual strength, but the ideas can apply to your other needs as well. I will choose only a few words that have a high calorie count. You may find others that are needed in your diet.

I Don't Understand

The words I choose are, "I don't understand." These words have a high calorie count because they speak an important message. Replay some of the tapes in your memory to hear again how you and others have said, "I don't understand." Listen to what it means when the words are spoken between husband and wife, parent and child. "I don't understand" means

37

that is a possible tension point, a potential problem in the relationship. Think what it means at work or at school when someone says, "I don't understand." Someone has reached a limit. Someone needs help. Unless the words are heard and unless there is a response a problem will develop.

This sermon is concerned primarily about your relationship with God. Replay those tapes again and hear the ways you've said "I don't understand" to God. The words are said in many ways, but they still have the same calorie count. Why does God let babies die? people starve? wars destroy? Or you may have a specific question about an issue in your life. Why did I lose my job? Why the problem in our family? Why the accident, the illness? Why, God? I do not understand. I mention these questions, not to make you feel guilty about asking them, but to help you identify that point where there is a potential problem in your relationship with God. Your failure to understand can lead you to God rather than away from him.

Other words in the text have a high calorie count and are related to the words, "I don't understand." The people in the Temple were amazed at Jesus' intelligent answers. His parents were astonished when they found him in the Temple. To be amazed or astonished is another form of not understanding—without the anxiety. We also want to look for points of amazement and astonishment in your life. Each of those points shows a place where you can grow in your awareness of the unlimited power and love of God.

The phrases "I do not understand," and "I am astonished or amazed," have high calorie counts in a conversation because they express a need. They are not casual, space-filler words. They identify an area of limitation for the speaker. They indicate an area of potential trouble or potential growth.

I Do Understand

To reach a point you do not understand you must travel through areas you do understand. When you come to the limit of your understanding, it is good to back up and retravel through the part you can grasp. The climax of our text is a point of non-understanding that we can share with Mary and Joseph. But to reach that point let's also share with them the part of the story we do understand.

Each year Mary and Joseph went from Nazareth to Jerusalem for the Passover. We can understand that. They could worship in their home and in the synagogue, but for the special season they went to the Temple. We worship each Sunday here, but for the special seasons of Christmas and Easter, we pull out the stops on the organ, we light the lights, bring in the flowers. We're doing something special. Their annual trip to Jerusalem for Passover was special. But this year's trip was extra special. Jesus was 12. He had completed his Bar Mitzvah, a custom similar to our confirmation. Now Jesus could go into the Temple with Joseph. It was a father and son thing to do and each took special pride in their being together. Parents and children can understand that.

The group from Nazareth traveled together in a caravan, the equivalent of chartering a bus today. When it was time to go home, the Nazareth crowd met at their campsite and headed north. Mary and Joseph traveled for a day without seeing Jesus. We can understand that. Boys that age are always ahead of, behind or beside, but never with the group. But boys that age always show up for supper. When Jesus was not with them for the meal, they felt their first pang of anxiety. We can understand that.

The next morning, Jesus' parents started the day's trip back to Jerusalem. They found him on the third day. That could be one day out, one day back and one day looking. Or it could be three days of searching. Where would you look for a 12-year-old boy in a large city? Start at places where there are trees to climb, water to splash, rocks to throw or animals to chase. But they didn't find him.

On the third day Mary and Joseph went to the Temple—maybe to look for Jesus, more likely to pray that they could find him. There he sat taking part in a discussion with the learned people of the day. The scholars were amazed at the boy with a Galilean accent who could not only answer questions but also ask questions.

According to custom, the father should have gone forward to reclaim the son. But at such a time, emotion rather than custom ruled. Mary ran forward. How easily we understand her words! They are words that are a part of parent-child conversations in every generation. First she said, "Son, why have you done this to us?" Notice the *to us*. Every parent has said and every child has heard that. Parents feel that each word and action of a child is done for the effect it will have on parents. The feeling is part of loving your children. Of course, children don't see it that way at all. It's a part of growing up.

Then catch the next line. Mary says, "Your father and I have been terribly worried trying to find you." Notice she speaks for her husband too. Parents like to start their statements of correction with, "Your father and I, your mother and I." It gives them a majority. Two parents—one child. We understand all of this.

This Bible story, and many others, tell us things we can easily understand. It shows us why God sent his Son to be a human being with us. Jesus the baby, Jesus the boy, Jesus the man, is a person we can identify with. He helps us say, "I do understand." I understand because his life relates to mine. Jesus the person helps me understand myself. He helps me understand others.

The Limit of Understanding

Jesus' reply to his mother are his first words recorded in the Scripture. If you have a Bible with his words printed in red, his answer would be the first appearance of red ink in the New Testament. He said, "Why did you have to look for me? Didn't you know that I had to be in my Father's house?" Then Luke tells us, "But they did not understand his answer."

Why were they looking for him? Because they hadn't seen him for three days, that's why. He's 12 years old, and Bar Mitzvah or not, he still needs a mother and a father. And what's this talk about his father's house. His father's house is in Nazareth. Joseph may have been a carpenter but he was not the contractor who built the Temple. This was not Joseph's house. If Jesus wanted to be theological and talk about the heavenly Father he could have said, *"our* Father's house" but he said *my* Father's. The first words printed in red and he already claims a special relationship to God. That's the kind of talk that got him killed.

Let's try to understand Mary and Joseph's failure to understand. These are people who had already stretched their ability to understand far beyond most of us. An angel had told Mary she would have a baby even though she was a virgin. After some explaining about the Holy Spirit, she understood. Joseph was the man who found his fiance was pregnant. He didn't understand until an angel explained. Then he understood.

However, the birth of Jesus did not remove the limits of their understanding. What Jesus said in the Temple again brought them to the point beyond which they could not understand. But the things they did understand helped bring them to that point. Their inability to understand their Son did not break their relationship with him. He didn't reject them because they didn't understand him. They did not reject him. The text says, "So Jesus went back with them to Nazareth where he was obedient to them." Also please note that Mary did not ignore the things she could not understand. Luke tells us, "His mother treasured all these things in her heart." She treasured the mystery of that which was beyond her understanding.

Now for us. Think about your relationship with God. Review the part you understand and reach out to the part you don't understand. Find the limit of your ability to understand. I understand God loves me. I don't understand why. I understand I am going to heaven. I do not understand what heaven will be like. You can list many more things you do understand and also many more limits on your understanding. God does not end his relationship with you because you do not understand him. You do not have to end your relationship with God because of your inability to find a final answer to each question you or others ask.

Christ has come to those points in your life where your understanding has reached its limit. By the power of the Holy Spirit he has already expanded your ability to receive the grace and love he has given you. He is still with you both to increase your understanding as you face the troubled areas of life and also to increase your astonishment and amazement as you glimpse the glory of God through the limitations of the human mind.

We have seen the baby in the manger and the boy in the Temple. Each one starts in our reality. Because God is with us in Jesus Christ we have the beginnings of an understanding of God. But we do not stop with the baby or with the boy. We travel with the man to the cross and the tomb. That trip shoves the point of our understanding up. We see him die to pay for our sins. We understand our guilt is gone. We see him who was dead and is alive again. We understand that we can die and still live.

Jesus Christ has put a high calorie value in our words—words such as love, grace, death, forgiveness, life. Test your spiritual diet to see if you are receiving the strength he gives you in those words. Grow in the understanding of the grace he has given you.

ELDON WEISHEIT
Fountain of Life Lutheran Church
Tucson, Arizona

The Shock of Christmas
John 1:1-18

I have a friend who was a very successful executive in a large corporation. As he was approaching 45 years of age and the last of their children went off to college, he and his wife made the decision to sell their home, give up their astronomical income, in order that the husband could go to seminary to become a pastor in the United Methodist Church. Their decision sent a shock wave through their friends, and his colleagues in the corporation could hardly believe it. Why would any one as successful and prosperous as he leave it all for the hardships of three or four more years of education and the modest income of a pastor? What a shocking act it was!

The prologue of the Gospel of John announces a far more shocking

41

act, however. These thunderous words with which the Fourth Gospel begins sent out a shock wave through the human community which is as forceful today as it was to the original readers. What John declares is that the event of Christmas is shocking to the human mind. Christmas is shocking, says the Gospel for today, in what it tells us about ourselves, and what it tells us about God—so shocking that we can hardly believe it.

Christmas Tells Us Something about Ourselves

In the beginning was the Word, and the Word was with God, and the Word was God. . . . And the Word became flesh and dwelt among us, full of grace and truth.

In that first Christmas the divine Word of God became human. Became one of us! The divine invaded the human. The divine Word became its very opposite—human flesh and blood!

The shock of the Christmas event is that God's Word has come to the world as a human being, and with that act God has revealed to us something about ourselves. The divine cannot become human! The Holy does not become the mundane! Human flesh cannot embrace the divinity of God's Word! It is unthinkable! It is incomprehensible! What a shock this Christmas event is—shocking in what it implies about our humanity.

That the Word became flesh and dwelt among us as a human means that this lowly humanity of ours has been sanctified once and for all. Never again can we think of our humanity as dirty, offensive, and defiled, for God has sanctified it in the very act of incarnating his own Word. If God can inhabit this human flesh that we share, then surely it is something sacred and honorable.

When I was a teenager, my church made it quite clear that dancing was not the sort of thing you did in the church building. Of course, we all danced at school and at private parties and thought nothing of it. But we would never dare to suggest that the youth group dance in the basement of the church. So, when the new, young sponsors of our group announced that we should have a square dance in the basement of the church, we were understandably worried. What would the old, staid members of the church council think? Surely this would terminate the short tenure of these new and vigorous sponsors of the group. We came that evening to the church ready to be told that the dance was cancelled; but to our surprise everyone was there, and things were ready to begin. To our amazement when the first dance was announced, who should be the first couples on the dance floor but our pastor and the president of church council with their spouses! Much relieved we went about having a delightful evening. We knew that it was now okay to dance in the church. The very presence of the pastor and the church council president in our midst that evening signaled that this activity was acceptable.

We may wonder at times if our humanity is okay—acceptable to God. Or, is it something of which we must be ashamed and continuously repentant? When God became a human in the form of that tiny baby in the manger, God *danced* amid our humanity. The Christmas act declared that human flesh and blood are made holy and good—holy and good enough that God's Word himself might become embodied in it.

Shocking although it may be, Christmas is the celebration of God's act in Christ and therefore the celebration of our own humanity. The embodiment of God's Word as a human being in this history of ours recalls the fact that our humanity is a result of God's creative work. We can, therefore, live our humanity with dignity and pride and never again can we allow human existence to be denigrated or abused. Christmas shocks us with the announcement that our humanity is sacred and holy.

Christmas Tells Us Something about God

And the Word became flesh and dwelt among us, full of grace and truth; we beheld his glory, glory as of the only Son from the Father. . . . No one has ever seen God; the only Son who is in the bosom of the Father, he has made him known.

The shock of Christmas is that God would be in this world of ours among us (his own creation) as a person. The means by which all was called into existence is now a human infant. What can it mean that God's powerful, creative Word is introduced in the world as a human being?

The Word of God through which all existence came into being is now the power of one single human personality. God is among us not as sheer incomprehensible power, but as the simple power of love. God does not enter our lives with lightning bolts and marvelous miracles. Instead we find God in the simple, quiet, personal caring and loving of Jesus of Nazareth. God has chosen to take the way of *the power of weakness.* Our minds are sent reeling at the fact that the Lord of the universe is the unobtrusive but persistent power of love in one who is so utterly weak.

A recent television movie entitled, "Bill," starred Mickey Rooney. Rooney played the role of Bill, a 50-year-old mentally retarded man working at a country club. He meets a young man who is interested in making a documentary film on retarded adults, using Bill as his subject. His interest in Bill is purely as a subject of his film, and he has every intent of exploiting Bill's innocence for his own profit. But the more he works with Bill the more captivated he becomes by Bill's simple, friendly caring. So overwhelmed by Bill's love is he that, when he moves his family to another part of the country, he must eventually bring Bill to the same city. What the story does so forcefully is to portray the power of love in one whom we would call weak. Bill had no power—physically he was powerless. He had no social, economic, or political power. He was absolutely weak in all the ways we conceive power. And yet he had a tremendous capacity for friendship—simple caring and loving. And because of that love he was powerful in his weakness.

In Christ, God has come among us as a weak and helpless human being. In Christ, God's power is the power of weakness—the power of love.

Christmas Tells Us Something We Can Hardly Believe

The Word was in the world, and the world was made through him, yet the world knew him not. He came to his own home, and his own people received him not.

So shocking is Christmas in what it tells us about ourselves and about God that we can hardly believe what we are hearing! Our humanity is sacred and holy? God's power is the power of weakness in love? Who can believe it? Who could receive some one who was so utterly incredible?

What is so incredible about this Christmas message is the extreme to which it suggests that God will go in order to make us his children. Can we ever comprehend the fact that God would become his opposite (a tiny human infant) for the sake of humanity? Sometimes in our wildest moments of romance, we will exaggerate how far we will go in our love of another. Like the romantic young man whose note to his beloved read something like this: "Darling, I would climb the highest mountain and swim the deepest sea for you! Your ever loving, Jim. P.S.—I'll be over to see you tonight, if it doesn't rain." So far and no farther will our human love go.

Hence when God's love goes to the extreme of the Christmas act, we can hardly believe it. Surely there is some mistake, some misunderstanding. Is there such a love as that? A love that discards all power for the weakness of love? A love that moves the lover to become his very opposite in human flesh?

One of the greatest love stories of the 20th century is the story of King Edward the VIII of Great Britain. He was a very popular monarch; and at the age of only 42 it appeared that he would have a long and successful reign. But one fatal flaw prevented his ever fulfilling that promise. He came to love an American woman, a Mrs. Simpson, who was in the process of divorcing her American husband when she and the king met. They courted for a time, and with each passing week the scandal grew among the English people. How shocked they were! It was unthinkable that their King should be courting a commoner, an American at that—a *divorcee at that!* The public opinion in England would never allow it, and the outrage of the people swelled to furious proportions. King Edward then was faced with a terrible dilemma: If he were to continue to reign as king of England, he would have to break off his relationship with Mrs. Simpson. Or, if he were to continue his relationship with the woman he had grown to love, he would have to give up the throne. In one of the most extreme acts of human love—one which puzzled but fascinated much of the world in 1936—Edward abdicated the throne. He gave up his office in favor of marrying a woman he loved more than power and pageantry.

As shocking as it may be, in that first Christmas the king of the universe abdicated his throne in order to become a human being and dwell among his subjects as one of them. This he did that we might know his immeasurable love for us.

ROBERT D. KYSAR
Christ United Lutheran Church
Gordon, Pennsylvania

THE EPIPHANY OF OUR LORD

What Do You Want to See in the Star?
Matthew 2:1-12

Two people settle into their seats at orchestra hall. She can hardly wait for it to begin. He cannot wait until it is over! The violins lift her into a seventh heaven. The violins wouldn't lift him anywhere.

We listen to the radio in our house. Upstairs, the youth listens to a certain station. We listen to what they call, "dentist chair music." It all depends on who is listening.

We see, we hear, what we are expecting to see and to hear.

I walk into the art gallery and look at the paintings of a certain artist. I am convinced that he has fooled the public. "Those are tire tracks on that canvass!" I complain. The more sensitive artist sees what is there as an expression of life as it is.

Much more than we care to accept, we are influenced greatly by where we are at the moment, what is going on inside of us, as to how we will react to anything that comes before our eyes or touches our hearing.

45

King Herod heard that the Messiah had arrived! Such an honor! Not only was Herod a great king, fearless and strong, who somehow had brought order out of chaos, he was the king on the throne at the time God sent his Messiah. What would Herod do? He would start a celebration! If only such a reaction were true. Herod went head hunting after this new arrival! To Herod, anyone, even the Messiah of God, was a threat to him if he came to be king. His history was to get rid of his competition, even if it meant the murder of his own family, and it often did. God's Son was a threat, so Jesus became marked for death in Herod's eyes.

The Wise Men saw Jesus differently. Two clues tell us how they saw Jesus:

The first clue is that they followed the star to Bethlehem. Jesus was to them more than a little child lying in a manger. He was the climax of their studies. He was what they found on earth when they looked into the heavens.

But he was more than this. Jesus was the object of their love. Somehow, as they looked into the heavens, they saw the vision of the Prince and they came to him! They knelt before him with gifts of gold, frankencense and myrrh. He was the object of their studies and the subject of their love.

To Joseph, Jesus became a problem. Mind you, we hear no complaints from Joseph. After his brief encounter with the angel before the birth of Jesus, he does not speak to us again. But Jesus must have been a problem. Joseph was not able to return immediately to Bethlehem because, first, Mary had to recover. Then there was the hurry-up trip to Egypt when they were warned that Herod was about to strike in all of his fury.

I often have wondered two things about Joseph. First, did the running around shorten his life? Joseph simply disappeared from the biblical record after they returned finally to settle down in Nazareth after the twelfth year of the life of Jesus. Secondly, did Joseph live long enough to learn what the manger and the star and the virgin birth, and the Wise Men and his changed life all meant? It all depends on who is looking and who is listening as to how we see the Christ who has come to us!

Who is this Jesus Christ!

The late Kent Knutson said it so powerfully in 1972. "He is Lord! He is Savior! He is your friend!"

But what does that mean?

It again depends on who is being asked that question. For one person he is the fulcrum for his curse! For another he is that someone you call on when all else fails. For another, he is the one who is your strong right arm when you want your will done. For another, he is the one who gives credence to what you are saying. To another, he is the God you hold in awe.

To one he is the God who is your good old buddy and each of these views are equally sad.

It is the message of Epiphany, the season we now celebrate that gives us a center upon which we can build, one that does not change! Epiphany says that Jesus is the light of the world! That is one of those "it doesn't matter who is listening and looking" statements.

Jesus is the light in the world and that is good because the world is in darkness. That is a good statement for us to hear. It says that the light does not come from the star of Bethlehem. The light does not shine down into the manger. It shines out from the manger.

The world is in darkness. That is one of those statements that depends on who is listening and looking. Only you can say what the darkness is. The darkness may be poverty. But another will say that it is not only an economic darkness. There is a darkness that is much worse. It is the darkness of racism on all sides of the street.

Another says that darkness means using up all of our natural resources and polluting all that which is held in reserve. That is our darkness.

To a child in war-torn Central America, the darkness is government troops driving through his village one day and rebels coming through it the next. To a responsible person, darkness is people voting not their consciences but their pocket books. Darkness depends on who is listening, who is watching.

Hatred. Greed. License to do what you please. Alcohol. Drugs. The darkness is all things, all these things and more that Satan, the prince of darkness, places before us to keep us from seeing what happens underneath the star of Bethlehem.

What is the word? Jesus is more than a threat to your life, but make no mistake, he is indeed a threat. He is more than one to study and even bring gifts to. He is more than one who will trouble you with a life that may not even be as secure as it was before. He is a light that has begun to shine in the darkness!

This is the Epiphany word. He is forgiveness. He is hope. He is encouragement. He is a word of love. He is what you need him to be. He is all things to all people. This is when the Lord's Christ becomes exciting! When he meets *our needs!*

When you look down at the little child in the manger, look at the one who will meet you at your point of darkness, who will never change his love for you.

J. THOMAS HOUSHOLDER
Edison Park Lutheran Church
Chicago, Illinois

His Baptism and Ours
Luke 3:15-17, 21-22

Today we remember a baptism—the baptism of our Lord. It is entirely appropriate to also remember baptism in the life of our congregation. But just what is it about baptism that makes it worth remembering?

The Occasion?

In this congregation we are privileged to experience baptism often. We are used to such occasions and we do them well. There are procedures to be followed—forms to be filled out, the request of a date, a candle to be inscribed with name and date, a pastoral call to be made.

There are people to be invited—
- the pastor, who sees to it that everything goes smoothly.
- the congregation, which never seems to tire of embracing these new members.
- the parents, a bit nervous that the child they are still getting to know might not be at his or her best.
- the sponsors, proud to have been asked and rather serious about the responsibility.
- grandparents, who will beam proudly from the second pew, and take hundreds of pictures.
- occasionally brothers or sisters, who don't fully understand what's going on but who are demanding in their curiosity.
- and of course the baby—whether asleep or awake, placid or screaming—the star of the show, the center of attention.

There are important words to be said—
"Do you promise . . .?"
"I do."
"Do you believe . . .?"
"I believe. . . ."
"I baptize you in the name of the Father, and of the Son, and of the Holy Spirit. Amen."
"We welcome you into the Lord's family."

And there are meaningful actions—
the sign of the cross.

the splashing of water.

the lighting of a candle.

the introduction of the baby to the congregation.

No matter how many baptisms we have, each is an occasion. We are good at that. Not even the most loudly wailing baby can mar such occasions. I suspect that many of us experience in the baptismal ceremony a blend of solemnity and informality it would be hard to beat—personal yet dignified, the best our liturgy has to offer.

Somehow that's always been the way I've thought of Jesus' baptism—personal, yet dignified. John the Baptist may have been a rather strange figure, but he and Jesus were cousins. They met one another with dignity, both men of stature. Then John stepped aside, leaving Jesus clearly set apart. The scene is as familiar as baptisms in our church.

The Vision and the Voice?

But that's not the way Luke tells the story. In his account, John has already been slapped in jail by Herod. And Jesus is lost in the crowd. "Now when all the people were baptized, and when Jesus also had been baptized. . . ." In fact, the occasion is almost missing entirely. Luke treats Jesus' baptism as an accomplished act.

All we're left with is an event which, as described, is rather embarrassingly like a grade B movie.

- Jesus in prayer (Who could fault him for piety?)
- the opened heaven (Can't you just see the clouds slowly part letting one strategic shaft of golden light zero in on Jesus' bowed head?)
- a vision in the form of a bird (a dove at that, and probably pure white)
- and the topper—a voice from heaven (Surely Charlton Heston with maybe the Mormon Tabernacle Choir as back-up?)

The most dignified occasion would have trouble rising above such a scene. Luke has ignored the trappings of ceremony, and has left us, uncomfortably, in the presence of a vision and a voice. We are not even given the comfort of that being a private religious experience on the part of Jesus or John, as the other gospel writers allow. Luke makes it clear that the vision and the voice were a public designation of just who this is.

The words spoken—"Thou art my beloved son; with thee am I well pleased"—echo the Servant Song in Isaiah 42:

Behold my servant, whom I
uphold,

49

> my chosen, in whom my soul
>> delights.

They are the words by which the servant is introduced to the nations. They are words which call to mind that the servant is to be a suffering servant. Perhaps they are the words which Jesus had in mind when he spoke of his death as a baptism.

In this congregation we have made a practice of introducing the newly baptized baby to the congregation. That introduction carries with it a faint echo of that voice from heaven. It is an introduction of one who, through baptism, is identified with Jesus in life and death.

The Power and the Task?

It is not enough to introduce the servant, something must be said of his authority and his task:

> I have put my Spirit upon him,
>> he will bring forth justice to the
>>> nations.

It is no easy task to bring forth justice in the world, to bring an end to human suffering, to create unity and dispel disharmony. It is a task that calls for power; not the power of the state, or technology, or reason alone, but the power of God.

It is a power that is inclusive, not exclusive. One of the prerogatives of the powerful of the world is to limit contacts to what pleases or benefits them. God does not act with such limits. "God shows no partiality." Through Christ, God's power is opened to all, opened for their advantage, not God's. Jesus is Lord of all so that all might benefit.

Peter's sermon in Acts 10 makes both the source of the power and the task explicit. ". . . God anointed Jesus of Nazareth with the Holy Spirit and with power; (and) he went about doing good and healing all that were oppressed by the devil. . . ." "Going about doing good" sounds pretty innocuous until one reads the Gospels and discovers just how this Christ touched and continues to touch the lives of people. It is a touch that rescues and heals and reconciles. It happens through the words and works of love.

Remember

Today we remember baptism—his and ours. We remember the occasion, but as least important. We remember the vision and the voice as announcement and introduction. We remember the power and the task; the gift of the Holy Spirit—the same Spirit that empowered him—and the assignment to follow in his way.

The occasion may one day slip from your memory. You may forget the date, lose the certificate, the gown may fall away into dust. If so, you will have lost little. There will still be his baptism to give you vision, the voice to remind you of who you are, the task to which you have been called, and the Holy Spirit to empower you. In that we can live.

Pour your Holy Spirit upon us: the spirit of wisdom and understanding, the spirit of counsel and might, the spirit of knowledge and the fear of the Lord, the spirit of joy in your presence. Amen. (LBW, p. 124)

KAREN G. BOCKELMAN
Bethlehem Lutheran Church
St. Cloud, Minnesota

SECOND SUNDAY AFTER THE EPIPHANY

Eve, Mary, and Women in the Church
John 2:1-11

At a recent annual convention of the American Psychological Association, several women speakers claimed that organized religion is in conflict with full freedom for women. Manhattan psychotherapist Aphrodite Clamar said the "rise of the women's movement poses a direct challenge" to churches and synagogues traditionally dominated by men with women in subordinate roles. She said, women are no longer willing to be subservient . . . or to be satisfied with inferior status. "Churches and synagogues will have to change their traditions or more and more women will walk out" (New York, AP).

In his book, *After Eve,* Alan Graebner echoes: "The Church is one of the most obstinate anti-woman institutions in our society. Piously preaching love and the commonality of sinners before God, it has established beliefs, attitudes and practices demeaning, even crippling, to women. As an institution it has traditionally distinguished itself fighting in the reactionary rear-guard against the advances in women's rights."

The Wedding at Cana

The setting for today's Gospel was a marriage in Cana in Galilee. The mother of Jesus was there as was Jesus and his disciples. When the wine

51

gave out, Jesus' mother said to him, "They have no more wine." Jesus' response—which makes the story very difficult to understand—was, "O woman, what have you to do with me? My hour has not yet come." She seems to ignore that confusing statement and goes ahead as if Jesus had not refused; and Jesus does what she requested. This picture of Mary as an active participant in the ministry of Jesus does not correspond to the oldest Gospel tradition (Mark 3:31-35) where we find Jesus strongly rejecting intervention by his mother. And even at the wedding in Cana, Jesus carefully disassociates himself from his mother's interests and gives priority to a later "hour" dictated by his heavenly Father. When the hour comes for Jesus to pass from this world to the Father, he will grant Mary a role that will involve her, not as *his* mother but as the mother of the Beloved Disciple, now Jesus' brother. What this means is that the Gospel tradition excludes Mary in the ministry of Jesus as his physical mother but has Jesus interpret *who* his mother is later in terms of full discipleship.

John's Gospel chooses two scenes to convey this clarification: the wedding at Cana and the hour of Jesus' death. The Johannine community apparently was already experiencing equality between men and women in the church, as evidenced by the several instances in the Gospel of John in which the importance of women is obvious. Paul's dream that there be no distinction between male and female was realized in John's community though this was not always the case in the Pauline communities.

Why has there been so much confusion—even pain—associated with this matter of the place of women in the life and ministry of the Church? A look at the larger biblical tradition may shed some light on our present question. Let us begin with the first image of woman in the Bible: Eve.

Eve

The biblical picture of Eve is rooted in the two creation narratives at the beginning of Genesis. In the priestly account of creation in Genesis 1, it is stated that God created humankind in his own image male and female. Both sexes were representative of the likeness of God, and God saw that it was very good. In the traditional reading of the second creation story, the male is created first, then every beast of the field and bird of the air, and then the female is made from one of the ribs of the first person. Feminist theologian Phyllis Trible has thoroughly analyzed this passage and suggests that the first creature should be pictured as neither male nor female but as "earth creature" who is unfulfilled by itself, and is unfulfilled by other helpers *(ezers)* or companions, so the Lord God forms the earth creature into male and female, affirming the equality of one to the other. She notes too, that in the traditional reading of the passage, the woman has been understood to be the male's helper or *ezer* in a subordinate way. But of the sixteen times the word *ezer* is used elsewhere in the Old Testament, it implies a superordinate rather than a subordinate relationship. For example, God is often the *ezer* or helper of Israel. As such, the term suggests a superior rather than an inferior position.

But what about the Fall of humankind? Was it not woman who yields? Does she not bear the greater guilt because of some innate weakness? If that is so, then it could also be said that the male did not demonstrate strength or dominance in the life situation, but was weak and slothful. Dr. Trible would say that a pro-male, anti-woman bias is expressed in the biblical tradition and the same has been preserved in translations that have been done by male scholars.

The Hebrew/Judaic tradition in which the image of Eve was preserved served to legitimate a patriarchal society. It pictured God often with such male metaphors as warrior (man of war), king, lord, master, shepherd and father. Examples from the laws and history of Israel illustrate that women were valued less than men, female infants less than male. Women were considered more as property than equal partners to men. Females had fewer, if any, legal rights. Even genealogies were traced through males, as if only males "begat." Female biological functions were considered more unclean. Ritual bathing following the birth of a female was twice as long as after the birth of a male child. We are told that in the ancient Jewish tradition, women were confined to the house but could go out to attend the synagogue. There from a balcony or side room, she and the children could watch the males study Torah and say the prayers. A rabbi was not to speak to a woman in public. In fact, the daily prayer of Jewish men was a threefold thanksgiving, one of which was to praise God that he had not created him as a woman. It is fairly safe to say that the biblical roots preserve a negative view of Eve and her daughters. This deeply etched picture has not been easily changed.

Mary

The most prominent woman in the new community who could also be seen as the counterpart to Eve is the mother of Jesus. By humbly bearing the Messiah of God, she undoes what "disobedient" Eve brought on the human race. She exemplifies the female virtues of submission, tenderness, quietude and obedience. As such, the image of Mary became a model for later centuries of female Christian devotion.

The Gospel traditions portray Jesus as having departed from the male religious conventions of his time. He goes out of his way to speak to women and treats them with respect. A miracle story gives details of how a woman with a seemingly incurable issue of blood is healed by touching the fringe of his garment. On the occasion of his visit to the house of Mary and Martha, he chides Martha for choosing to be about that less important business of serving tables, a function typically assigned to the woman of the house, and he compliments Mary for attending to the weightier matter of listening to his teaching.

Women were first to witness the empty tomb and it was to a woman, Mary Magdalene, that Jesus first appears, instructing her to go and tell his disciples of his ascension to the Father. Particularly in the Johannine community we discover a prominent position given to women as disciples of Jesus. And it was at the foot of the cross, when Jesus' hour had come, that Jesus grants Mary what she was denied at Cana as his physical mother, namely to be his disciple. John's Gospel includes women as bona fide disciples by telling us that Jesus loved Martha and Mary and that Mary Magdalene was one of his own sheep whom he called by name. But it is especially as his mother and the beloved disciple stand at the foot of the cross that they are designated as models for Jesus' "own," his true family of disciples.

A case can just as surely be made that Paul opened the door to women in the life and ministry of his churches. Specific women are mentioned in his letters and greetings. In what sounds like a great crescendo to his claim that through faith rather than through Torah all are God's people, he states:

> There is neither Jew nor Greek, there is neither slave nor free, there is
> neither male nor female; for you are all one in Christ Jesus (Gal. 3:28).

Women were expected to pray and prophesy in the service (1 Cor. 11:5) although it was advised that they cover their heads. In another passage (1 Cor. 14:33b-36) it appears that Paul denies women the right to speak in church, saying that they should be subordinate, and ask whatever questions they have to their husbands at home.

Apparently as Christianity evolved into an institution during the second and third centuries, women were required to be submissive, quiet, not to teach or have authority over men, because they were the daughters of Eve. Their lot was to gain their favor from God by bearing children in faith, love, and holiness (cf. 1 Tim. 2:8-15).

Whether it was due to struggles with heresy, for theological or cultural reasons, Christianity reverted to sexism in dogma and practice. The influence of certain philosophical notions about the nature of the material world caused some of the early church fathers to mistrust the physical dimension. Deep suspicion of the body grew out of the separation of reality into matter and spirit. As a part of the material world of evil, the body and its functions were misunderstood and mistrusted by some male theologians who projected their preoccupations on to women, for women represented the body, sensuality, and evil. Women were considered to be dangerous to the religious life. Tertullian wrote:

Do you not know that you are Eve? . . . You are the devil's gateway. How easily you destroyed man, the image of God. Because of the death which you brought upon us, even the Son of God had to die.

The image of Eve (or woman) as temptress was strong. At times the notion of original sin was identified with sexual passion, and sexual passion with woman. Centuries later, the most highly respected Christian medieval theologian, Thomas Aquinas, considered woman defective and accidental, a male gone awry.

In the midst of this kind of thinking, the Virgin Mary was raised to a semidivine status. Doctrines about her as being sinless and sexless began to develop. She was elevated to a religious pedestal somewhat beyond the scope of ordinary discipleship assigned her by Jesus at the foot of the cross.

The Protestant Reformation attempted to free women from these two distorted images of woman. Convents were closed and the religious woman was offered wifery and motherhood. The Protestant stress on the vocation of family pressured the religious woman to find her proper place in the home as wife, mother, and housekeeper. Meantime, the church remained a male bastion perpetuating an image of woman that, for the most part, kept her from full participation in the life and ministry of the church. It has been largely during this century that women have gained full voting rights in our congregations and only recently the privilege of the ordained ministry. But even more important than either voting or ordination is the removal of those deep distortions and stereotypes that have prevented both females and males from their fullness as God's people.

Today's Woman

So here we are at this moment in history struggling for wisdom, obedience, and grace sufficient to meet the challenge of a new day for both women and men in the church. Women stand on the threshold of new possibilities of freedom and opportunity, not only in society but in the church. Our seminaries report that enrollment is moving toward an equal number of female and male students. Similar things could be said about some of the advances that have been made in other parts of our common life. There is, to be sure, much left to be done.

Yet, mother, sister, wife, and daughter, are released from the old Eve image as the source of humanity's iniquity. And they are no longer saddled with the divinized image of the stained-glass Mary. Women in the church are not assigned to inferiority or superiority, but full humanity. We honor the Lord of the church, who has called both females and males into full discipleship, not by casting each other into the role of scapegoat for the human plight, nor by placing one or the other on an artificial pedestal, but by announcing in word and deed the gospel of full discipleship in Christ for all.

WILLIS GERTNER
University of Wisconsin
Eau Claire, Wisconsin

THIRD SUNDAY AFTER THE EPIPHANY

Liberating Good News
Luke 4:14-21

Good-news, bad-news stories have been around for some time. One of my favorites tells the story about the Pope, who one Sunday announced to the huge crowds of the faithful gathered in St. Peter's Square, "the Lord spoke to me last night while I was praying, and gave me some good news, and some bad news." A hush fell upon the crowd as the Pope continued, "The good news is this: The Lord has promised to return by next Sunday." At that, a loud roar of approval went up from the crowd. But then the Pope continued, "He also gave me some bad news. The bad news is that he is real mad!"

Thankfully, the Gospel for this Sunday is sheer "good news," and we want to do all we can to hear it as such. It is not good news about the end of the world, as some might like to hear, but good news for the present, good news that has to do with our life right here and now. This good news centers in Jesus Christ, the Liberator, so we will call it "Liberating Good News."

But in what way is this good news liberating, and in what way is Jesus Christ the Liberator of humanity? Is he a Liberator, as some have dared to suggest, in the mold of a Zealot freedom fighter or a modern-day Che Guevara? Or is he only a Liberator of humanity's inner captivity to the powers of sin and death? Or is he in any way the symbol of hope for the poor and oppressed? There are the kinds of questions alive today, and we want to struggle with them as we look at our Gospel more closely.

The Setting in Luke's Gospel

This story of Jesus' Sabbath visit to his hometown synagogue in Nazareth plays a key role in Luke's Gospel. Mark and Matthew have it later

56

in Jesus' ministry, but Luke uses it to introduce Jesus' mission and message. It serves as Jesus' Inaugural Address. Previously Jesus had been baptized by the Holy Spirit and tested in the wilderness. Now he is ready for his life's work. So Luke tells us that Jesus returned to Galilee in the power of the Spirit, and began to teach and preach.

That sets the stage for this dramatic scene of Jesus' visit to Nazareth. It doesn't take much imagination to put one's self into the drama. This is Jesus' hometown. Everyone knows he is the carpenter Joseph's son. This is the synagogue in which he learned to worship and pray, sing the psalms and memorize the Scriptures. Now he returns, and word has gotten around that Joseph's son is quite a teacher. The synagogue is packed. And they honor Jesus by asking him to read the Scripture. He responds with the reading from Isaiah: "The Spirit of the Lord is upon me . . . to preach good news to the poor . . ." And when he finished, he sat down to interpret the words, as rabbis did. His hearers are rapt with attention. Now they can hear for themselves what he's like. And Jesus began by saying, "Today this Scripture has been fulfilled in your hearing."

At this point, however, the story begins to take a different turn. If you continue reading beyond today's lesson, you will find that although they first speak well of him, some ask, "Is not this Joseph's son?" and within a short time they are enraged and take mob action to do away with him.

Quite obviously, Jesus' words, "Today this Scripture has been fulfilled in your hearing" are not what they had expected to hear. They had hoped to hear a moving homily about the prophet Isaiah and the exiles to whom he spoke. But when Jesus claimed personally to possess the Spirit, and when he further claimed to be the very One in whom the prophetic words were fulfilled, *today,* that became the offense and bone of contention. Who does he think he is?

And that is exactly the question toward which Luke is driving his readers. There is much human drama here. But Luke's purpose far transcends the human setting. In the words of Isaiah, Luke has found a vehicle for expressing who Jesus is and the purpose of his life. And what Luke would have us see is that Jesus is the Spirit-Anointed Proclaimer of good news to the poor. That's what his gospel is all about.

The Good News Mission of Jesus

But what is this good news? That is the crux of the matter, and it is something we need to be very clear about.

In his recent book, *The Christian Challenge,* Hans Küng, the provocative Catholic theologian, offers this moving description of what the mission of Jesus was about:

From the first to the last page of the Bible, it is clear that God's will aims at man's well-being at all levels . . . in biblical terms at the salvation of man. God's will is a helpful, healing, liberating, saving will. God wills life, joy, freedom, peace, salvation, the final great happiness of man, both of the individual and of mankind as a whole. And this is the meaning of all that Jesus proclaims.

One could summarize this to say that Jesus' life embodied good news for humanity. He took up, as it were, the cause of humanity. But again, what is this cause of humanity?

A. *Good News for the Sinner*

Surely at the heart of the good news for humanity embodied in the words and deeds, the death and resurrection of Jesus, is the message of God's unconditional love and mercy. This is God's good news for sinners. And in Luke's Gospel, even more than the others, we see Jesus putting this kind of all-embracing, forgiving and inviting love in action. He welcomes sinners into his presence, he invites them to be his followers, he even sits down and eats bread and drinks wine with them. The pious don't understand. They call him a "glutton and a drunkard, a friend of sinners." In response, Luke's Jesus tells those three marvelous parables of the Lost Sheep, the Lost Coin, and the Lost Son, all of which portray the over-whelming joy of the Father when the lost are found. Or Luke preserves the touching story of the woman who interrupts a banquet by casting herself at Jesus' feet and pouring out her tears of sorrow for past sins and tears of gratitude for that past forgiven. The scenes in Luke's Gospel present real people, trapped in their way of life, miserable and confused, without hope or love, who suddenly encounter the liberating good news of a God who accepts them as they are, seeks their welfare, wipes away their tears, and offers them the opportunity to get on with life again—this God present in the words and deeds of Jesus. Surely this is the heart of the good news for humanity brought near in Jesus.

We must pause a moment and make this personal. Do you and I know this God of mercy, who finally pours out his love for us on the hard wood of a cross? To know in the biblical sense is to experience personally, to have gotten in touch with the reality itself. To know in this personal way is first to know something about the truth of ourselves—our hidden life, our real motives, our inner self behind the mask. It is to lay ourselves open before the God who knows us better than we know ourselves, and to put an end to our excuses. And then it is to hear the lifegiving word of his forgiveness as we are, the good news we can begin again and live daily in the assurance of his love and power. To know this is to be in touch with the liberating good news that can make us whole.

B. *Good News to the Poor*

But we must look once again at our Gospel for today, and listen to the words from the prophet Isaiah, which interpret Jesus' mission.

> The Spirit of the Lord is upon me, because he has anointed me to preach good news to the poor, . . . release to the captives, . . . sight to the blind, liberty for the oppressed, . . . the acceptable year of the Lord.

Who are the poor, captives, blind, and oppressed? There is little doubt that the prophet had in mind the exiles, the remnant carried off to Babylon. And he was announcing to them the liberating news that their time of captivity was over, their moment of freedom was at hand.

But how do these words apply to Jesus' mission? It would be tempting to forget altogether their social and political context in Isaiah, and to reinterpret them in a purely religious manner. And this is, in fact, what has usually been done. The poor are heard as Matthew's "poor in spirit," the "captives and oppressed" as those burdened by sin and guilt, and the "blind" as the spiritually ignorant.

However, before we try this old way yet again, let us see if Luke's portrait of Jesus may lead us in another direction. It may be that we are trying to preserve a portrait of Jesus that is safe and comfortable, but not the Jesus proclaimed in Luke's Gospel.

Listen to some other clues about the mission of Jesus in this Gospel. In the very first chapter, in the birth stories, Mary sings the praises of a God who chooses those of low position in life and humbles the great. According to the Magnificat, "he (God) has put down the mighty from their thrones, and exalted those of low degree; he has filled the hungry with good things, and the rich he has sent empty away." Surely Mary's God is the God of the poor and lowly.

Another clue may be heard in Luke's Sermon on the Mount. Whereas those blessed by God in Matthew's sermon are the "poor *in spirit*" and "those who hunger and thirst *after righteousness*," the blessed in Luke are simply the "poor, those who are hungry and those who weep now." Moreover Luke also includes in his Sermon the prophetic words of woe spoken by Jesus against the rich, the full, and those who now laugh. Once more we hear the message of God's favor toward the poor and the powerless, and his word of warning against the affluent and powerful.

One final clue. We have already observed Jesus' love for the sinner in Luke's Gospel, but to this we must add a long list of other persons who lived on the edge of society and who became the special object of our Lord's ministry. These include the hated Samaritans, the outcast tax collectors, the common people, the mass of villagers and peasants who were like sheep without a shepherd, and especially in Luke's Gospel the oft-forgotten women and children. Real people, all of them, living on the margin, but now invited to participate in fellowship with Jesus.

What do these clues teach us about the mission of our Lord? Do they not provide for us the fuller context in which we need to hear those opening words of the prophet Isaiah as they define for us our Lord's life and work? Do they not illumine for us the mission of our Lord as one dedicated to the cause of humanity; the sick and the suffering, the poor and the powerless, the despised and the dispossessed?

When Jesus announces that the Spirit is upon him to preach good news to the poor and captives and blind and oppressed, must we not include these suffering poor within the good news of his ministry? Surely this Jesus *is* the Liberator of the poor, the friend of the powerless, the bearer of God's liberating hope for all the sufferers of the world.

And just as surely we, as followers of this Christ, need to embrace this social dimension of his ministry. In the same way that we have heard the good news of God's unconditional love for us in the story of Jesus, so we also need to hear the good news of God's liberating love on behalf of the weak and the helpless in the same story of Jesus.

And our task then is to identify ourselves with the cause of the needy, and to share in his mission of love and mercy for the hungry and sick and imprisoned and oppressed, to be, that is, good news to the poor.

What this might mean personally for you, your family, or our congregation is something each of us is called upon to wrestle with and decide. But let me offer you two examples that may help.

The first is from Luke's own Gospel, the chief tax collector, Zacchaeus. Remember what happened to Zacchaeus after he had his life-transforming encounter with Jesus? He decided to give one-half of his income for the poor. From a life bent on greed and gain, he became the friend of the poor. That's quite a change.

The second is a contemporary example. He's a lawyer, with a working wife, two children, and a reasonably affluent life-style. But he spends one day a week at the welfare clinic offering legal advice to persons without charge, and his family has decided to get by on one car, as well as adopt financially a hungry child through monthly stipends. That's quite a change too.

Jesus brought liberating good news. Those persons are right who say this good news is at heart the assurance of a gracious, forgiving God. But those persons are also right who say this good news embraces God's liberating love and care for the human family's suffering and poor. Both belong to the mission of our Lord proclaimed in today's Gospel.

Let us pray: Almighty God, you sent your Son to proclaim your kingdom and to teach with authority; anoint us with the power of your Spirit, that we too may bring good news to the afflicted, bind up the broken-hearted, and proclaim liberty to the captives; through your Son, Jesus Christ, our Lord.

WALTER E. PILGRIM
Pacific Lutheran University
Tacoma, Washington

So You're Thinking of the Ministry?
Luke 4:21-32

The introduction to the sermon could be used as an introduction to the entire service and the theme and thought of the day. The preacher could then just refer to this commentary, summarize it, or use an entirely different introduction.

In the Name of Jesus. Amen. It is more than a month ago since we celebrated the festival of Christmas, the birth of Jesus Christ. Like the huge rings that go out from the center of a pond when a rock is thrown into it, Epiphany can be thought of as "the spreading out of Christmas." This little baby of Bethlehem, to whom angels sang hymns of praise and who shepherds came to visit is the Son of God. Epiphany expands this truth. This little child, born at Bethlehem, to poor parents, is also the Savior of the *whole world,* everyone's Lord. He has, I suspect, touched your life in one way or another. People who are called into the family of God are ministers. The word minister usually brings the image of a pastor, but that's not the way I am using it here. To put it simply "you are called into service ... the service of the Lord" by virtue of being a Christian. I hope that you are thinking of this ministry at this moment. Shake yourself a bit! Settle into the pew (perhaps not too comfortably) and think with me about ministry. (pause) So you're thinking of the ministry?

We Do Not Make the Choice

A. If We Choose, We Can Also Select

You don't hear any bells ringing. You don't notice any sirens going off. There is nothing terribly spectacular about thinking of the ministry.

61

You're thinking of the ministry! So what? A lot of people pride themselves in being able to make their own choices. Unlike a lot of other things in our lives, you and I don't actually make the choice for this ministry. The twelve disciples were all individuals who were separately called into service by their Lord. In most cases, a person would be impressed by a rabbi and then follow that rabbi and become his disciple. The disciples, as you and every other Christian, are called into ministry by God's choice.

Jeremiah felt this choice very strongly. He felt that the responsibility had been laid upon him. The audience, at least most of them, who heard Jesus that day in the synagogue, were quite sure that they were counted among the faithful by their own choosing. Because of this idea they could also then go on to believe that they were superior to others as well as very safe in their own religious beliefs. Let's not be too hasty in separating ourselves from these people, quickly concluding that there is no way that we could be like this. That can be fatal to faith.

After Jesus—as was the custom with the visiting rabbi—read to the congregation from the scroll in the synagogue, he sat down and "the eyes of all in the synagogue were fixed on him" (Luke 4:20). In their own way they were thinking about ministry. At first it all seemed to be so very cordial. But then Jesus began to open those words a bit further. There was much more to what he said than they first imagined. This is so often true when we hear the word, especially when we listen only superficially.

When Jesus began to uncover the self-righteous limiting that the hearers were doing, then their acceptance turned to anger and extreme indignation. Who was this young rabbi who dared to try to teach them and who spoke such irreverent words? They were fully convinced that their life, their religious life and confession was of their choosing. Since it was the result of their own choosing they could also select their own priorities of how that ministry was to be carried out. They could also decide to whom they would extend this ministry. Jesus recalled the experience of Elijah who was assisted and helped by the widow of Zarephath. Please note that she was a Gentile. Jesus recalled the healing of Naaman, the leprous Syrian army officer. In both cases he was talking about events that reached out to normally "unacceptable" people and they were examples that were entirely the gracious act of God. They did not find God. God found them and embraced them. The problem with believing that we do our own choosing for the ministry is that we then believe that we can also do our own *selecting* of priorities for ministry. If you have the right to choose your ministry, then you have the right to select what it is in this ministry that you will do. If you have the right to choose your own ministry, then you have the right to decide with whom and for whom this ministry is to be exercised. This is not the way it is for you and for me as we think about our ministry.

B. God Sends Us

We are chosen for our ministry and with this choosing goes the sending. Did you get the feel of all of this when you heard about Jeremiah this morning? He stammered and stumbled because he felt that he wasn't equipped for the kind of ministry to which the Lord called him. But God chose and God equipped and God sent him out. Paul reminds us that "God appointed in the church teachers . . ." (1 Cor. 12:28). For Luke, in the Gospel, these events were the inauguration of Jesus' ministry. It was a ministry that would involve rejection as well as triumph. God's concern for everyone is seen in the ministry of Jesus Christ. The initiative is God's. Even the psalm today has this flavor as the writer speaks of "taking refuge in God" (71:1) and asks to be "set free" (71:2) so that he can "recount your mighty acts (71:15) and "your righteousness . . . yours alone" (71:16). The more determined we are to control our own destiny and to claim the ability to be the center of our lives, the more we will have difficulty with "being chosen and sent."

There is something in the very spirit of our society that objects to the idea, especially in religion, that we are not the choosers and therefore cannot be the selectors either. God sends us out and the fuel of that sending is his love. Important as all of the other gifts are, and as commendable as knowledge, sacrifice, and good performance are, they find their meaning and their power only in the love that we experience in the sending by God (1 Cor. 13).

So you're thinking about the ministry! I hope so! This is a most important part of our Christian confession to consider. It no longer leaves our commitment to the folly of our own selection, nor to the weakness of our own abilities. As strange as it may seem to you right now to think of yourself as one who is sent, it is the focus for this moment.

God Designs the Ministry

A. So Impossible It Can Be Offensive

God designs our ministry. If any one of us was to design this ministry we would do it in such a way that we can fulfil it with whatever gifts we have at hand and to our satisfaction. The problem with the congregation in Luke 4 was that some of them had their own design for ministry. It was one with which they were satisfied. They felt quite comfortable with it. But the design of our ministry often seems so impossible. Jesus was met with indignation. Many of the people refused to accept his design for ministry. They wanted to put him to death. Now that's not a very encouraging motivation.

The "agape" that 1 Corinthians 13 is speaking of is the kind of life that is built on sacrifice, humility, courage, and even suffering. The design of this ministry is so impossible that to the average person, and even to the committed it can become offensive. "We sometimes become quite upset when the church or one of its spokesmen suggests that our private lives are filled with selfishness and pride and indifference to human need. We protest when church councils speak out against abuses of social justice and economics and politics. We are indignant when it is pointed out that the American way is not necessarily God's way" (*Proclamation, Epiphany*, p. 33). We have learned to look for the final payment in terms of success and glory. Sometimes this happens and sometimes it doesn't.

For these reasons it isn't hard to understand why Jeremiah should suggest that God had the wrong person. It is for these reasons that we would prefer to choose our own kind of ministry rather than listen for the call and the prompting of God who says, "Behold, I have put my words in your mouth. See, I have set you this day over nations and over kingdoms, to pluck up and to break down, to destroy, and to overthrow, to build and to plant" (Jer. 1:9-10).

B. So Valuable It Dare Not Be Missed

Just because the ministry is God's design we dare not miss it. Whether you can feel a bit of what Jeremiah felt when he turned down the call to ministry because he felt he wasn't fit, there certainly have been times in your life when you felt inadequate. It is at those times when we look for other ways to go or when we look for a ministry that will not be so demanding. Take another look! Demanding as the love pictured in 1 Corinthians is, and as valuable as it is for those who receive it, at the same time the real blessing comes to the giver. Where you and I might well have left the synagogue in a "huff" over the ill reception, Jesus continued to include these people in his call. The blessing of God which is ours in ministry is too valuable to be missed.

Since we're thinking about ministry, recall once how often people reject their ministry, ignore it, walk away from it for some very insignificant reasons. It could be nothing more serious than the introduction of a new book of worship. It could be the insensitive speech of someone else that turns them away. "If this is the way the church is I want no further part of it." Consider the indignation of the people in Luke 4 and see there what they missed because they insisted on their way and on their own righteous judgments.

It Takes God's Leading

A. Patient Listening

Are you still thinking about ministry? Perhaps you say, "That's all well and good for Jeremiah because the Lord came and touched his lips, but how am I supposed to find that kind of courage?" *It takes patient listening.* We just don't listen very carefully sometimes. In the debates that go on in politics, religion and business, and sometimes the combination of them all, there's little listening taking place. The moment someone departs from your particular point of view, you don't listen, you gear up for battle. This isn't very good soil in which the Holy Spirit can work. Yet sometimes that's the way we hear the word too. If we want to know God's leading, then we have to be patient listeners to this word, to his Word, and to one another. Imagine what could have happened if instead of trying to destroy Jesus, these people could have overcome their pride and arrogance and said, "We can't see your point of view at all, but we want to hear you out." If you're thinking about ministry, then check your listening. God sees us and speaks to us just as we are and not as we think we are.

B. Faithful Ministering

There's another step in following God's leading. If you're thinking about ministry then there's only one thing to do and that is to exercise it. God does not intend to have his people sit around and feel guilty about what they are not able to do. He does not find glee in having us compare our love to the model of 1 Corinthians 13. God intends for us to be in ministry. He intends that we use the power of his love as we experience it in Jesus Christ and then act. You will notice that it is faithfulness, not success that is the key word. Love was the banner of victory for Jesus, but that banner led him through rejection and even death before triumph.

When you come to the Lord's Table today, rejoice in the fact that the Savior is there with you, giving you his body and his blood and then you can take heart to go out to be "his holy communion." This is ministry. This is the ministry we should be thinking about.

Where are you then right now? Thinking about ministry? Detached? Satisfied? Uninterested? Whatever your particular mood or place at the moment, I would urge you to consider these good words. Give them their chance. Risk their great power. God bless you as you go out as he guides you into ministry.

ALFRED BULS
Bethel Evangelical Lutheran Church
University City, Missouri

Taking God at His Word
Luke 5:1-11

Because this Gospel is an ideal proof text for evangelism we tend to miss much of what it says. If somehow the words toward the end, "henceforth you will be catching men," were omitted, the passage still would be of compelling importance for the Christian life. We will concentrate especially this morning on two verses under the heading "Taking God at His Word." "And when he had ceased speaking, he said to Simon, 'Put out into the deep and let down your nets for a catch.' And Simon answered, 'Master, we toiled all the night and took nothing! But at your word I will let down the nets.'"

Recognizing God's Word

"He said to Simon, 'Put out into the deep and let down your nets for a catch.'" One of the primary problems of taking God at his word is knowing when God speaks. Many of us live with a private fable that runs, "I can't know God's word now, but if I had been there then . . . ." There are many things wrong with this idea, the chief of which is that it's probably not true. I suspect that most of us with a high degree of education, a scientific mind set and our late 20th century sophistication would be numbered not among the disciples but among the scoffers and the skeptics.

Peter, faced by this remarkable carpenter from Nazareth, had no written guarantee that he was the Messiah, that this was God speaking. Indeed in terms of the religion of his day and of most of the Scripture that he had available, he would have concluded otherwise. In view of Peter's later career, the conviction that this was the Lord was ambivalent and variable at best. Perhaps it was his preaching, or that he was caught up in the enthusiasm of the crowd—whatever it was, Jesus' words confronted Peter with authority and he obeyed. The Old Testament story of the calling of Isaiah reflects that same kind of response to the authority of God's Word. "I heard the voice of the Lord saying, 'whom shall I send, and who will go for us?' Then I said, 'here am I! Send me.'"

Today we live in a world where many of the images of authority have been fading. A generation ago the very word "mother" brought tears to the eyes. Now a word about motherhood, unless it be a critical one, is likely to be regarded as schmaltz. The very concept of patriotism, of loyalty to country and flag, produces among many people a large measure of cynicism. The fading image of religious authority has come to apply not only to the pastor but to the Bible, the church, and to God himself.

Part of the problem may be that we think we know something of God's word, concerned as it is with quaint ideas of sheep and sowing seed and vineyards and chosen people—and we have found it irrelevant to most of life.

We need to recognize that there are different levels to taking God at his Word. Most of us have remained pretty close to the surface. Finding God's Word generally means turning to the Bible and looking for a specific prescription to every ill, a ready-made solution to every problem, and then following biblical instructions no matter what. For example, the Jehovah's Witnesses, finding a rule about the drinking of blood in the book of Leviticus, concluded that it forbade transfusions. Or some of our fundamentalist brethren have found God's Word most clearly enunciated in rules about drinking and card playing and sex, and have little time left for matters of love and justice. Or—and here I need to add a "mea culpa—I, too, am guilty"—in our Lutheran insistence on theological purity we have often misread Luther's doctrine of the two kingdoms to mean that the church and individual Christians must limit our concern to churchly affairs. So in Germany, Hitler seized power almost unchallenged by the church. And here in America we have hesitated overly long in proclaiming God's Word in terms of racial tensions and in the threat of a nuclear war.

Certainly the answer must lie in dealing with God's Word on deeper levels than simple prescriptions and rules and pretailored solutions to problems of which we are not yet aware. There is a depth in God's Word that meets the real world of commerce and unemployment, of education and science, of clubs and sports, of friendship and politics, of status and wealth, of race and technology, of poverty and international tension. Taking God at his word in this world is far more complex than simply finding biblical rules and following them.

Hearing God's Word and Following

There are no simple, easy solutions. We can only make a beginning, but a beginning that starts in a different direction. To hear God's Word for today we need to read the Scriptures not for rules and regulations, not even to gather a few basic principles like honesty and purity. We need instead to see the person behind and under and through the Scriptures. Faith and trust are always in a person. The Christian sees that person as God revealed in Jesus Christ.

So Peter came face to face not with rules and regulations and instruc-tions about how to fish but with a person who called him, made demands upon him, tested him, and loved him. And so the biblical witness—writers set down the record of their experience with God and his word for them. And we are confronted with a call and demand and guidance of a person, of the Christ, who is as truly Lord of the World today as in Peter's day. It is to life in this real world around us that God's Word calls us and in which we find God. Dietrich Bonhoeffer, the German martyr theologian, caught the vision most clearly.

> Whoever evades the earth does not find God. He finds only another world; his own, better, more beautiful, more peaceful world. He finds a world beyond, to be sure, but one that is not God's world, that world which is dawning in this world. Whoever evades the earth in order to find God, finds only himself.

So in this alienated, cynical, sophisticated world in which you and I live, we need to listen carefully as God's Word calls us as truly as it called Peter. It comes not in rules and prescriptions and prefabricated answers but as we come face to face with the Person of God as he calls out to us in Scripture, in the Christ who came not as king but as servant, and in the world of need and unrest which he came to serve and to save. His call is insistent—"Come, follow me, put out into the deep and follow me."

FRED E. RINGHAM
Mount Carmel Lutheran Church
Minneapolis, Minnesota

SIXTH SUNDAY AFTER THE EPIPHANY

Genuine Revolution
Luke 6:17-26

When I was a college student back in the radical, unsettled sixties, watching the burials of King and Kennedy, with Vietnam a daily re-minder of manufactured death, part of the campus language, the lexicon of that time, was talk about the coming revolution.

That was the campus byword, the "Revolution" soon to come.

When the college administration interposed bureaucratic regulations to which we took offense, we'd say, "Wait until the revolution."

Whenever things seemed unfair, unjust—"Wait until the revolution."

Whenever the politicians lied to us and leaders seemed remote—"Wait until the revolution."

That was something of the dream. A coming political reality where all things would be put right. Social justice, equity, peace for all, plenty for the poor, power to the people . . . all of it just around the corner. "Just wait," we'd say to each other, "just wait until the revolution."

There aren't many of my generation who speak of the revolution today. Most of us are now good Democrats, or good Republicans, or at the very least, thoughtful Independents. Some sell insurance, some are lawyers, some operate computers, some sit in Congress, others administer government programs. Not a few have been born again. And some stand in pulpits.

But no one speaks of the revolution anymore.

Whatever it once meant, it is now nothing more than the shattered mythology of a period noted for polemics and protest.

Trouble was, we looked for the wrong revolution.

We weren't seeking the genuine signs of revolution—genuine signs such as those found in this morning's Gospel.

How blest are you who are in need; the kingdom of God is yours.

How blest are you who now go hungry; your hunger shall be satisfied.

How blest are you who weep now; you shall laugh.

How blest you are when men hate you, when they outlaw you and insult you, and ban your very name as infamous, because of the Son of Man.

On that day be glad and dance for joy; for assuredly you have a rich reward in heaven; in just the same way did their fathers treat the prophets.

But alas for you who are rich; you have had your time of happiness.

Alas for you who are well fed now; you shall go hungry.

Alas for you who laugh now; you shall mourn and weep.

Alas for you when all speak well of you; just so did their fathers treat the false prophets.

(Luke 6:20-26 NEB)

The revolution has come, though we call it by another name.

Echoing John the Baptist: "Behold, the kingdom of God has come upon you. Repent and hear the Good News."

The blessings and woes reported by St. Luke contain within them a radical revision of priorities where the rich are sent away empty and the hungry are filled full; the proud and arrogant are pulled down and the humble and poor are raised up; where those who laugh with the pleasures of the world will lose it all and weep, and those who weep will find a time of delight.

There have been attempts to spiritualize this message from Luke . . . to say, for example, that the poor spoken of are not the economically poor but merely the poor in spirit—to say that the hungry are not those of the earth who hunger daily but merely those who hunger after God's Word—to say that the rich and mighty who are given this awesome warning are just those who think and act like tyrants and not those who run roughshod over the weak and trod upon the helpless.

There may be some value in spiritualizing what Luke has reported, but to do so and then leave it there would be unfaithful to the biblical witness.

Composed largely of the urban poor, the early church attracted the poor, the slaves, the socially rejected, and they would have understood Jesus in a social and political sense, as well as in a spiritual sense.

At the time Luke reports Jesus' message, first century Palestine was victimized by acute economic and political unrest. The land was held mostly by absentee landlords and the farmers were little more than serfs. Urban poverty was as bad then as it is today. The whole of the homeland was held in the grip of an occupying army. Adding to the strife, the Jewish faith was splintered into competing sects, some of which sought accommodation with the occupiers while others waged terrorism and called for revolution. Before the century would end all of these factors and more would explode into armed rebellion and the destruction of Jerusalem herself. There is little reason to believe that those who first heard this message from Jesus were not themselves victims of the oppressive Romans and absentee landlords and the stifling taxation.

In such a setting, the words of Jesus would resound loudly and gladly in the ears of the Christian poor. For them the Christian Gospel meant that ultimately the blessed of God were not the rich and powerful who tyrannized the poor. Rather, the poor themselves were the holy ones of God.

Reformers of all times have advocated social revolutions which would redress the grievances of the poor against the rich. Generally, such revolutions would be limited to no more than leveling class distinctions by making the poor sufficiently rich and the powerless sufficiently powerful.

But the words of Christ, for all their political and economic implications, are not some kind of manifesto which the poor of the world can hurl against the rich. Instead, we come to the heart of the Gospel: blessed are the poor, the meek, those who mourn the sorrows of the world; blessed are the wretched and the abused of the earth . . . blessed are these for they shall inherit God himself as their father.

The social reform envisioned by Christ is nothing less than God's intervention into the affairs of human history. It extends far beyond mere human visions of this or that political utopia—it goes to the very heart of what it means to be under God's protection and love.

We have here Christ crucified, beckoning us to recognize not political revolution, not redistributed wealth, but the comfort of God who by his saving act has truly conquered all the oppressive powers of the earth. In Christ, we discover and proclaim the God who has blessed the poor, the humble, who gives sight to the blind and sets at liberty all those who dwell in darkness.

But in speaking these words, Jesus also speaks harsh truth. It was a harsh message then—an even harsher one now.

The image of a God who sends the rich away empty and promises sorrow for those who laugh now is an awful message for those of us, myself included, who live outlandishly comfortable lives compared with most of the world.

It is a message that strikes at the very core of our suburban, consumeristic life-styles, judging and condemning each of us individually.

Understand this message . . . God will send the rich away, but the humble and the poor he will comfort.

By the standards of this world, into which category do you fall?

The nations of the earth spend far more on the engines of war than on the elimination of hunger. Hatred makes warfare and hunger commonplace. The United States exports $14 billion worth of armaments to foreign countries each year, more than any other nation on earth, including the Soviet Union.

In the great nations of the earth, missiles are harbored underground awaiting the word to go and kill the peoples, and more is spent each year in an unending cycle of deadly "peacekeeping." As President Eisenhower said, "Every gun that is made, every warship launched, every missile fired represents a theft from those who hunger and are not fed, from those who are naked and are not clothed."

The Western nations—with less than one-third of the world's population—consume two-thirds of the earth's resources.

Our consumer living frustrates ourselves and those about us because of our possessiveness and insatiable demands upon the resources of the world.

The average family, my own included, spends more on an automobile in one month than most Third World families spend on food in one year.

The poor, the unsettled, the disinherited of the world weep because their children die of malnutrition and warfare.

And Lazarus sits at the rich man's gate begging crumbs, if not justice, while the dogs of war and selfishness lick his wounds.

God's light shines for the world. But we sit in darkness.

The message is harsh.

But is it not also a message of immense joy, an announcement of Holy Revolution?

Who is there among us to dispute what Christ has said?

Who is there among us who does not wish to see the humble uplifted, the hungry filled?

When pictures of dying children flash across our television screens, who among us is not possessed of a desire to extend a healing hand if that were in our power?

You and I, we believe this proclamation of Christ. We believe it and that is why we are gathered here today . . . we gather to proclaim the Christ who proclaimed comfort to the poor.

I am not naive enough to believe for one moment that if we dispose of all our goods, alter our diets, drive 10-year-old cars, that the poor will be one wit better off than they are now. But this knowledge does not in the least excuse our ignorance of their plight, nor does it allow us to continue in our own self-indulgence at their expense. On the basis of Luke's Gospel, to align ourselves with God and Christ means to align ourselves with the poor and the hungry and the humble.

It is quite clear, as we see ourselves the Chosen of God, we must also see ourselves with the poor.

Given all of this, how then shall we reconcile our wealth with the message of Christ?

We cannot.

There is no way we can ever reconcile it all.

But perhaps, just perhaps, as with so many other things, we simply live in ambiguity, knowing we are under God's judgment while nonetheless living in confidence that his kingdom shall come to us as well.

All of this means that

• we will do our good works knowing we never do enough

• we will contribute to the American Lutheran Church Hunger Appeal knowing we can never contribute enough

• we will give to Indian Concerns knowing we never give enough

• we will help supply the area food pantry knowing we will never supply enough

• we will live, in other words, knowing that in the end, the very End, we have only the mercy of God in which to place our trust.

We have signs of that mercy already.

We have the Sacrament of Baptism which called us to him before most of us knew it.

We hear of his mercy in the words of absolution spoken in confession.

But most especially, we see and taste and sense his mercy in the Supper of our Lord.

In this Meal we have a fleeting glimpse of the coming kingdom, for in this Meal the poor find fullness and the rich forgiveness.

In this Meal the humble and the mighty find equal space and all have place at the Lord's Table.

In this Meal rich and poor, mighty and low, come equally before God as forgiven sinners and Jesus continues his habit of eating with known outcasts.

At this Table we Christians locate our commitment to the handicapped, the teeming refuse of foreign shores, the poor, the dispossessed, with all who hunger and thirst for the justice of God.

It is here, and only here, that Lazarus gets well and children live.

RUSSELL E. SALTZMAN
Emmaus and Immanuel Congregations
Kennard and Orum, Nebraska

SEVENTH SUNDAY AFTER THE EPIPHANY

Good for Nothing
Luke 6:27-38

I've got this problem. I don't look much like a preacher, and sometimes I don't act much like one either. Consequently there are many times when I am not regarded as such. Just the other day, for instance, while I was making my rounds at the local nursing home, I visited an elderly woman who is both a bit forgetful and even harder of hearing. And so, leaning close to her ear, I sought to re-introduce myself to her for perhaps the third or fourth time. "I'm Pastor Nestingen," I explained in a voice much louder than necessary, "from up at the Greenfield Lutheran Church." Unfazed, however, she shot back immediately in a stern and most patronizing tone, "Oh, you think so, do you?"

Now apparently that's the kind of excusable abuse every preacher must learn to live with, regardless of whether its source be the well-meaning, even if somewhat blunt little old lady at the nursing home or the resident ne'er-do-well whose constant claim that the pastor actually works only a few hours a week really gets under your skin. My standard reply to such painful parishioners is usually something to the effect that ". . . the worst thing about doing nothing is that you can never take a day off!"

Snappy comebacks notwithstanding, however, I'd probably be the first to admit that I'm somewhat more sensitive than most to such veiled insults. Indeed, I often find myself feeling the part of that frenetic comic,

73

Rodney Dangerfield. For I, too, am engaged in a lifelong search for some semblance of respect, if not for me personally, then at least for my profession.

It all began, as a good Freudian might say, in my youth. Not that my potty training was somehow inadequate, but it was simply all that negative reinforcement I received. I mean, I feel like the guy who, much to the surprise of those who knew him best, decided to go into the ministry. His mother responded by saying, "Oh, I'm sure he will make a fine pastor. After all, he does seem to know so much about sin!" Not what I would consider a sterling recommendation by any stretch of the imagination. When I am asked to produce the credentials of my calling, I often respond, tongue-in-cheek, "Well, you know, my parents always wanted me to be a doctor so they could be sick for nothing. But I fooled them! I went and became a preacher so they could be good for nothing!"

An Otherwise Offensive Phrase

Good for nothing?? Yes, to be good . . . for nothing!! This is what Christ is calling us to do on this day in those Gospel words excerpted from his Sermon on the Plain. And it is this same twist of a phrase, once so ably pressed into service as a poignant put-down, which now describes with equal audacity the strange, new standard of Christian excellence set before us this day. For it is in the words of this otherwise insidious insult that we find captured a Christian corrective to the inadequacy of a morality which merely mimics the ways of the world.

Jesus is serving notice on the reduction of all matters religious to a preconceived notion of human give-and-take, the accommodation of God's will for you and for me to a prefabricated personal code of ethics. There'll be no more carrot-and-stick approach to ethics in the kingdom, and Christians will no longer conduct themselves on a business-as-usual basis. All so-called incentives to good behavior, all ulterior motives must be set aside. It's not tit-for-tat or you-scratch-my-back-and-I'll-scratch-yours. For Jesus says in so many words, "You've heard of being good for something. Now let me tell you about being good . . . for nothing!"

But wait a minute. It's not as if Jesus intends to suggest for the Christian something in the same sense of what we might mean when we cast aspersions on another's character by stating succinctly, and yet usually after the fact that we knew all along they'd never amount to much. Nor is this understanding of the Christian life to be misconstrued as the cowboy's ultimate insult wherein the worst that can be said of someone who fails to pull their own load is that they are simply a waste of good food.

No, and yet nevertheless what Christ says, and says quite clearly today is that we as Christians are expected in some strange way to set our sights on a kind of unconscious Christianity, the character of which is defined by its willingness not only to love for nothing, but also to do good for nothing and even to lend for nothing as well. Ultimately, in fact, this is the goal, this is the purpose of today's text: that we would arrive at some understanding of the delightfully divine inner illogic of merely being good . . . for nothing. Christ has now loaded an otherwise offensive phrase with a completely new and different meaning.

To Love for Nothing

But now let's get down to cases. For what does Christ himself ask of us, not just once, but three separate times? To begin with he asks, "If you love those who love you, what credit is that to you?" After all, he adds, "even sinners love those who love them." And I say, "Ain't that the truth!" For the world duly demonstrates that even the lowest of the low share in a certain comradery and fellowship. Even sinners fear, love and trust those who fear, love and trust them back. Therefore what must set us apart as Christians from the rest of these is our willingness to love both God and one another, not for what we can get out of it, but rather both literally and figuratively for nothing.

Thus the situation for us as Christians should be like unto that of the husband who, for no apparent reason at all, came home one evening from work, presented his wife with a dozen red roses, gave her a hug, and said those endearing words, "Honey, I love you!" Whereupon she immediately burst into tears. "What on earth is the matter?" he wondered. "What a day!" she complained. "First the washer broke down. Then Junior fell out of his high chair. And now you've come home drunk!"

Yes, and so shall there be some rather strange reactions to the Christian set free by Christ's call to love for nothing. It will be as the sentiments expressed in a slightly altered version of a by-now famous Broadway musical standard: "A bell is not a bell until you ring it. A song is not a song until you sing it. Love in your heart is not put there to stay; love is not love until you give it away" . . . for nothing!

To Do Good for Nothing

But again Christ wonders, "If you do good to those who do good to you, what credit is that to you?" What credit indeed, especially as the verse concludes "even sinners do the same." And here again the same principles seem to apply. For despite the fact that the world has sought to re-write the Golden Rule to read, "Do unto others before they do it unto you!" nevertheless the situation is such that even sinners are more happy to meet a kindness halfway. What must distinguish Christians from all others, then, is an alternative agenda to do good, not with a mind to favors repaid in kind, but again, both literally and figuratively, for nothing.

It is as the story oft told of a stranded motorist. Having found his way to the door of a nearby farmhouse, he had intended to call the nearest town for a tow truck. But the farmer would not hear of it, and was more than obliging in restoring the stranger's car to running condition. In turn, the thankful motorist tried to offer the farmer some money for his troubles. He refused to accept it, of course, but as the motorist persisted in his offer, the farmer finally said to the man, "Look, mister, I'm feelin' pretty good about having helped you out. And if I took your money, you'd buy that feeling back from me. So with all due respect for your generosity, I'll have to insist that it's simply not for sale!"

Yes, and there is something to be said for the Christian who would adopt a similar attitude toward doing good deeds. For Christ has already labored to liberate us from the need to keep a running tally with our neighbor, from the built-in profit margin implicit in our every good deed. No, but this is not the way with the kingdom. Good works only intended to help us get ahead with God are not, by definition, good works at all. Rather we must simply plunge ahead, doing good that we might be good . . . for nothing.

To Lend for Nothing

But finally now Jesus concludes that "if you lend to those from whom you hope to receive, what credit is that to you?" And once again he re-affirms the fact that "even sinners lend to sinners, to receive as much again." But the truth of the maxim almost goes without saying. For in matters of our material possessions and money, even Christians have more business sense than common sense. Yet perhaps it is in this regard that we shy most of all from taking up a peculiar Christian identity as we fail to see that our investments would pay ever higher dividends as we venture in faith to lend for nothing.

All of which might simply serve to put one in mind of that story concerning the man who dragged his wife of many years into divorce court. "Money, money, money!" he complained to the judge. "That's all I've heard about since the day we were married. Not a day has gone by that she hasn't hounded me about it. I tell you I'm sick and tired of it, and I won't have it anymore!" The judge, somewhat sympathetic with the man's plight, nevertheless tried to maintain his objectivity. "Tell me, sir," the judge began, "What is it that she does with all of this money?" "Well, your honor," the man replied, "I couldn't rightly say. You see, the fact of the matter is that I haven't really given her any yet!"

And so it might be for us as Christians. We live with the nagging doubt that selfless giving is only for the foolhardy in faith when the fact of the matter is that we really haven't tried it yet. We are certain that generosity pays off only for those who can afford it, and again it may only be because we have no intention of being generous in the first place. So the kingdom is not cost-effective! So what? There is certainly nevertheless low overhead and an even lower price tag hung on our salvation, and it all happens for us as we are led to lend . . . for nothing.

To Be Good for Nothing

To love . . . for nothing. To do good . . . for nothing. To lend . . . for nothing. Ultimately to be appraised by Christ himself as good . . . for nothing. This is the clarion call of today's Gospel, and the mark of faith which, when exhibited, will differentiate the Christian from the rest of the world. For as Christ sums up, "Love your enemies, and do good, and lend, expecting nothing in return;" so we begin to glimpse the superiority of both loving and lending, both doing and being . . . good for nothing. For this is the essence of real and radical Christian living as we become engaged in a kind of unconscious Christianity, doing whatever we can, whenever we can, for whomever we can, automatically and as a conditioned-response to God's grace.

Indeed, we would liken it unto the little boy who'd been in and out of trouble all day long. Finally in frustration Mother asked her young son, "Why can't you just be a good little boy?" The precocious youth, a con artist at heart piped up, "Oh, but Mommy, I'll be good for a nickel!" But Mommy, never at a loss for words herself, simply stared and then observed, "Why don't you be like your Daddy, and be good for nothing!" Yes, and that's it. For this is what Jesus is inviting us both to do and to be today. He is saying, in so many words, "Why don't you be like your Father in heaven, and be good . . . for nothing! But now let me warn you, once again, . . . the worst thing about doing nothing is that you can never take a day off!

ROLF NESTINGEN
Greenfield Lutheran Church
Harmony, Minnesota

Toward Becoming a Whole Person
Luke 6:39-49

One of life's essential struggles, often not clearly recognized, is the thrust toward becoming a full and complete person. In our more reflective moments we have the feeling that we are not what we could be. An innocent question in a child's book of riddles sets us up: What is the biggest room in the world? The answer: Not a palace or a stadium but "room for improvement"! Of course! Deep in our hearts we know there is more to life than we have made of it, more to faith than we have ever exercised, more to love than we have ever been willing to commit ourselves.

Perhaps you don't think about this much at all. You like to take whatever comes and do what you can with it. No one is perfect, so why not come to terms with yourself? Be satisfied with what you are! But life won't let you off that easy. There is a pull between your best self and your worst self, between doing the right thing and what is more convenient and comfortable. It is what the apostle calls the conflict between flesh and spirit, between the old man and the new man. You cannot bow out of that and head for the spectator's benches.

Have you not had to scale down your dreams, settling for a lot less than you thought you would have to, and feeling quite dismayed at what happened? How about those plans you could never bring off, or the future that once seemed endless but now keeps getting shorter and shorter? Events put your life in disarray and there isn't enough time to set things right.

A Vermont farmer, a confirmed bachelor for many years, finally took the bold step and got married. Months later he was asked by one of his friends, "Did you do as well as you thought?" "No," he replied, "but come to think of it, I'm not sure she did either!" There is a difference between the man you thought you married and the husband you got. Perhaps you got more than you expected. In any circumstance, marriage is a union of two incomplete persons. If we are at all earnest about life, we feel deeply the striving, the yearning toward becoming a whole person.

In "church language" we are treading at the edges of a subject called sanctification—the ongoing process by which God makes us holy in heart and life. This yearning to be more than what we are is the place where the Holy Spirit takes hold to move us toward the "measure of the stature of the fullness of Christ." This is the burden of the Gospel for this Sunday —Luke's selection of statements by Jesus—that light up the narrow contours of our lives and inspire us to move toward what we by the grace of God can become.

The Place of Beginning

If in fact we are restless with the way we are and yearn to move toward greater wholeness, we are summoned first to be honest with ourselves. It takes courage to look at ourselves truthfully, with all masks stripped away. It is the place of beginning.

With characteristically extravagant language to make a point, Jesus asked, "Why do you see the speck that is in your brother's eye, but do not notice the log that is in your own eye?" It is a human trait, common to us all, that we can see faults in others we fail to see in ourselves. Our own blemish may be ten times greater, but it is easier to pass judgment on others. Some are so insecure in themselves that they are compelled to put the other person down in order to enhance their own feeling of superiority.

Jesus insists that we be forthright and honest with ourselves, face up to our faults and sins, and remove the log from our own eye, before we try to correct another.

This is what is involved in repentance. It is the courage to identify and claim ownership of our sins, to see them with deep regret and inner shame, and then in a faith-inspired act, thrust them into the welcoming mercy of God!

This demand of Jesus for honesty has a sharp edge and cuts across our whole society. In the January, 1982, issue of Harper's Magazine, Sally Helgesen has published an essay on "Theoretical Families" in which she notes the keen interest in "pro family" legislation among certain political leaders. A "Family Protection Act" is proposed containing some thirty laws and prohibitions that some conservatives believe "will restore an America that probably never was." The author then goes on to point out that the bill is sponsored by a Senator who recently divorced his wife of twenty years to marry a woman half his age. Two of the bill's original sponsors have been arrested on morals charges while a third advocate was convicted for bribery! Obviously, there are many sincere and solid people concerned for shoring up the life of the family in our society. But how easy it is to see the specks of sawdust in the eye of another while ignoring a whole rubbish pile close at hand! Like charity, honesty begins at home. No one can become a whole person without it.

The Source of Integrity

It is important to remember that growth toward wholeness is nourished at the center of our lives. It is inner health that gives shape and form to our visible deeds. You don't look for bad fruit on a good tree, for figs from a thorn bush, nor do you pick grapes from a bramble bush. "The good man out of the good treasure of his heart produces good, and the evil man out of his evil treasure produces evil; for out of the abundance of the heart his mouth speaks."

It may be that the way we dress makes a good impression in an interview; carefully chosen words can make us appear confident and competent, but if it is all fabrication covering a hollowness inside, the game will soon be over. If we are trying to put our best foot forward, do we not have to use the other foot once in awhile? Integrity is not a garment we wear for appropriate occasions. It is the outward expression of an interior experience of the shaping presence of God. There forgiveness has swept the room clean, unworthy motives have been purged, what was once dead has come alive, and it all begins to show in a life-style marked by grace and love. The good tree bears good fruit. The hands do what the heart feels. The feet go where the mind directs, and actions grow out of convictions deeply held.

This is why the thrust of the gospel is toward the re-creation, re-formation, and the renewal of each individual person. It reveals the action of God in creating a new man and a new woman. It is the good tree bearing good fruit that makes the difference. The church is to be the "forest of good trees", an integral part of the landscape, its fruits bearing witness to God's creative and renewing powers. Out of the abundance of the heart the mouth speaks, the mind thinks, the words flow, and the feet move toward the tasks that need doing. Wholeness is nourished from the center. It grows from the inside out!

Wholeness Made Visible

Clearly, God has a role marked out for those who are eager to make more of their potential as his servants, set in this place at this time. They are to be like the city set on a hill which cannot be hid, the lamp that lights up the whole house. Jesus comes at it from the other side: "Can a blind man lead a blind man? Will they not both fall into a pit?" Of course! It is the one who sees who can lead the way. It is the person who has been ruggedly honest with himself and dealt with the frailties and foibles of his own life, who has been made secure by the grace of God to stand openly before the world. It is the person whose inner life has been transformed by grace and set free from hidden tyrannies, whose life in the world is a witness to the continuing creative and redeeming activity of God. As men and women get their act together, as their brokenness is healed, and the fragmented pieces of their lives are fitted into place, they become whole persons and the territory around them is brightened.

Is not this about where we are? We are not yet what we can be, but God is not finished with us. The Holy Spirit draws us into the process of becoming holy in heart and life. As we are stretched and pulled toward wholeness, the truth of what God is doing among us becomes more visible. And the unbelieving world is startled by the discovery that he who once became man in Jesus Christ and walked among us, is among us still, embodied in those who name his name! They may not look like him, at least as others picture him, but their words are marked by his accent, and their actions extend his remarkable effort to embrace the whole world with his love. Whole people committed to holy tasks are disciples who have become like their Teacher! May their numbers ever increase!

RAYMOND W. HEDBERG
Arlington Hills Lutheran Church
St. Paul, Minnesota

A Glimpse of Glory
Luke 9:28-36

Next Wednesday is Ash Wednesday, the beginning of Lent, the season of our remembrance of the suffering and sacrifice of Christ. Today is the last Sunday in the season of Epiphany—the season of the manifestation and revelation of Christ to all the world. This is also the Sunday of the Transfiguration of our Lord—a Sunday for the celebration of the glory of God revealed in Jesus Christ. It is almost a kind of ecclesiastical Mardi Gras—a time of final celebration before entering the penetential season of Lent.

There is much that we can't understand about the transfiguration. What actually happened? We can't be sure. There is much mystery here. Jesus himself in Matthew 17:9 speaks of it as a vision. We have no final word on the physiology, or physics or the psychology of this event.

But we do know that it had a profound impact upon Peter, James, and John and that it seeks to have a similar effect upon us. We can't go back and enter into their experience, but through this text their experience

81

seeks to enter into our lives so that Jesus can be for us now, in some small measure at least, what he was so powerfully for them then.

"They Saw His Glory"

For one thing this text seeks to move us to reverence, awe and wonder. "They saw his glory" (Luke 9:32). They were so moved that they wanted to build some booths there to make the place into a sacred shrine. Through this text we are invited to catch at least a glimpse of the glory they experienced.

This story of the transfiguration reminds us of the experience of Moses in the theopany of the burning bush. Remember how he came upon a burning bush that was not consumed and that a voice spoke saying "Do not come near; put off your shoes from your feet, for the place on which you are standing is holy ground" (Exod. 3:5).

On this Epiphany Sunday as we ponder the revelation of the glory of God in the transfiguration of Christ, we too bow in awesome adoration before God's holy presence. This is a time for trust and thankfulness. It is also a time to sing with reverent praise "Holy, Holy, Holy, Lord God Almighty!"

We are all tempted to take great wonders for granted. The story is told of a mother who was taking her little girl on her first train trip. As they rode across the countryside, the little girl was so excited that she kept jumping up and down and pointing out the window "Look mommy! There's a bird! There's a cloud! There's a tree! There's a cow!" Sensing that her daughter's exuberance was distracting the other passengers, the mother apologized "Please forgive my little girl's excitement. The world is still wonderful to her."

I hope the world is still wonderful for all of us—the singing bird, the opening flower, the glory of a starlit night, the waning moon, the rising sun! We look out into the starry night and behold a tiny bit of the vastness of a universe so far beyond our ability to understand or comprehend. And there is mystery too in little things, so tiny and yet so vast in wonder! Lifeless creation teems with potential for life. The building blocks of life are built into it—life of grass and flowers and trees and bugs and beetles and bees and birds; the life of trout and hummingbirds and collie dogs and crocodiles; the life of eagles and elephants—creatures large and small beyond our counting! There is mystery here and wonder beyond our ability to comprehend or to express. As I try to capture and convey a little of this awesome wonder, I sense my limits as did Jennie Armstrong who wrote these lines:

82

I tried to write a song today
But bird's song led my thoughts away . . .
A bobwhite calling to his mate
A wild rose blooming at the gate . . .
A babbling brook among the flowers
Freshened by the morning showers.
I cannot write a song today
My thoughts have traveled far away.

There is so much mystery, so much at which to wonder in the living things around us. But then we think of the mystery of another conscious, creative living being—we think of the mystery of our own lives. Atoms and molecules of air and earth and water coming somehow together into self-awareness. Molecules aware of themselves and of others. Molecules that can think and dream and fear and hope. Molecules that can sing and create a symphony. Molecules coming together to be loved and to love. Now we move beyond awe to reverence—to what Albert Schweitzer called reverence for life. Does it sometimes happen to you as it does to me, that when visiting with a friend or spouse or child your thoughts are distracted from the conversation as you just look at that person and are struck by awesome wonder of what it is to be a human being. Each one of us is a universe of living mystery as great in wonder as all the mystery of the vast lifeless universe itself.

Yet the mystery of creation around us and of our own being is but the beginning of mysteries. On this day of Epiphany transfiguration our awe and wonder, our reverence, is not just for creation nor for life, nor even for human life. Today we rightly sing "Holy, Holy, Holy, Lord God Almighty!" Today we pray as we have prayed so often, and often so thoughtlessly, "For thine is the kingdom and the power and the glory forever." Today we bow down to worship God with joy and thankfulness and also with reverence and with awe.

To speak of God is to ponder one who, though he has promised always to be with us is yet always far beyond us. "For my thoughts are not your thoughts, neither are your ways my ways, says the LORD. For as the heavens are higher than the earth, so are my ways higher than your ways and my thoughts than your thoughts" (Isa. 55:8-9).

This theme of the greatness and glory and holiness and majesty and mystery of God is one that runs through all of Scripture. Today it is condensed and focused in the disciples' experience of the transfiguration of our Lord. It expands our thoughts and enlarges our imagination. It is beyond us, but it is not beyond the possibilities and power of God who is "able to do far more abundantly than all that we ask or think." And so we say with Paul "To him be glory in the church and in Christ Jesus to all generations forever and ever" (Eph. 3:20-21). That word glory is the word from which our word doxology comes. To glimpse the glory of God is to be moved to sing the doxology:

Praise God from whom all blessings flow;
Praise him, all creatures here below;
Praise him above ye heavenly host;
Praise Father, Son and Holy Ghost.

We especially praise God this morning because his power is not limited by the littleness of our faith. When doubts and fears assail us, we thank God that he is indeed able to do more than all that we can ask or think. We thank God that he has given us this mysterious and in so many ways unbelievable gift of life. We thank and praise him for having permitted us to glimpse his glory with Peter, James, and John in the transfiguration of our Lord.

"Listen to Him"

Having pondered the glory of God in the transfiguration of Jesus we are tempted to sing the doxology and to go home, but having paused to praise we are now prompted to listen. That voice that spoke to those three disciples now speaks also to us "This is my son, my chosen; listen to him!"—listen to him! We are not just to praise him, we are to hear him.

Jesus is God's word to us. The word of God in the most basic sense is not in words but in a person. "And the word became flesh and dwelt among us, full of grace and truth; we have beheld his glory, glory as of the only son from the father" (John 1:14).

Jesus is God's word to us. "In many and various ways God spoke of old to our fathers by the prophets; but in these last days he has spoken to us by a son, whom he appointed the heir of all things, through whom also he created the world. He reflects the glory of God and bears the very stamp of his nature, upholding the universe by his word of power" (Heb. 1:1-3).

Jesus is God's word to us. "Listen to him!" This year don't just give up something for Lent, add something to Lent. Read the New Testament. Read the Gospels. Read them as you read the front page of a newspaper. Read the New Testament letters. Read them as you read the editorial page of the morning newspaper. Read, not out of legalistic obligation but in eager anticipation especially of seeing and of hearing Jesus.

We have heard so much of Jesus, a lot of it second hand through pastors and teachers, that we think we know Jesus quite well. But no one knows all there is to know of Jesus. There are surprises, perhaps even revolutions, waiting to break through into our lives from new encounters with Jesus through the New Testament.

As we confront him, he challenges and corrects as well as comforts us. His ways too, are not identical with our ways. In him we are not to be "conformed to this world". But we are to be "transformed by the renewal of [our minds], that [we] may prove what is the will of God, what is good and acceptable and perfect" (Rom. 12:2).

We are often so captured by, and conformed to, the ways of the world around us that we don't even realize the extent to which our lives are out of harmony with the way of Christ.

An African and an American pastor were visiting together. The African told of certain marriage customs that were practiced in his congregation in Africa. The American pastor was so shocked that he asked "How can your people do those things and still claim to be Christian?" To which the African pastor replied, "As Americans you wonder at some of our practices, so we wonder at some of yours. How can you so satiate yourselves with wealth and wastefulness and still claim to be Christian?"

Whether we live in Africa or in America our challenge is not just to keep up with the Joneses next door but to let the love of Christ so control us that we are more and more conformed to him. Therefore we listen to him to learn of him that we might more and more live with the heart and mind and will revealed in Christ our Lord.

Forward with Jesus

With Peter, James, and John we have glimpsed his glory. We listen to him and now we seek to move forward with him. Those disciples wanted to settle down and make the place into a sacred shrine. Not so for Jesus. He had work to do. He was on the way toward the cross and the disciples were to move on with him. The vision was over and "Jesus was found alone" (Luke 9:36).

So now for us, we are given no perpetual vision of glory, no assurance of endless ecstasy. But we are given the abiding witness of Jesus. He has promised to be with us in our unfolding venture of living. He leads us on from visions of glory back into the details, even the dreary and dreadful and sometimes dirty details of our daily life.

As we follow him we discover that we too are being led on the way of the cross. That cross is not only the sign of God's suffering and saving love. That cross not only marks the cost of our eternal salvation. That cross tells of the way we are created to live. That cross shows the price of Christlike living in a sinful world.

The vision of glory is not given for our escape but for our encouragement and strengthening. Having glimpsed his glory we are to find our strength not in ourselves, not in our own wit and wisdom, not in the might of our money nor in the power of our nation but in the power of God who transfigures and transforms and empowers our lives to carry forward his will of love. As we have beheld his glory so now by his grace let us follow him even in the way of the cross.

LOWELL O. ERDAHL
University Lutheran Church of Hope
Minneapolis, Minnesota

Saved from the Time of Trial
Luke 4:1-13

Temptations to Take the Easier Way

One of my responsibilities as a father is the supervision of our children's piano practice and lessons. I am thrilled with them over the mastery of a piece of music, but I also feel anguish with them as they struggle to learn a new selection. The prospect of having to learn new notes, fingering, and dynamics is accompanied by a temptation. The temptation is to not bother with the new piece, to be satisfied with the old, familiar ones and not struggle with the new, harder one. The temptation is to take the easier way.

All of our days are filled with temptations to take the easier way: Shall I read this latest novel by John Irving or just watch "Dallas" on TV? Shall I pull on my jogging suit and run four miles this morning or just pull up the covers? Shall I talk out this conflict with my wife or walk away and hope for the problem to pass? We face hundreds of such situations each day in which the choice is not between what is good or evil, rather between what is harder and easier. The temptation is always strong to take the easier way.

Is this so serious? These seem like insignificant temptations. What's the concern? Helmut Thielicke helps to raise our concern about "harmless" temptations with this comment in *How Evil Came Into the World,* "The Tempter always operates in disguise. He hides behind a mask of harmless, indeed, pious benevolence. All temptations in life begin in sugared form. 'The people never know the devil's there, even though he has them by the throat,' says Mephistopheles in *Faust*." The harmless temptations are the most dangerous kind.

Jesus' "Harmless" Temptations

The Gospel for today describes one of Jesus' encounters with the tempter. The devil offers Jesus temptations which seem harmless. They are not temptations to do evil. The devil just encourages Jesus to choose an easier way to show the world that he is the Spirit-filled Son of God. Listen to these "harmless" temptations.

"Command this stone to become bread." Not a bad idea. A lot of good could come from such action. Changing stones to bread could be a giant step toward meeting the needs of millions of starving world citizens. If used properly, this bread-making power could provide a marvelous humanitarian service. Jesus was tempted to choose this way.

Or how about this way: "Accept the authority of all earthly kingdoms." Another worldwide suggestion. With Jesus in control of the world's political, military, and economic power, disarmament would be swift, peace would be certain, and an equal distribution of wealth would be immediate. This plan deserves some thought.

Or another way for Jesus to serve as the Son of God: "Dive off the temple tower and let God perform a dramatic rescue." This event would show that God can be manipulated to do what we want and need. He is at our service. Such a message would be appealing to the masses, for we like to hear that God will keep us successful and happy. This way would certainly attract the crowds and enlarge Jesus' following.

The appeal of these temptations was increased by their contrast to the way God has chosen for Jesus to fulfill his mission as Son of God. Jesus' temptations came just after his baptism in the River Jordan by John. This symbolic death in baptism served as a clear sign of the way God would bring to completion Jesus' appointed task—by another death—a death on the cross. Aware that the cross awaited him, Jesus surely was tempted to take some other, easier way. Such temptations did not cease, for Luke notes that the devil did not give up, rather "he departed until a more opportune time."

The Last Temptation of Christ

As Jesus drew nearer to the pain and horror of the cross, the temptations became more intense. Such is the point of view of Nikos Kazantzakis in his re-creation of Christ's life and passion in *The Last Temptation of Christ*. Kazantzakis portrays Jesus as tempted even as he hung on the cross. Kazantzakis' Jesus imagines what life would have been like had he chosen another way. In his coma-like dream Jesus gets married, fathers many children, enjoys the company of friends, and works as a kindly carpenter until he is a white bearded old man. The dream concludes as Jesus is confronted by his disciples. They were decrepit old men. Peter degenerated from a rock to a "sponge full of holes," and the others were spiritless men with "bloated bellies, dangling backsides, and double chins." Long ago they had given up the fight, and their destiny shriveled into meaninglessness. In their company was an angry Judas who bellowed the truth about the *un*crucified Jesus: "Traitor! Deserter! Your place was on the cross. That's where the God of Israel put you to fight. But you got cold feet, and the moment death lifted its head, you couldn't get away fast enough." The rest of the disciples joined in the chorus against Jesus, "Coward, Deserter, Traitor!" Jesus' dream was a horrible nightmare. His life had been wasted, for he fell to temptation and avoided the cross. He chose an easier way, and it proved to be the way of failure.

He Was Tempted as We Are Tempted—to Avoid the Cross

The author of Hebrews brings us into the temptation experience of Jesus with these words: "For we have not a high priest who is unable to sympathize with our weaknesses, but one who in every respect has been tempted as are we, yet without sin" (Heb. 4:15). Jesus' constant temptation was to choose another way than the cross. Our temptation is similar— to choose an easier way than the way of the cross.

All of God's sons and daughters have crosses to bear. We all can think of people who carry heavy crosses: the woman whose aging parent needs daily care; the husband whose wife has suffered at home with multiple sclerosis for 18 years; the parents whose daughter is plagued with severe mental illness; a young man who carries the weights of a friend who has no other friend. If you know people who don't have crosses, then you likely don't know them very well, for each of us in our own way has been given a cross.

But under the strain and pain of our crosses we are tempted as was Jesus. We wish for another way—an easier way. We say that there must be a happier way for us to live as baptized children of God. Some other way would have been better than this one. Instead of accepting the cross and experiencing the benefits of cross-bearing, we long for some other way. And so we are tempted as Jesus was tempted.

Kazantzakis' Jesus awakens from his nightmare to find himself on the cross. He is relieved as are we to discover that his uncrucified state was only a miserable dream. He was not a coward, a deserter, or traitor, for he was crucified. He accepted God's way. The closing words of the *The Last Temptation* lift high the central feature of our faith:

> Temptation had captured him for a split second and led him astray. The joys, marriages, and children were lies; the decrepit, degraded old men who shouted coward, deserter, traitor at him were lies. All—all were illusions sent by the Devil. His disciples were alive and thriving. They had gone over sea and land and were proclaiming the Good News. Everything had turned out as it should, glory be to God! He uttered a triumphant cry: "It is accomplished!" And it was as though he had said: Everything has begun.

Jesus died on the cross. He was faithful to God's plan. He did not fall to temptation. Oh, that we could say the same for ourselves. Too often our crosses become too painful, and we run from them. We fall to the temptation for an easier way. When we fail, our comfort is found in the Jesus who did not run away from the cross. He will bear the weight of even our crosses. He will do that forever if necessary, or long enough for our faith to be strengthened and our trust in God to be renewed so that we can pick up the crosses again and fulfill God's purposes for our lives. Our cross-bearing is erratic and uncertain. Jesus accepts all crosses. He bears them faithfully. He will not fail us.

Saved from the Time of Trial

We pray in the Lord's Prayer, "Save us from the time of trial." The time of trial and temptation will indeed come to us, and we cannot avoid it. Again and again we will be tempted to avoid the way of the cross. We may often fall to such temptations. However, we may be confident that we will not be destroyed by the temptations or by our failure. For Christ Jesus has declared God's victory over all temptations. His death on the cross establishes forever that love is more powerful than apathy; sacrifice is greater than selfishness; good is stronger than evil. Jesus' death on the cross proclaims that God's gracious plans for his chosen ones will not be defeated. Christ is crucified. He is faithful, loyal, obedient. Our prayers are answered. We are saved from the time of trial.

LOWELL J. TIMM
Capitol Drive Lutheran Church
Milwaukee, Wisconsin

Courage, Christian!
Luke 13:31-35

You never know when you'll need it, and sometimes we just need to hear the word to realize that we have it. Some of you may need to hear it now so I will say the word. Courage.

Courage, Christian! Courage—it can be yours for the right reason, for the right cause.

Courage. Prophets like Jeremiah had it and the Gospel for this day reminds us how Jesus prophetically demonstrated courage. Now understand, courage or bravery or whatever heroic determination is called—is not always a matter of being fearless. Sometimes it's just the opposite. Often courage is a matter of going ahead and doing what's right in spite of being afraid. That's what makes it courage. So . . .

Courage, Christian! It Can Be Ours in the Face of Danger

In the Gospel we heard Jesus was warned by some well-meaning Pharisees that he would be killed by Herod unless he fled. Instead, Jesus, apparently knowing what he was getting into, sent a message to Herod by these same Pharisees that was not exactly calculated to reduce the danger.

Of course, as Christians, we've been warned too that it's dangerous to follow someone named Jesus. Now maybe some have not read the label of their baptism, where it indicates something about persecution, hardship and suffering . . . but it's there. Perhaps, if some haven't appreciated the danger of baptism, that's because all our pomp and circumstance as a church can cause the sharpness of the Gospel to be dulled and the danger of following Jesus, covered up, and then we may find ourselves imperiled by a going-through-the-motions Christianity.

I remember a few years ago addressing a group of pastors and spouses, and in passing, I referred to the scandal of the Gospel and I could see in several faces that just didn't register. A scandal? When I added the word *skandalon* from the Greek, at least the clergy seemed to get the idea. Sometimes it's hard for us with our safe and traditional lives to understand the sense of stigma and danger that comes when you truly follow Jesus. You see, following Jesus will mean eventually going beyond the respectable limits of the world that expect Christianity to be comfortable and an experience where you get what you want out of it, and certainly something that shouldn't bother you and the way you live.

We really never will realize what kind of Christians we are until we face danger. Danger of any kind, if it's recognized, usually gets a response—either we panic and run or we stand and we fight.

Would Jesus panic? Would he be put off by the threat of the bully Herod? It was real enough, but apparently, seeing himself as one of the prophets, with some undisguised irony he said, "It cannot be that a prophet should perish away from Jerusalem." Do you get it—I'm here already and I am a prophet at least, and this is a good place to die! Jesus expected to suffer and die.

Danger. Will we be put off by it? Sometimes we are. Sometimes we run instead of fight the good fight of faith. There are all kinds of illustrations that we could tell about that—the temptation to laugh with everyone else at the jokes about the Poles or Blacks, or the expectation that we'll give in and cut corners at our work like everybody else. But this story presents us with a new opportunity to find our courage in the face of danger and danger's threat of suffering.

In this life we are going to suffer. It's part of living in a sinful world. But there seem to be two categories of suffering. Sometimes we suffer because we are untrue to Christ, and we call that sin. And sometimes we suffer because we are true, and we call that faith. The question, however, is not how we can avoid suffering for Jesus' sake, but how shall we endure it and the answer is . . . courage.

Courage, Christian! It Must Be Ours for the Sake of Duty

One's true duty is not a matter of routine or a mindless following of some inexplicable direction which once may have had a meaning, but now is carried on only with the hollow ring of "It's my duty," or maybe the more hollow ring of "It's your duty."

Jesus saw his duty and because he saw it, it must have strengthened him to then be able to say, "Go, tell that fox, 'Behold, I cast out demons and perform cures today and tomorrow and the third day I finish my course.'" Jesus would not be deterred.

Ah, the focus of that third day is on his duty. A duty chosen by the Father and accepted by the Son, so that in spite of all the danger, there could be a resurrection . . . for more than one. And because there is, we now can do our duty of proclaiming Christ and him crucified. But that is the scandal—Christ crucified—and we just might be nailed with him if we don't go along with the jokes or the cheating.

His story must be told. And, as you know, in this congregation that's what the Meaning of Life Class is really all about. It comes down to a story of a scandal that we try to tell in six weeks.

Part of that scandal also includes praying that people will accept an invitation to come and listen to the story and believe it as they've never believed it before and if they've had faith before, to see it grow and if they haven't, to find faith for the first time.

Will we do our duty? There are many parts to it . . . prayer, visitation, sharing names with people who might be invited, so that the story can be spread.

Now, whenever we do our duty, we find that this courage that we wondered if we had, has a power behind it . . . or the duty couldn't be done.

In Jesus's case the power seems to be in his compassion, reflected in the words, "O Jerusalem, Jerusalem, killing the prophets and stoning those who were sent to you, how often I would have gathered your children together as a hen gathers her brood under her wings and you would not!" Surely that longing gives more meaning to those familiar words "For God so loved the world that he gave his only begotten Son."

In our case, the power to do our duty involves what we might call bi-directional compassion. It's where I gratefully experience how God has had mercy on me, the worst sinner I know, which, in turn, causes me not just to think, but to feel, compassion for others so that I have the courage to do my duty as you must too, and thereby keep the great commandment, which is to "love the Lord your God with all your heart, with all your mind, and all your soul and your neighbor as yourself."

Courage, Christian! Our Destiny Involves Justice

But where is justice to be found? Well, there can be no justice without some kind of judgment, but the trouble is . . . so many judgments turn out to be unjust. The confessed killer feigns insanity and after a few months of psychiatric care, he is released. At the same time, another man is released from prison after 22 years when it is finally discovered that he was innocent all along. The only justice that we can ever be sure of comes from the one who, as we confess in the Creed, comes "to judge the living and the dead."

Now Jesus gives more than justice, linking himself with the prophets like Jeremiah, he not only pronounces judgment, "Behold, your house is forsaken," he himself suffers the ultimate injustice. Here is the only innocent one ever and he suffers his unjust death so that such an injustice might become the avenue of mercy for others. That is to say, the cross of injustice for him becomes the cross of mercy for us. With such mercy from him, our destiny is to contribute to his justice by having mercy on others and making all our judgments honest.

The courage to make such contributions of honesty will redound to his praise—a praise of Jesus which is sure to come in all sorts of forms.

By quoting in our text the 118th Psalm, "Blessed is he who comes in the name of the Lord," Jesus was thereby identifying himself as the rejected one (you'll see that in the psalm), the rejected one who becomes "the head of the corner," that is, the support of that house which will be forsaken unless he becomes part of it. "Blessed is he who comes in the name of the Lord" was also a phrase anticipated prematurely on the lips of so many as Jesus neared the end of his journey by entering Jerusalem on that day we now call Passion Sunday. In a sense, we also now on this day, give him anticipatory praise as we await another day of judgment and we give him this praise, by being brave enough to suffer for his sake.

If you have the eyes to see, you will find such bravery in faithful people as they meet the enemy called cancer and its danger and resist for Jesus' sake . . . not for their own. You will see it in so many of the elderly, struggling to maintain their dignity for his sake in nursing homes or living alone with failing hearing, failing eyesight, failing energy, but not a failing faith.

Perhaps the real key to faithful courage is found in freedom. Someone has said that real freedom is having nothing left to lose. I thought about that, and it occurred to me that it needs just a little addition. And I think it's supplied by Paul in the third chapter of Philippians when he says, "I count everything as loss because of the surpassing worth of knowing Christ Jesus my Lord. For his sake, I suffered the loss of all things and count them as refuse in order that I gain Christ and be found in him."

That's freedom and that's where courage is born and that's what you and I were baptized into—so that as part of our destiny and his, doing our duty in the face of any danger—we will have just what we need—Courage, Christian, courage!

W. Eric Rauch
St. Paul Lutheran Church
Berea, Ohio

THIRD SUNDAY IN LENT

Repent or Perish
Luke 13:1-9

On July 8, 1741, Jonathan Edwards preached his famous sermon, "Sinners in the Hands of an Angry God." Here are some parts of that sermon.

93

The wrath of God burns against his enemies. . . . The pit is prepared, the fire is made ready.

Hell opens its mouth wide to receive them.

There is nothing between you and hell—but air.

God holds you over the pit of hell, much as one holds a spider or some loathesome insect over the fire . . . for God abhors you; God is dreadfully provoked; his wrath towards you burns like fire.

O Sinner! Consider the fearful danger you are in; it is a great furnace of wrath, a wide and bottomless pit full of fire and wrath, that you are held over in the hands of an angry God.

Outdated Message?

How do we as twentieth century Christians respond to that sermon preached nearly two hundred and fifty years ago? Out-dated, you say? Totally irrelevant, you respond? A completely wrong view of God, you suggest? Only an interesting piece of American history, you reply?

Well, consider then an older piece of history—biblical history. The One we call Lord and Savior was approached by some unidentified persons who seemed eager to pass along a current news item. They asked Jesus if he had heard about the Galileans whom Pilate had slaughtered while they were in the very act of making religious sacrifices. Imagine their sudden uncomfortableness at Jesus' response. He asked if they were suggesting those Galileans were worse sinners than they themselves simply bcause they came to such a gruesome end. As the news-bearers' ease turned to dis-ease, Jesus continued, suggesting they didn't know how to interpret such happenings. The message they should hear in such occurrences is simple: "This should make you think of your own end and your need to repent, today! For if you don't you will also perish."

Jesus continued. He went on to say that there was another current event being talked about those days. Had they heard about the construction workers building Pilate's aqueducts in Jerusalem who were crushed to death when the tower fell on them? Surely they didn't think those workers were worse offenders against God than other people living in Jerusalem. Rather, such events should be seen as "pointers" to the destruction that threatens all people in Jerusalem, unless they repent. And that includes each of them standing in front of Jesus that very moment. Instead of looking at such events as museum articles or mere facts to gossip about, they should see those events pointing at their lives. Such events should open their eyes to see if they themselves are living and acting as he, Jesus, is living and acting toward others. For unless they turn around one hundred eighty degrees to re-orientate their lives to God, they themselves will perish.

Misdirected Message?

Well contemporary Christians, how do you respond to those words of Jesus? Do we reply that they were addressed to others? Do we suggest that the people to whom Jesus addressed his words were among those who eventually saw to his crucifixion? Do we respond that the events and their implications were directed to people living in another time and another place with little relevance to us today?

Well, consider then some rather recent news. A headline from this week's local newspaper read: "Air Ambulance Crash Kills Three From Methodist Medical Center." Did you talk about that tragic incident this week? I wager it wasn't about those three medical personnel being worse sinners than you or I. But—I also assume the odds are rather slim that the suddenness of their death stirred you to think about the possibility of your own sudden death, and whether or not you are prepared to meet your God, and whether or not you are living the kind of life which is patterned after the life of our Savior?

No, I rather doubt those were your thoughts. Yet that is what Jesus and Luke in today's Gospel are suggesting. "It is a time of violence and tragic death," they are saying. Such times, they suggest, call for alertness and faithfulness to the Christ-like life. "For unless you are bearing the fruits of love and concern and self-giving for others, your last moment may suddenly come upon you only to find that you are unprepared." That is what Jesus and Luke are saying to you and me and all who read these words.

Now do you see that this message of repentance does apply to us? It is an urgent message. There is no room for "business as usual" as we consider its implications.

Grace-Filled Message?

That's what the little parable in this passage states as well. Jesus told about a certain landowner who planted a tree in his orchard. Each year the owner came looking for some fruit from its branches, only to find it empty. Finally, after three years of finding it still barren, the owner commanded: "Cut it down. It's just using up the land." But the gardener pleaded for one more year. The gardener said he would personally continue to dig around it and put more fertilizer on it. Because of this personal plea, the owner consented to let the tree alone for one more year.

When you and I hear that little parable, we should respond: "That's good news!" And it is. The landowner (clearly God) gives time to repent, to bear fruit, to re-orientate our lives so they bear the fruits of faithfulness and love and sacrifice . . . as did the life of our Lord. That's grace! That's God's love in action, suggesting he will give us "more time" to re-orientate our lives. That's the reason some worshippers sing with introspection and joy the verse in the *Lutheran Book of Worship* that precedes the Gospel in Lent: "Return to the Lord your God, for he is gracious and merciful, slow to anger, and abounding in steadfast love."

Open-Ended Message?

Is that our only response to the little parable of the fig tree? Did you notice it is an open-ended message? We don't know how the story ended. Did the tree bear fruit after an overdose of fertilizer and tender care? Or was the tree still fruitless after another entire year and therefore cut down?

Should not you and I see in this little parable of the fig tree a warning, an urgent warning? Better still, should not you and I ask ourselves: "How have we responded to an overdose of God's grace?" After all, that is the goal of repentance. Repentance is not the end. Rather, as Martin Luther says in his Small Catechism regarding baptism and its implications for daily life: "A new self should arise to serve him." The Prayer of the Day in *LBW* puts it this way: "Help us to hear your Word and obey it, so that we become instruments of your redeeming love."

"Service"—"obedience"—"instruments of redeeming love"—that is the goal of repentance. That is why Luke in his Gospel always associates the word repent not with guilt, sorrow, self-hatred or fear, but with fullness, joy, confidence, new relationships, fresh starts. Yet Luke, like Jesus, always leaves the message open-ended. For we must decide if we will repent, if we will respond, if we will re-orientate our thoughts and actions toward Christ Jesus, and the thoughts and actions of his life.

Once-in-a-Lifetime Message?

Now you and I may have done that once. We may have repented. We may have publicly declared our intentions "to live among God's faithful people . . . to proclaim the good news of God in Christ through word and deed, to save all people, following the example of Jesus, and to strive for justice and peace in all the earth" as the order of Affirmation of Baptism in *LBW* states.

But remember, this business of repentance is not a once-in-a-lifetime thing. Repentance must occur daily. Like marriage vows which are spoken at one particular time and which must be renewed daily if the marriage is not to crumble, so our repentance must be renewed and put into practice, daily.

Community-Orientated Message?

The early Christian church clearly understood this. The early church realized how difficult it was to see the implications of repentance and to put the fruits of repentance into practice. That is why by the early third century there was a delayed process of baptism. Adults were enrolled for an entire year as candidates for baptism and brought into the Christian community. There was a prolonged time for the candidates to turn from the darkness of their old ways to the light of the Christ-like life. The early church gave serious attention to repentance. Since those coming from pagan backgrounds brought their old ways with them, they needed the community to demonstrate over and over again, what it means to turn to the light of Christ.

Thus sponsors had an important roll with the baptismal candidates. They had to show what daily repentance meant. And that is also why some parents take great care in choosing baptismal sponsors to this very day. They too want their child to have help in seeing what it means to live the discipline of a repentant life. The roll of the baptismal liturgy in the early church was also a help. In that liturgy, the candidates literally turned around. They would face the west for the renunciation of the devil and the powers of darkness (symbolized by the west and the setting of the sun). Then they would turn one hundred and eighty degrees to the east (the place of the rising sun of light) and confess the creed. So in some baptismal liturgies today, there is movement: from the waters of the font, to the altar and then facing the congregation (which proclaims its welcome of the newly baptized into its midst and into its priesthood).

Life-and-Death Message?

Do you see it now? Do you sense how this matter of repentance is life and death business? Repentance is not relegated to the so-called hell-fire and brimstone preachers of the past. Repentance is up-to-date, personal, crucial. Repentance involves our total response, not just once, but day in and day out as long as we live. Repentance involves our life-style.

So the final question today's Gospel would ask us is how many calamities and atrocities and disasters must we hear about before we discover the joy of total obedience to the Lord Christ in and through the Christian community? Or to put it somewhat differently: How many Lenten seasons do you personally have to hear the message of the cross and to give your life over daily to the One who hung upon its beams?

RICHARD REHFELDT
Windsor Heights Lutheran Church
Des Moines, Iowa

Home Is Where the Heart Is
Luke 15:1-3, 11-32

The Prodigal Son probably vies with the Good Samaritan for most popular and best known of the many parables that Jesus spoke. Both of them capture our special interest because they so dramatically and succinctly picture the love of God *for* us and *through* us. Today's parable emphasizes the "for us" of God's love.

The story of a prodigal son finally returning home to a waiting father includes more than the account of a shiftless and ungrateful son. His elder brother emerges toward the end of the story and, he too, helps to flesh out the portrait of God's love. We learn that love is there for the despicable as well as the dependable. It is a lesson that they needed very much to learn, as do we: "Home Is Where the Heart Is."

Neither boy appears to be very likeable. They are hardly "chips off the old block." They are selfish and insensitive to each other, with an added bit of nastiness toward their father. The one can't wait to get away, the other can't wait to see him go. The one demands his share of the inheritance (a pre-paid part of his father's estate), the other is willing to wait around as his share grows in value and ultimately becomes his own. Jesus tells the story to a group of tax collectors and sinners, as some critics on the fringes listened in, so all could better understand the forgiving love of God toward prodigals and toward "perfectionists."

The Younger Brother

The boy after whom the parable is named, the Prodigal, believed that "home is where the action is." The family domicile was too filled with boredom and routine. He had fastened his eyes on greener pastures. He wanted his home to be out there in the world of action and excitement. He felt life had to be more than this narrow circle of family and a few friends.

In youthful enthusiasm he propositions his father for the chance to strike out on his own, staked by his share of the family fortune. Already we see evidence of the father's patience and love; for, despite fatherly prerogatives of ordering the boy to stay home, he respects the lad's desire for identity and independence and even adventure. The wisdom and experience of age perceived a potpourri of potential dangers in such a cockeyed venture. Yet the boy had to have the opportunity of learning first-hand, perhaps even the hard way, that life is more than "action."

It didn't take him long to get on his way! Jesus says that in a few days he "took his journey into a far country, and there squandered his property on loose living." Even if he had had high-minded goals, his life became a round of mere games. Soon reduced to desperation and working at swilling swine to survive, he began to come to his senses. He was learning that "home is *not* where the action is."

The Elder Brother

The elder brother stayed behind, believing that "home is where the hearth is," a haven, a security, a safe *place* which would eventually be his very own. He seemed at first glance to be the better of the two boys: settled, dependable, devoted to duty, a no-nonsense participant in the family enterprise.

But seeing him in action upon receiving the news of his long-lost brother's return tarnishes the positive picture we might have had of him. He disliked his wayward brother so much that he bitterly resents his return; he complains to his father of being short-changed for all his faithfulness, unhappy that the old man wants to celebrate the prodigal's return. He can't bring himself to call him "brother," preferring to sting him with the words, "this son of yours." But underneath it all is a resentment of his father's love for an unworthy son. Like the laborers in the vineyard, he "begrudged his father's generosity." Love was alright when it extended to the respectable, the faithful, the deserving (like himself). As for his brother, "He made his bed; let him lie in it." He resisted sharing the love he had known with anyone so undeserving.

The Father

And therein lies the contrast and the beauty of the third character in the parable: a waiting father who demonstrates that, indeed, "home is where the heart is." Each boy needs his love and he handles each boy gently and patiently, offering that which neither deserves nor could claim. He refused to invoke parental authority to settle the score, reprimanding the wayward for his profligacy or the whining one for his jealousy and anger. Instead, each son is met with a love addressing his peculiar and acute need of the moment.

The prodigal son, returning with a heavy heart and a guilty conscience and a wounded pride, is swept off his feet by a father's love which had patiently waited for his return. Jesus tells us that the father ran to meet him; spotting him at a distance, he couldn't wait any longer to embrace his long-lost son. Though the boy had hit the bottom, the father lifted him up. Though the boy had stupidly and selfishly squandered his inheritance, the father welcomed him back home. Though the boy had disowned his family, the father restored his membership. The boy learned again that which he had earlier despised and partly forgotten: "Home is where the heart is," a heart beating with love for him.

Us

For those of us who—like the prodigal son—come to our senses and want to come back home, we are assured of a Father's welcome and the forgiveness and the grace we need for restoration of our membership in his family. In fact, that's part of what the church is all about: to share the forgiving and reconciling love of God with one another and with any who return "from the far countries of action and prodigality."

The other boy saw more duty than delight in manning the home fires. He had stuck it out and now didn't want any competition for the attention or the affection of his father. Yet as he vented his anger and pouted because of the fuss being made over his returning brother, he, too, met the meaning of "heart" in the home. His father didn't rebuke or ignore him in the ecstasy of reunion; he rather reminded him of the added blessings they had been privileged to share in their joint ownership of "all that is mine," alleviating any fear of being short-changed in the future. And then he underscored the reason for celebrating: "this, your brother, was dead and is alive; he was lost, and is found." It is not what the prodigal had done, but that he had returned, which compels them all to make merry and to be glad.

For those of us who, like the elder brother, have tried to stay and do our duty here within the family of God, the story urges us to be grateful for the love we've known and shared for many years. But it also reminds us "to rejoice over each sinner who repents." Our acceptance of the returning is a mark of our understanding and appreciation of the love of the Father which we have experienced and the inheritance he has promised to all who love him.

These are basic qualities of God's love for us all. Jesus himself becomes the bridge over which we prodigals return home. Through him we know that "home is where the heart is." And for those of us who, like the elder brother, await the arrival of returning sisters and brothers, it is again Jesus and his love which enables us to receive and to welcome, to join in celebration at every "family-reunion" which takes place here in church or wherever his people gather.

DALE D. HANSEN
St. Luke Lutheran Church
New York, New York

God's Doing a New Thing
Luke 20:9-19

The hero of Puccini's opera, *Tosca,* sings an aria about a "Strange Harmony of Contrasts." And there is a strange harmony of contrasts in the First Lesson and the Gospel appointed for today. Careful listening and reading of these lessons reveal a strong wave of optimism in the First Lesson, and a dire note of pessimism in the Gospel. And we need to see the interaction of the two—the theme of grace in the word from Isaiah and the bitter contrast of judgment in Luke. For in seeing this contrast, we'll discover some of the conflict and stress in the Christian life as our journey presses on toward the upward call of God in Christ Jesus, and is accompanied by the minor chords of judgment and the major resolutions of grace.

I have called this sermon "God's doing a new thing," and the title telegraphs the good news of where God comes down, and where we come out. Let's get at it!

A Sorry Story

This Gospel text is a sorry story. And as we read it we can say, "Treachery is old! Ingratitude is old! Cheating and conniving are old! What's new about that?" Well, the Gospel really describes the world's brand of good news—such as it is. For the world will tell you that if you're going to make an omelette, you're going to have to break a few eggs. If you live in the academic world, you know that the slogan is publish or perish. If you live in the world of commerce, the slogan is produce, or a pink slip. Get lost. In the world of marriage, it's live up to my expectations and meet

101

my needs, or there's the door. But here in this Gospel text the greed, the callousness, the hardness of those tenant farmers is so crass, so bold, so old, it almost turns your stomach.

It's old all right—but when the victim of the swindle, the greed, the cheating is *God himself*—well, it may not be new, but at least it's news!

The meaning of the parable is so thinly disguised that Luke tells us that only the presence of the people saved Jesus from harm the moment it came out of his mouth. And in this word that speaks to each servant being more shamefully treated than the one before until the son himself is killed, we hear an echo of Jesus' word we spoke of just a few Sundays ago, "O Jerusalem, Jerusalem, killing the prophets and stoning those who are sent to you! How often would I have gathered your children together as a hen gathers her brood under her wings, and you would not!" Time and again God sent his emissaries to his people, only to have them beaten, wounded, and cast out. And prophetically, Jesus saw his own end drawing near as he sensed the sullen rejection in the hearts of his listeners.

A Persistent God

And yet—even in the face of the heartlessness of his pople—God insists on doing a new thing! In spite of this ultimate rejection, God persists even to death and through death to free his tormentors by offering them release from the guilt of their own infamy. God *is* doing a new thing. But the way he goes about it is a far cry from what we might expect. Rather than surrender the grip of his love for his people in the face of their open hostility, God is willing to surrender his very life blood to open the door to reconciliation and hope for the very ones responsible for his misery. God's heart has been set from eternity to provide deliverance for the very ones that reject him, and by their rejection of him he is established as the head of the corner—the cornerstone of hope even for his mortal enemies. There is absolutely no limit to what he will do to deliver the people he has chosen to love.

To Make Things New!

And that, my friends, is a new thing—so new, so radical, so uncompromising in loving determination—that we have trouble comprehending it. For when God says he is doing a new thing, he doesn't mean he's merely inventing the latest model and offering it as kind of heavenly afterthought for all the old things. The new thing God is doing is recreative. The last word of Revelation is: "Behold, I make all things new!" And in that making he constructs a wholeness, a completeness that transcends the shallow and the inadequate and the trivial for which we all too often settle. But until that newness breaks through in our lives and awareness in Christ, it remains hidden from those whose gaze is transfixed by the passing parade of the temporal and, therefore, temporary. For us to catch the vision of the new thing God is doing, we have to cut deeply into this Gospel lesson—as painful as that may be.

An old teacher of mine used to say that we have to locate ourselves in the parables if we are to understand them. And where are we in this one? As we look around the precincts of this story, where do we find ourselves? It takes great courage to confess it—in fact, we dare only confess it when we know we confess to a Father who forgives—but who among us has never turned his back on Christ? Who among us has not left a commitment unfulfilled—failed to love when love was hard to find—slid out from under a sticky situation where our love and comfort and support might have brought newness into an old and broken relationship? Isn't this *our* story as well?

Except for an oh-so-thin polish of socialization, aren't we participants with those who are so confounded willing to grab all the good we can get for ourselves, and who seldom have the courage or commitment to reach out and touch someone? Wherever we turn there are appeals for help that go begging—simple kinds of appeals like a pint of blood for a Red Cross drive, a sack of groceries for a community food shelf, a few hours a month to drive meals to hungry folks who need the help that home-delivered meals provide. The list could be a lot longer, and is really only a prelude to the giving of ourselves in loving concern for the hurting people of our families, our parish, our community. But we are too busy—too preoccupied—too tired—too bored. (Or, we just plain forget.) And so again and again the life and love that our Lord seeks to offer through you and me who share membership in his body here on earth is stymied.

If the Shoe Fits . . .

Now, *who* do those merciless tenants in that vineyard represent after all? Don't we, in some measure, share identity with them?

But bleak as the picture may be, it's not all black. Newness—and its awareness—almost always occurs in crisis. The religious leaders to whom this parable was first spoken were at the flashpoint of crisis. And the crustiness of their oldness would not let the newness break through. Through this whole lesson there is an unremitting theme of judgment—absolute disaster—that waits for those who fail to see the new thing God is doing in Jesus Christ breaking into their lives and into their worlds. To reject the stone means that the stone will fall on them and crush them.

A Groundswell of Hope

But for those who refuse to cling to their boldness, and who look with eagerness for the signs of newness, there is the reward of seeing the new thing God does in them and for them. No, the picture is not black. Bleak maybe. But for every cause that needs response that was listed a moment ago, there is always a small but faithful band who will rally to bring a sense of newness to those in need. In the pressures of pastoral duties, I'm sure my colleagues in ministry would agree that there is always a groundswell of newness that is emerging that gives us both joy and hope. Part of that groundswell is with us today as we rejoice in the people who join our fellowship to share with us the task of bringing a continuing sense of newness to the body of Christ in our congregation.

Part of that groundswell is found in the faithful partners in our common ministry who, with few complaints, shoulder the many responsibilities of leadership. We detect and rejoice in newness that comes through them—and the newness that we see happening in them. All of this testifies to the glory of God who, at the cost of his own life, offers himself so that we can together find and do the new things he has in store for his people.

Centuries before Christ the people of God were a captive band of homesick, miserable exiles who languished in distant Babylon, crying for their lost homeland, their destroyed city with its magnificent temple. The crushing despair of defeat had weighed on them for decades, and in their captivity in Babylon they dreamed of the lost glory of their once teeming city and crowded temple. But the prophet came to them and said, "Forget about the past glories when everything was coming up roses. Behold, God is doing a *new* thing!" God lives above and beyond the death of the ancient city with all its splendor. He is a creative and active God who reaches out to bring into being something new, the something ultimate, that will have a beauty of its own because it comes from his hand.

To us who walk by faith as his people in this place, God reminds us that he has made a promise to us. And his promise lives through the agony of rejection and death, and rises each day anew in hearts filled with hope, and tells us to look around and see it happening right before our eyes in our own fellowship of faith. God *is* doing a new thing in and among his people. God keeps his promise. Do you believe that? So do I! Let's live in that promise. And act on it.

PAUL K. PETERSON
Gloria Dei Lutheran Church
St. Paul, Minnesota

"Into Thy Hands"
Luke 23:44-49

The final moments on Golgotha were wrapped in eerie silence. The unbelievable was happening—Jesus of Nazareth was dying.

As we look back over the tragic sequence of the events in this 23rd chapter of Luke, we discover that we have been swept along by them . . . we are involved. Perhaps nothing ought to have been said, or written. There are certain moments in the Gospel history when music must take over. Mere words cannot contain, or control, the story line.

However, the early church did not remain silent in the aftershock of his cross—nor dare we in our time. What happened during those final six hours speaks of the human situation, and of God's response in cosmic terms. This generation desperately needs that divine/human dialogue. For strangely enough, this moment of death speaks most profoundly of life.

The disciples desperately tried to stop Jesus' mad rush to Golgotha, but they were not successful. Now it had all come to this, and they stood around, beaten, discouraged, and despairing men.

What a setting—the bleak hill, the jeering crowd, the air itself charged with electricity. There was great darkness when Jesus died. It was almost as though the sun itself could not look upon the deeds that human hands had done. Scripture tells us that the temple veil was torn in two; that our Lord cried out with a loud voice in that final moment—"It is finished." And so it seemed to be, that not only this life of promise was finished, but that the hopes and dreams of people for a new world had seemingly been overcome by dark forces.

But then, his words came, "Father, into thy hands I commit my spirit." Quoting from the 31st Psalm, he added but one word, and what a word it was—"Father." It was this verse from the Psalm that a Jewish mother taught her child to say the last thing at night. Just as we were taught as little children to pray: "Now I lay me down to sleep . . . ," so a Jewish mother taught her child to say before darkness settled upon the village: "Into thy hands I commit my spirit." Thus Jesus of Nazareth died like a child falling asleep in his mother's arms.

God-Forsaken

The identification which people of our age are able to make with that final moment on the cross is not accidental. It is alarmingly contemporary.

105

Just as despair was no stranger on that cruel hill, despair has not been a stranger in this so-called enlightened century. Men and women of the twentieth century often feel like God-forsaken people in a God-forsaken world. Sometimes we have felt in our personal lives the "withdrawal of those everlasting arms." At other moments our sensibilities have been assaulted by a century of wars, the horror of the Holocaust, the strident sounds of terrorist voices, and the Damoclean sword of nuclear war. We have become calloused by tales of cruelty and terror, and like Macbeth, "We have all supped full with horrors."

Is it any wonder, then, that we ourselves often feel "hostage to meaninglessness and despair"? The final despair for religious people is the suspicion that God does not care, or worse yet—God is not even there.

As the novelist Arthur Koestler wrote, "God is dethroned, and although the masses are tardy in realizing the event, they feel the icy draft caused by that vacancy. Man has entered upon a spiritual ice age."

The Parish and the People

Any parish pastor who has lived close to his people has felt that icy draft from time to time. We have sensed it when a young mother is taken, and her children and husband cry out, "My God, my God, why?"

We have felt it cut through to our bones when someone who has stood by our side, and held up our hands in the hard work of the Christian ministry begins to age in front of our eyes . . . to falter . . . and to despair. And their encouraging word is no longer heard, and the silence has made life once more almost absurd.

One of the strengthening experiences of my parish life here in Madison was the frequent visits of my father from Milwaukee. He came, certainly not only to hear his son preach, or to share the latest clergy jokes, but to visit and love and laugh with his grandchildren and his lovely daughter-in-law. But now, for over a decade, those visits have stopped. The kind words and laughter are no longer heard. And the icy draft is not something that you have to read about in Koestler's book.

"Carry On in Your Work . . ."

However, death does not have the final word, either on Golgotha, or in your life and mine. Every sermon I preach to my challenging congregation is hammered out in a study where the picture of my father looks over my shoulder . . . and I remember. And if I should need to have my memory further jostled, I can open my desk drawer, take out an envelope which reads "To Robert and Carl, to be opened at the time of my death."

In the last paragraph, which although meant only for our eyes, I have shared with my people in Madison, he wrote: "If it should happen, I have no fear. I go with the promise of forgiveness of my sins through faith in Christ as my Savior. Carry on in your work. . . ."

The Christian faith is always passed on person to person. It is never the result of cleverly devised television presentations by glib preachers. Nor is it the child of ritualistic recitations, or dogmatic assertions. It is always born in the crucible of human personality—"That which I have heard, I pass onto you." And because we know the life of the One who first spoke these words in the midst of death, its authenticity is not doubted. And we are given strength. We feel that God is with us in death as well as in life.

"A Gift" Is Given

Certainly, Golgotha is not an invitation to debate the probabilities of immortal life, nor is Good Friday meant to appeal to the heroic in us so that we might emulate his great example of courage and fortitude. Rather, Scripture tells us that what we received on Golgotha was a gift.

Here we have the amazing unfolding of God's love for us—and we desperately need to know that God loves us and forgives us. Most of us are aware of the guilt that torments our sleeping and waking hours. We cannot stand ourselves, let alone one another. Then suddenly we perceive that this good Man, who seems to be dying for no reason, has shaken us down to the very roots of our being—"My God, this was all for us!" Intuitively we realize that he has taken upon himself my guilt and yours. And in the taking, he has freed us.

In his dying, he has assured us a place in the presence of a loving Father forever. Good Friday made sense to the early Christians only when they saw God's hand in it. The writers of Scripture tell us that God has always borne this terrible burden for his people: "The Lamb who was slain from the foundations of the world," is how they put it.

The Death of a Brother

Not only does the cross assure us of forgiveness, but gives us back our hope. Just this past week I received a phone call I never thought I would have to answer. A caring pastor on my brother's staff in Austin, Minnesota, informed me that Carl had died suddenly from a heart attack while playing handball. At first I could not believe it; he was younger than myself, and I had always tucked away in the recesses of my mind the image that he would attend my funeral, and bring comfort to those whom I had left behind. But now the calendar had given a bizarre twist, and I would attend his funeral . . . and comfort his loved ones.

For over twenty-five years, we had the joy of sharing the Christian ministry together. His buoyant spirit, his physical vitality, his "Martin Luther-like humor" gave rich evidence of his love of life and people. The tree had been so tall, and now that it had fallen . . . the space in the sky was unbearably large.

My family and I made the sad pilgrimage to the church he had served so well. Surrounded by loving, stunned, and grieving people, we heard again the great Scripture passages of hope. We heard a young pastor eloquently speak of Carl's service, of his love for his people and his family, and above all of God's grace. The music is always the difficult moment in any Christian funeral service. This time, however, the strong sound of "Beautiful Savior" and "A Mighty Fortress Is Our God" lifted our hearts and pointed us to Christ's cross.

What we had proclaimed in different ways, in different times, and in different places to our people began to come through to me as I listened, not as a preacher, but as a brother. For his family and mine, it was a moment of sharing the ultimate conviction that human existence has meaning. And that meaning is ultimately found in the cross of Jesus Christ, for we "have preached Christ crucified, a stumbling block to the Jews and folly to the Gentiles, but to those who are called, both Jews and Greeks, Christ, the power of God and the wisdom of God."

"He Will Be All Right!"

I asked myself as I returned to my study the next day to prepare to meet my people, "What was it that sustained us in this dark moment?" Two things came together with overwhelming clarity. We loved Carl and we also loved one another. Thus the sharing of that moment of blinding grief was made more bearable.

But even more important than a strong and loving family was a strong and loving Savior in the midst of a loving people. We were part of that people, we were part of a greater family—the people of God in a church called St. Olaf, and another called Bethel.

As I sat in my study, I reflected on the response of my young son Eric, who then was only seven, to the death of an older man in our parish. As I left for the funeral on that particular day, Eric asked where I was going. I told him I was going to conduct John Haugsland's funeral. Eric had known this older man, and had loved him. He looked up and said, "Will he be all right, dad?" At first brush, the question seemed inappropriate; then suddenly, I saw the clarity and beauty of it. I turned back and laid my hand on his shoulder and said, "Yes, Eric, he will be all right." Turning back to the game he had been playing, Eric said, "That's good."

God knows how good it is. As humans, we know the pain of our humanity and the vulnerability of our lives. We are sinners, and we need to be forgiven; we are mortal, and are threatened by an enemy that would extinguish those with whom we love and share. But because of Christ, there is for men and women of faith the ultimate assurance. As Christ bowed his head and said, "Father, into Thy hands I commend my spirit," so may we. And we are able to say to one another and to all others who will listen when the anxiety in a little boy's heart seeks for assurance, "Yes, Eric . . . Carl, too, will be all right."

ROBERT G. BORGWARDT
Bethel Lutheran Church
Madison, Wisconsin

MAUNDY THURSDAY

A Covenant for Us
Luke 22:7-20

The Covenant: Something to Celebrate

We just heard the reading from Jeremiah which speaks of a relationship between God and Israel in terms of a covenant: "Behold, the days are coming, says the Lord, when I will make a new covenant with the house of Israel. . . ."

The Gospel took us into the Upper Room and the event of Jesus eating the Passover meal with his disciples, the night before he was crucified. Of course, it was during this meal that Jesus instituted the Holy Communion. He blessed a cup of wine and some bread with prayer and shared them with his followers. When he passed the cup of wine, he said "This cup which is poured out for you is the new covenant in my blood."

The Second Lesson from Hebrews mentions both the former and new covenants, particularly in regard to how Christians should live their lives in the new covenant.

This word "covenant" is the key word in our worship today. Let us remember that many covenants are mentioned in the Bible, but we can put lights around the one that the Lord made with Abraham: that he would bless Abraham and his descendants, making them into a great nation, and that through Abraham's seed, all families would be blessed. The Lord kept that covenant alive when he took his people by the hand and brought them out of slavery in Egypt and when he established his Law with Israel at Mount Sinai. But in the years that followed, Israel worshipped other gods, failing to trust and worship the Lord only.

This is how Jeremiah interpreted the downfall of Jerusalem in his day. Judah had broken God's commandments and had committed injustices in the government and market place. So he looked to the future, to a new era and a new covenant. The old covenant does not need to be renegotiated. Something new and unique would take its place. The new would not be defined in terms of regulations and outward observances. It would be an inward reality of the heart. The knowledge and grace of God would be given by the Lord himself to each person, not only to a prophetic elite, but to all people.

It is not difficult to understand why Christians in the early church and down through these succeeding centuries have interpreted these words of Jeremiah as words which referred to Jesus Christ. He would be the one through whom God would establish a new relationship—the Way through which God would put his word within people, making his truth and love known in each person. So on the night of Jesus' betrayal, just as he is about to die and be raised from the dead in God's glory, he gives the Holy Communion to his followers: "This cup which is poured out for you is the new covenant in my blood." Jesus is inaugurating a new age, the new creation, the new birth, the new heart. And he gives it for all people—for us who are gathered on this holy night. As we gather to eat and drink, we remember and we proclaim his death and resurrection. We celebrate the new covenant which God has established with us. What blessing! What joy!

The Covenant: Something to Do

Now, the reading from the book of Hebrews sounds the word "therefore." We eat and drink this holy meal. We live in and regularly celebrate the new covenant, not only to receive God's grace upon grace, but also to do God's will. God has a purpose in the creation of the covenant. He has given us responsibility as we live in the covenant's blessing and joy.

Draw Near to God

First, according to Hebrews, we live in the covenant and celebrate it in Holy Communion so that we "can draw near to God with a sincere heart

110

and a sure faith." The book of Hebrews reminds us that Christ has acted as an elder brother in a large family. He is the firstborn, the pioneer, or the forerunner on our behalf. What Jesus did makes a difference for us. He entered the presence of God; he came with victory into the true holy place. He has torn down the barriers between us and God, barriers which people erected through sin and disobedience. He has made our access to God possible, which we acknowledge each time we pray and end prayers by saying, "through Jesus Christ our Lord. Amen." Yes, the new covenant which God makes with us makes it possible for us to know and love God.

I agree with William Barclay who said that the most precious thing in the world is a friend to whom we can go at any time, and never feel a nuisance; someone to whom we can turn whenever we need him; someone to whom we can talk about anything; someone who will never laugh at our dreams or mock our failures; to say it again, someone to whom we are never a nuisance. Who can this be but God our Father? And Jesus Christ has made it possible for us to draw near to him. All that we need to do is to take him at his word.

Hold On Firmly to the Hope

Second, we Christians living in the new covenant can "Hold on firmly to the hope we profess . . ."

We, like Christians of every age, have the constant temptation to abandon our commitment to Jesus Christ in the midst of all of the other things and ideas of the world. The early Christian community was shocked with a terrible sense of betrayal by those who broke ranks. We have become calloused to the indifference which people show Christ, including friends and even ourselves. Living in the new covenant means activity and work: holding firmly to our confession of faith in Jesus Christ. "Keep meeting together," the writer of Hebrews reminds us. Keep on studying the Bible. Keep on joining together in Holy Communion. Keep on praying.

I remember reading about the Poet Shelley.

Every morning he sat down at about the same time and wrote. Frequently it was the chore of writing words without meaning or greatness. But when the moment of inspiration struck and he made contact with the eternal, he was ready to capture whatever came at that moment. Shelley is remembered for his great poetry, not for his daily scribblings. But his great writing would not have happened without his daily scribblings. (From *Forward Day by Day,* 1977).

So it is in our life of faith. To hold firm to our faith and hope, we need to practice our religion daily. That means setting aside times for study and prayer. That means gathering with other Christians to worship at least once a week. That means working in schools and government and business for justice. That means striving to see in others the authentic person whom God created in his love, instead of people who always fall short of our selfish expectations, so that we can relate to them in Christ's love.

Do Not Turn Backward

Third, according to God's word in Hebrews, living in the new covenant we Christians are not to turn backward. Faith is reaching forward. Jesus Christ lived, died, and rose again so that we could be right with God through our faith in him. But our salvation will not be complete until Christ comes again on the Day of Resurrection. In a sense, we are like the ancient Hebrews. We have been freed from slavery; we have been brought through the sea; now we must journey on, looking ahead to the promised land. Christian faith and hope is that posture of looking ahead, not backwards. This Eucharist is a time to remember our Lord's death and resurrection, but it also is a time to anticipate his coming again.

Or, to put it in biological terms: all organic life grows by a form or principle of its own unfolding, and it comes to maturity if it is not damaged by outward forces. The greatness and the misery of our human lives is that we can fail to grow by refusing to cooperate with the life process. Throughout our lives, God stands, calling us into a future which he has planned for us in Jesus Christ. By our own act, we can turn back and not trust and rely on him. Or, we can look to him, discovering his power and Spirit working within us to propel us into the future.

Just this week I was chatting with a 91-year-old man. I asked him how he was feeling. He replied by saying that he felt pretty good as far as his physical health. "O sure," he said, "I have my good days and my bad days. But the hardest part for me now is waiting." "Waiting for what?" I asked. "Waiting to go home with the Lord."

He wasn't shrinking backward. With faith and hope he was straining forward. That is the posture of the Christian who daily lives in and celebrates the new covenant, even as we do today in this holy meal. With God's promise, we look to the future with hope. Now that is something to celebrate!

DAVID LINDBLOM
St. Stephen Lutheran Church
Minneapolis, Minnesota

"It Is Finished"
John 19:17-30

"We do not want to stone you because of any good deeds, but because of your blasphemy" (John 10:33 TEV).

Among some Christians a favorite question for speculation and discussion is the activity and whereabouts of the devil. The answer that is useful to me, but usually shortens the conversation is this one: "If you want to catch the devil, I am going to tell you where you will most surely find him—seated in your own arm chair if in it you are alone!"

Such is the reason and realism of Good Friday. Jesus died on the cross because his life was on a collision course with the powers that be. He antagonized the religious establishment. This created the possibility of civil unrest which prompted fear in the heart of the government. "What should we do? If we let him go on in this way, everyone will believe in him and the Roman authorities will take action and destroy our Temple and our nation." Such is the realism of this tragic event. And it is scary! For the powers that be were made up of well-meaning people; people who honored age-old traditions; people who respected their institutions; people who wanted to protect their own way of life. It is important to remember that those responsible for the crucifixion of Jesus Christ were not the irresponsible riffraff of society. If this were the case, evil could be controlled by more strict law enforcement and building bigger prisons. The cross of our Lord clearly but uncomfortably demonstrates the evil that is alive in the heart of what we call goodness or respectability.

Such is the realism of this Calvary drama. It says to us, "As good people, who for the best of reasons killed Jesus, so also today this radical nature of evil within us has the power to make us hate, persecute, suspect, and even kill.

Even this very Gospel is evidence of what we are talking about. For here the Jewish leaders bear more responsibility for Jesus' death than the Roman Government. Consequently down through history, it has been the source of vicious and unbelievable persecution of Jews, much of its ugly head revealed on Good Friday. We are sincere when we say, "It is too bad that in the economic readjustment that needs to happen, the poor have to suffer." We contemplate the fate of the refugees in similar fashion. "It's not their fault, but we just don't have any more room and no more jobs." And that is how Mr. Evil does his work. Not in other people, but in me.

"If Russia would just be a Christian nation?"

"If people wouldn't be so greedy?"

"I don't want that people should suffer."

"It's too bad." "It is unfortunate." "I wish the world were not like this." "But since it is, this is probably the best way in the long run."

"It is expedient. . . . "

The Good Friday tragedy is the eternal reminder that evil is real, that Pilate is every person, and that the religious establishment is every person. "We do not want to stone you because of any good deeds, but because of your blasphemy" (John 10:33—TEV).

> *No one takes my life away from me, I give*
> *it up of my own free will* (John 10:18—TEV)

But the lesson of realism is not one of pessimism. John does not minimize the power of evil that put Jesus on the cross. But for him this is not the most important word and certainly not the last word from the cross.

For in John's description of the crucifixion, evil did not win the day. Jesus did not die as victim, but as victor, not as a helpless sufferer, but as king. It is in this insight that John's carefully crafted Gospel and account of Jesus' death is so strikingly different from the other evangelists.

Each step of the way Jesus is in charge. His arrest is described in this fashion: "Jesus knew everything that was going to happen to him, so he stepped forward and asked them, 'Who is it you are looking for?' 'Jesus of Nazareth,' they answered. 'I am he,' he said." That is not the response of a frightened person being dragged to the sacrifice!

Or again, consider how he responded to the charges by the high priest: "If I have said anything wrong, tell everyone here what it was. But if I am right in what I have said, why do you hit me?" One wonders who is really being questioned!

Once more . . . notice the direct words to Pilate, "You have authority over me only because it was given you by God." Not exactly the words of a helpless victim, would you say?

From John's perspective of the cross, Jesus is in charge. Each step of the way it is he who takes the initiative. He carries his own cross to the place of crucifixion. And there is no mention of any help or any stumbling along the way.

Friends, there is something more happening here than just an unfortunate accident. There is something more involved here than just bad timing by the forces of history. Nor is the cross of Christ simply the focusing point of demonic sin. That something more Jesus made very plain when he announced to his disciples, "No one takes my life from me, but I give it up of my own free will."

So the cross was not forced upon him. He willingly accepted it. He did not lose his life. He gave it. He was not killed. He chose to die.

There is the Lamb of God who takes away the sin of the world (John 1:28—TEV)

But is that all that is going on here? A good person who is perhaps a deluded fanatic going willingly, knowingly and bravely to an agonizing death?

Early in the Gospel, John the Baptist points up the purpose of it all when he points out the Christ and says, "There is the Lamb of God who takes away the sin of the world."

And there you have the reason for the crucifixion.

But John is not content just to say it. In characteristic fashion he calls attention to our struggle with evil by highlighting it through such motifs as darkness vs. light; seeing vs. believing; judgment vs. eternal life. In all these descriptive and helpful comparisons he never loses sight of the cross. In John's Gospel the cross has the center stage. The cross is the hour that has "yet not come" but for which Jesus was preparing. This was the hour about which Jesus could say, "Father, save me from this hour," and yet in the same breath say, "For this cause I came to this hour."

This "hour" language vividly dramatizes the sense of divine purpose that had been the reason for Jesus coming and his life. "I am telling you the truth," he says, "a grain of wheat remains no more than a single grain unless it is dropped into the ground and dies."

No, Jesus' death did not come about by chance or bad luck. Rather his death was the aim of his life. It is in this death that the real purpose of his life is revealed.

"The Lamb of God who takes away the sin of the world!"

It is good news that John's Gospel builds this truth carefully and plainly. But it is also a central biblical truth. We can begin with the Christmas story where we hear the news, "You shall call his name Jesus, for he shall save the people from their sins"; to the Apostle Paul who preached to the Corinthians, "I delivered to you first of all that which I also received, that Christ died for our sins according to the scriptures."

Here is the purpose of the cross, the Good Shepherd giving his life for the sin of his people.

It is finished (John 19:30)

And that is why this Friday can be called "good." Here is the redeeming sacrifice. Here is the sacrificial Lamb. Here is the Good Shepherd who did not leave his flock, even in the face of death. This is what the cross is all about.

In these tragic events our God is at work. Against the dark background of evil the light of unbelievable love shines forth. Yea, the enemies of God become the means by which his purpose is fulfilled.

"It is finished."

This is Jesus' last word before he died. It is a quiet statement of victory; for Jesus is not just saying that his life is about to end, but with the ending of his life, his work is completed. Here is the announcement of the fulfillment of the purpose of this one called Jesus Christ. This is the Christ about whom John said, "Jesus knew that the hour had come for him to go to the Father. He had always loved those in the world who were his own, and he loved them to the very end."

My friends, this news is for you. It is for me. John, more than any other Gospel, wants to drive this point home. This is the tone and tenor of his entire Gospel, but most pointedly in his view of Jesus' death. The cross is the focus of John's Gospel. And he, more than any other Evangelist, helps us to see the cross through the mind and heart of God.

When you have doubts as to whether or not you are saved, open your Bible to John's account of the crucifixion and read the words, "It is finished." Everything has been done that needs to be done. When some well-meaning but misguided brother or sister hits you with the question: Are you certain you are saved? Are you really sure? Here is your answer! It is not based on our faith or feelings which can go up and down like a yo-yo, but on the certainty of Jesus Christ.

Many of us have trouble with this mysterious doctrine of atonement. This may be one reason too many of us are more comfortable with "cross slogans" than we are in trying to understand the various theories of why Jesus had to die. But there is clarity and simplicity in this announcement, "It is finished." I even can understand that. So can you. This is not a theory. Nor an explanation. It is not a definition.

Here is the announcement, that a task has been completed, and a purpose fulfilled. "Jesus knew that the hour had come for him to go to the Father. He had always loved those in the world who were his own, and he loved them to the very end."

"It is finished."

Is there not power here to do battle with the evil within us? Is there not love here that prompts us to question our self-serving solutions?

One thing more. I know you are thinking about it, asking the question that started it all. What about the evil in our hearts? What about the hurts that eat away at us and the fears that overwhelm us and the pervading sense of futility that surrounds us? Is not this Good Friday message just another nice pep talk for Jesus?

We are here on this Good Friday not just because something has gone wrong, but because something has gone eternally right. The cross of Christ was not an accident of history and its victim a helpless pawn. The cross is the result of God's plan to do battle with the evil of the world and within us. At the cross he tells us that his Son won this war. We still have to fight some battles. But there is power here to do battle with the evil within us. There is love here that prompts us to question and change our self-serving solutions. Between this hour and the hour when we die, we can live by faith in his declared victory, "It is finished."

Durwood L. Buchheim
Wartburg Theological Seminary
Dubuque, Iowa

THE RESURRECTION OF OUR LORD — EASTER DAY

The Prince of Life
Luke 24:1-11

This is the day the Lord has made! Let us rejoice and be glad in it.
For Christ is risen: He is risen indeed!

A Fact Beyond Words

The Easter Gospel according to St. Luke points us to the victory of our Risen Lord, the Prince of Life. But if we heed the account carefully, a prime element seems to be missing. All the scriptural accounts of the resurrection are a model of the indirect and discreet way in which God tells us of an event which cannot really be described in words. What takes place inside the tomb of Joseph is bathed in an indirect and puzzling light. We are not really told about the resurrection as such! No sensationalism or curiosity tries to tear aside the veil of mystery. The reason ought to be obvious. We cannot speak of the resurrection as we would describe a weather report, a business setback or an ordinary happening in daily life. Its meaning is far too great for that. Words cannot begin to capture its fulness. Therefore the Easter story begins with no matter-of-fact, clinical description of how the resurrection itself took place. No, it begins with the reactions and effects of this tremendous event on the disciples and the women who followed Jesus.

Look at the Disciples

It is not by accident that the women are the first at the grave of the Savior. They came to offer their sorrowful remembrance of the dead. None of the women really believed that he was risen. Their only thought was as St. Mark tells us, "Who shall roll away the stone for us?" They were seeking the dead among the dead.

The men were sunk in disappointment and bitterness. They did not even come forth from their hiding places to anoint his broken body. We know their trouble. Their view of things had been completely shattered. They were rudely awakened at Calvary. How could they have thought that this man alone was exempt from guilt and death and mortality?

But Jesus is not just one more mortal, claimed at last by death. He has not merely brought teaching as to how God and man can again attain peace and fellowship. He has advanced the claim he can authoritatively close the gap between God and ourselves, that he can restore the world deranged by pain, unrighteousness, and enmity against God, that he is more than a match for the awful majesty of death. If this is so, however, it is a true catastrophe if he himself is overwhelmed by death, if the hands of the wicked can throw this divine life, this supposedly divine life into the tomb. This is why the disciples cower in corners, hidden and afraid, with every fond dream of the kingdom of God now smashed to pieces.

The Prince of Life Is Risen

Then he appeared, he the Risen Lord Jesus Christ, he the Prince of Life. We do not know what really happened or how it happened. The event lies in a zone of silence. It is invested with a veil of mystery. We know only what precedes and what follows. What precedes is that the disciples are lost in hopelessness and depression. What follows is that new faith takes possession of them. We see how in a moment of absolute and terrible hopelessness there suddenly appears the Risen Lord with his greeting and gift of peace. He is not among the dead: he lives! The disciples are not immediately full of perfect understanding. Their doubts and faltering are real. But the new and greater reality of God's mighty work has gripped them and they are on their way to a transformed life. Whereas once they were mired in the deepest gloom, they are now overcome by the size of what has taken place before them!

But How Do We Know?

Now the question arises how we may be sure that we have a living Savior. Our own death seems not only inevitable, but so devastatingly final. It is one thing to sing songs about the empty tomb on a bright Easter morning, it is another to face the day when your body and mine will soon be in our tombs. I have seen and felt the emotions which come upon others when their last evening has come. A few dozen verses strung out in an ancient chronicle of the Gospels appears to be a thin thread that is supposed to reach from Joseph's Garden to today's world and our lives within it. If someone would actually come back from one of our suburban cemeteries today with a full-blown account of heaven and hell, we would like it much better, for here would be someone we could see and hear in person—this would be preferable to words about a resurrection.

Or would it? The Easter story teaches us that this is not the case.

The Resurrection Gospel Is the Living Word of God

The disciples could never have believed that Jesus had risen from the dead on that first Easter morning, but for the fact that they believed his Word. They had heard him say, "Your sins are forgiven," "Young man, I say to you arise," and "Lazarus, come forth." They had witnessed his signs and wonders throughout his ministry, but they were not brought to faith by these miracles. In the presence of the Risen Lord, however, all of these former events took on new meaning—the way figures in a stained-glass window leap to life once the sunlight shines in from beyond. That is why the Easter fact will never convince if the Man doesn't convince us himself. The empty grave will not win us to faith; only the Risen Lord can. When we meet Jesus of Nazareth we realize that here is someone who for love's sake united his lot with our human lot and keeps faith with us. The person who is gripped by this solidarity with Jesus Christ knows that he does not allow death to come between him and me, but that I am safe with him for all eternity. This may dawn on us but gradually. Perhaps right now you can only say that here was a man who walked the earth and loved with an absolute love with no regard for what it cost. This is true, of course, but it is still not the ultimate truth. As yet you have only touched the hem of his garment, but not yet seen his face. If we would come face to face with the full Easter truth, it means we must live within that Word of power and grace. God the Spirit works through the message of triumphant, forgiving love. The resurrection fact cannot take root in a life that is wilfully distant from the fountain of life and faith in God, the sacred Scriptures.

A Fact Revealed Only to Faith

Hence it is not surprising that only those who had accompanied him and lived in fellowship with him were witnesses of the resurrection. Only among them could there be a profitable fusion between what they had experienced with him and the awe-inspiring new thing which happened to them on Easter morning. The resurrection is a fact which is open only to faith, and it is a profound aspect of the Easter story that the disciples could not see the mystery directly but had to believe the word of angels and witnesses. The Word does it all!

But a Second Easter Approaches

The fact that it is revealed only to faith distinguishes the resurrection from the return of the Lord on the Last Day. The resurrection is certain only to those who are resolved to live with him, who are won by his words and his whole person, who give themselves unconditionally to him. Those who will not do this may pass him by; they may obliterate the bloody drama of Golgotha and the divine miracle of the third day; they may act as though these things had never taken place. But one day this dream will be over. One day the eyes which spurned him will have to see him as he is. One day the fists which clenched against him will open in a gesture of worship. One day the knees which were stiff and independent will bow before him. This will be the second Easter of his coming again. This will be the moment when faith may see what it has believed, and unbelief will have to see what it has rejected.

Living on the Resurrection Side of Our Crosses

Today we are asked by the Word of this Risen Lord whether we are ready to commit ourselves, to entrust ourselves to this Prince of Life who rules over all the powers of death. Only in this way can we have the certainty of Easter. Only in this way can we overcome death and the fear of death.

Perhaps our fears are not so much connected with death as with what can happen in life. Will I amount to anything? Will my work have meaning? Will my family life be an oasis or desert each day? Will some powerful undertow of secret sin drag me down to misery and shame? Will I keep faith with the spirit and message of this day even for one day or one week or one year? These and other unborn terrors can unsettle and disturb the soul. But in the Prince of Life is our hope.

Easter Is More Than a Day

The Easter faith, then, is not just an upward glance to satisfy our curiosity about the mysterious hereafter. It is a summons of the Prince of Life to the present hour of life. "Be reconciled to God. Seize the new life which is offered; bury your old life of sin in the grave where Jesus lay. Now is the accepted time; now his arms are open to you; now the Risen Lord is seeking companions."

Finally, all of us must stand before him. Be supremely careful, then, that your soul is in the one sure hand that can still the waves and open the graves, bind up the wounds and cancel guilt. Then the old enemy cannot cross the circle which the Savior has drawn around you. Then your coffin will be a couch on which you will awaken when the morning of resurrection dawns. Then the burial place, whether at home or in a distant place, will be a plot where you will sleep as a seed in the eternal sowing of God, to ripen on the day of harvest.

All of this because the Risen Lord, the Prince of Life, will one day look straight at you and say, "You shall not die but live."

F. Dean Lueking
Grace Lutheran Church
River Forest, Illinois

SECOND SUNDAY OF EASTER

Peace Be with You
John 20:19-31

How would you stage a resurrection? What would you pick for a location? How would you arrange lighting and music and special effects to bring out the glory of this unheard of event? By this point in John's Gospel, we have come to expect some special things from him in the way of staging and drama. John so often begins with a dramatic incident and then uses that incident as a backdrop for a powerful speech of Jesus about what he has come to do. When the Greeks seek out Jesus after his triumphal entry into Jerusalem, Jesus says, "The hour has come for the Son of man to be glorified." He speaks of the present hour as the hour of the judgment of this world and he predicts that when he is lifted up he will draw all people to himself.

Or before he goes to the Mount of Olives, Jesus promises the gift of the Holy Spirit, he speaks of how no man has greater love than the man who lays down his life for his friends as he is about to do, and he prays that his disciples might be included in his oneness with the Father. His words are full of grandeur, powerful and dramatic, and his speeches can run on for chapters at a time.

We might imagine, then, that when John tells the story of the resurrection it will be in grand and glorious style, with great fanfare and poweı-ful statements of victory. Yet, what does Jesus say here in the twentieth chapter of John when he appears to his disciples as the risen Lord? He says, "Peace be with you. As the Father has sent me, so I send you. Receive the Holy Spirit," and not a whole lot more. Jesus' words are so brief, just a few lines, and the scene is so quiet and matter of fact that we might wonder what on earth has happened. Is this the same story?

Peace Through Wounds

What has happened is that the high point of the story, the dramatic crisis has passed. For John the climax of the story of Jesus comes not at his resurrection but at the crucifixion. The hour of Jesus' glorification is the hour when he hangs on the cross, and in that hour everything that is of first importance happens. The time when Jesus hangs on the cross is the time of the judgment of this world. There sin's power over human beings is ended. There the ruler of this world is defeated and cast out, and from his position on the cross Jesus begins to draw people of all nations to himself, the ultimate goal for which he came. Because the crucifixion really is the climax of the story it was necessary beforehand to spell out in detail all that nailing Jesus to the cross would mean for him and for the world. But the resurrection happens more quietly. It is not the great moment of victory for Jesus, but it is rather God's confirmation of all that has happened in Jesus' death.

When Jesus comes to his disciples after his resurrection he says, "Peace be with you." Neither the doors which are shut nor the fear which keeps them huddled behind locked doors can shut out the presence of the risen Lord. Jesus says to his disciples, "Peace be with you," and then, as if to show them on what ground he can speak this word of peace, he shows them his hands and his side. "Then the disciples were glad when they saw the Lord." Jesus' wounds are most immediately the basis for his words of peace because they assure the grieving disciples that the one who stands before them is the same Jesus of Nazareth that they knew and loved and followed, the very same Jesus that they saw die on a cross.

But Jesus' wounds are the reason that he can say to his disciples, "Peace be with you," in an even more profound way. It is through the wounding of Jesus on the cross that the disciples, along with all people, have been reconciled to God. It is through Jesus' death on the cross that people can live a life that is free from the awful weight of sin and death. It is through Jesus suffering and death that people are joined to God like the branch to the vine, and through his wounds that everlasting life begins for all who believe. That is why Jesus can say to his disciples, "Peace be with you."

The Message and Mission of Peace

But Jesus has not come to the disciples simply to assure and comfort *them*. He has come to give them a message and a mission. He intends to send them just as the Father has sent him. Now, if the disciples are going to take up a mission that is anything like the mission of Jesus, it is obvious that they will need more strength and courage than they have ever demonstrated, so Jesus breathes upon them in the same way that God breathed the breath of life into man at the beginning of creation. Through the Holy Spirit Jesus breathes into his disciples the breath of a *new* creation, made possible through his death on the cross.

But what are the disciples supposed to do? What message are they to bring? Presumably the next verse sums up the essentials, "If you forgive the sins of any, they are forgiven. If you retain the sins of any, they are retained." But what kind of a message is that? Is that a message of peace? These words have had so much doctrinal freight hung on them over the centuries that it is difficult to grasp what their meaning in this passage might be. What has so often been emphasized about these words is not that the power to declare forgiveness has been given to the church, but that the church has the power to *withhold* forgiveness. Individuals and kings and even whole nations have trembled before this power of the church. So, when Jesus, who announces peace, sums up the mission of his disciples by saying, "If you forgive the sins of any they are forgiven. If you retain the sins of any they are retained," we have the feeling that we have come in on the middle of the conversation.

But our clue to the nature of the disciples' mission lies back in Jesus' statement that he sends his disciples *as the Father has sent him*. How has the Father sent Jesus? We find the familiar description back in chapter 3:

> God so loved the world that he gave his only Son, that whoever believes in him should not perish but have eternal life. For *God sent the Son* into the world, not to condemn the world, *but that the world might be saved through him*. He who believes in him is not condemned; he who does not believe is condemned already, because he has not believed in the name of the only Son of God.

God sent Jesus into the world with the message of his love, not so that the world might be condemned, but so that the world might be saved. There are those who are condemned, but they condemn themselves because they refuse to believe God's offer of love.

If Jesus sends his disciples in the same way that he was sent, then the accent of their mission cannot come on the retaining of sins. It has to fall on God's offer of forgiveness. If the disciples are to speak the message of Jesus who announces peace on the basis of his own suffering and death, then the stress has to come on the love of God that sent him into the world to suffer and die and on the release from the power of sin which that death has won for all who believe. If the disciples are sent as Jesus is sent, then they are sent not primarily to pronounce condemnation, but to bring the message of God's forgiveness in Christ. It is only those who reject this message who thereby condemn themselves.

Peace for the Skeptic and the Doubter

Just as we may be ready in our minds to sort out those who will be saved from those who will be condemned, we have the wonderful story of Thomas. The Gospel stories of the resurrection almost always include the fact there there were those who doubted the report, or even the appearance. Thomas is the classic, hardheaded skeptic who would rather face the tragic truth squarely in the eye than kid himself with fantastic dreams. We might expect that since Thomas had heard the word about Jesus' resurrection from the apostles themselves, and yet, refused to believe it, that Thomas might join the ranks of the condemned. But Jesus' love for Thomas is much greater than Thomas' skepticism.

Interestingly enough, Jesus does no more for Thomas than he does for the rest of the disciples. He comes to him with the words, "Peace be with you" and he shows Thomas his wounds and invites him to touch and to believe, and this is more than enough for Thomas. Thomas makes the most profound confession of faith in the entire Gospel, "My Lord and my God." Jesus does not reject this doubter, but he does what is necessary to bring him to true faith.

On the one hand, the story of Thomas shows us God's great love even for those who doubt, as so many of us often do. On the other hand, the story of Thomas encourages even the skeptics among us to believe without seeing: "Blessed are those who have not seen and yet believe." Thomas, after all, could not stand there forever, beholding the risen Jesus. What was important in the long run was that Thomas go out and live his life on the basis of his faith in the risen Lord. His encounter with Jesus was necessary so that he could become a witness to the risen Lord, and so that his witness could bring those who could not see to believe.

Peace for You

The witness of Thomas is there for skeptics like you and me who need the assurance that there *was* a witness to the resurrection who was every bit as hardheaded and tentative as we are. For, as the last verse assures us,

124

"... these (signs) are written that you may believe that Jesus is the Christ, the Son of God, and that believing you may have life in his name." Jesus comes to us, too, with the words, "Peace be with you." He comes through all of the doors which we have locked in fear of our enemies and stands among us with his word of peace. He stretches out to us his hands with the mark of the nails. He shows to us the mark of the spear in his side. Through these wounds he has made peace for us, too. Through those wounds he assures us of the forgiveness of our sins and holds out to us the gift of eternal life. He breathes upon us the Holy Spirit, the breath of his new creation, and he sends us out as witnesses to others with the message of forgiveness as the Father has sent him. Peace be with you. Amen.

MARTHA L. MYERS
Resurrection Lutheran Church
Marion, Iowa

THIRD SUNDAY OF EASTER

Nowhere to Rest
John 21:1-14

We love an even-keeled life. A few moments of excitement are fine but basically we want calm. After a war, we talk of reconstruction: After a historical event, we return to normal. After big events in our families we find quiet and straighten up our house. These are events, however, that do not allow a return to a normal world because they have given us another. The resurrection of Christ signals the invasion of a new world upon the old. The text before us reveals again the difference between the new and old. Nothing can be the same again.

The Case for Normalcy

The three years or so of the disciples' life were a whirlwind affair when we consider the quiet from whence they came. These men were raised near water and learned patience from it. They learned to appreciate planning and considered mastery before any venture. But those itinerant years which ended in Jerusalem were strange, too fast, too quick for a plan of control.

And so when those years appeared to be over, it was time to go back. In the vagueness of the moment, they went back again to the nets, the

125

currents, and the strategy. It was back to the old fishing hole. And time to fit it all together. To take stock. Think of that exercise of taking off to reflect and gain control once more.

You would think that after such events of healings, Christ's rejection, suffering, and crucifixion they'd be off and traveling. Certainly they'd be announcing all that had come to pass. You'd think they'd be eager; unstoppable by such awesome sights. They weren't.

But then there is that comfort factor; the even-keeled life. There is the sizing up of the situation and determining what is to be a reasoned response. Ever notice a dog as he wheels around twice to make sure its okay to settle? To get comfortable? We want the quiet upon an arrival at a destination. We want to kick off our shoes and lean back. For the resolution of tension is a requirement laid down in our bones. We are possessive of our castles and territorial ways. And after each storm we return to even keels.

Then too there is something of our ability to forget. For often to forget is to survive. It can keep us sane. What if everything were captured vividly before us—the number of steps you took this morning, the faces you have seen, the advertisements, the sounds, all crowding into your consciousness for a reasoned response, all begging for your reaction. We must and do forget to protect ourselves. We covet the calm.

Peter too. "Let's go fishing," as any fisherman knows, is a chance to get away from it all and enter a world of intuition and concentration on unseen depths. It is a new place which can release us from a flood of uncompromising moments. Time to derive fresh insights. Time to sort and integrate the newness into the old flow of life. Time to forget. No fishing trip is ever so simple as getting food. Or is it?

We can understand that choice. It is a return to a normal course and a routine path. We use those paths to save time and conserve our energy. Our normal routine demands no draining decisions. There are no new realities to beg our response. We understand what Peter did because it was quiet safety that was the hoped-for consequence of that choice.

So the struggle to be normal goes on. We sense there must be a niche for our lives. We struggle for meaning along with the masses who buy books on how to have happy marriages, who try to get to the kids' soccer games, who try to have a little "fun" on tight budgets and fall into debt doing it. We want to join the generation trying to celebrate health, a touch of prosperity, a few fun times and, oh, the house payment. Look at us trying to be normal! It may not be simple but we hope we can say—normal, common! And if we can, we have a sense of accomplishment. We're normal, we fit. We're not strange, alone.

That is the definition we strive for.

Hospitalization? Get better and return to normal. Resettlement? Get back to routines. Financial setback? Get on your feet again. When our normal train is broken we want it restored because we want the familiar and the manageable.

The events that led up to and included the crucifixion for these men were neither normal nor manageable. Death had emerged victorious. Each was now left to fend for himself as best he could. The words of the kingdom of heaven were now hollow echoes. The signs of forgiveness were now dubious. With the grave went those signs and wonders that God had visited his people. They were now left empty—trying to forget; trying to go back to whatever they left.

The Incongruity of the Resurrection

But none of them made it. The fact that they were not successful in going back is witness that the word of the kingdom's breaking in was sustained. They could not return because of Christ's resurrection!

The resurrection appearances were a regathering and reconstituting of these people under the kingdom's rule. And "they knew it was the Lord," the one who called them, as they ate there by the fire. And none dared to ask because it was really happening! They did not have the luxury of a maybe. It really was the Lord. They could not go back, nor can we.

Jesus' appearance brings them a new definition to interfere with the old perspectives. It brought them a community and definition to life that healed. They wanted the safety of their normal ways but there he was, standing on the shore bringing them back to wondering, straining, contending for this new kingdom revealed through him. They came back to shore and to the listening, proclaiming and defending. It was all earth-shakingly abnormal.

They would now continue what Christ began. And his beckoning them back meant more than a meal on the shore. It was a call back to the world of sharing grace and forgiveness. The carefree, the unplanned, the spontaneous and playful are fine but these were cut out for journeys into unknown places to encounter a reality that kept people from being truly human. Their witness would call it into question and challenge its authority. Their witness would disturb and would bring peace depending upon which one was there first. The shoreline appearance drew them back into the whole enterprise firsthand. On their lips and in their eyes would be the herald of the coming day. "Now may the God of Peace who brought from the dead that Great Shepherd of the sheep equip you . . . to do his will." That was it. They were equipped to run headfirst into the hallowed perceptions of the day.

This era of the kingdom's work does not let us return to the old ways and old views. We are cast into the new where now the old was like the first house we lived in, interesting, alluring, but empty. Remember the first house we grew up in? How we may try to return in fits of nostalgia, but we can never go back! The people, the times, and the smells are all gone. We are barred. The disciples could not go back because of those appearances in Galilee. We cannot go back to the games and the unreal world as well.

To attempt to drop out from the picture does not mean we're finished with it. It only means we'll be pulled back into it again. We'll run away only to run into it again. There is no way to be rid of this kingdom, for it will always meet us when we least expect. When we feel that there is no more hope. Like after a crucifixion.

Sure, the life of the church is marked by low levels of interest. There is a tiredness roughly the size of boredom more than once in a while. And we are hard pressed to find some new life to pump into it. Perhaps we do not realize because it could be intentional; to keep things safe and manageable. Often we create a safety zone in the community where we can live with relative peace and harmony, a place to rest.

But where there is an ebb there is surely a flood. For as there are those zones of self-created safety, there will come a ragged edge quite unplanned and unanticipated. We cannot hold onto safety very long. The turn of events can throw us headlong into the Gospel's grasp once more. The old ways finally cannot work. Sooner or later they will fail and we will be left empty and exposed. It is no coincidence that John records for us that they caught nothing that night. They didn't connect. They were still waiting when dawn arrived.

Those men were taken from safety as were the others and restored to a ragged edge of life. Serenity and waters lapping at stout planks were not to be their lot. They were restored to wanderings and subjected to the criticisms of an angry world. They were reconstituted, reshaped; to be used, pushed into debates, hurled into the toughest of spots. They would be defending, arguing, proclaiming for the sake of the reality of grace in Christ.

They would be used and finally die with only a promise. Resurrection unto eternal life. Life for them by all "practical" definitions was restless, out of synchronization with the rest of the world. They must have wondered if they could go on like that another moment! But they did. And that witness was felt from generation to generation. Each in turn has shared it with the result the Word goes on bringing hope when all other hopes have failed.

But how can we ever get along with an era that has established safety and control as its reason for existence? How can we mingle, blend, and laugh with the commuters and joke with the diners? There is sand in our shoe. We don't feel quite comfortable. We don't move well within a world of pretend because we have been given a new definition to life. There is a certain agony in that. It is like not quite having a place to rest or as we have heard it said before, "The Son of man has nowhere to lay his head."

We are now fed with the sights and smells of a new era to assure us we are there. We are fed with a wondrous food that takes us back again to the sights and sounds of the critical event. And we would say, "this is just what I remembered." And we are taken back by a meal. "Given for you." That food takes us out of the world of fabrication and rationalization. It takes us out of dead reckoning and flying by the seat of our pants. This food puts us into a world of sanity and dependence and lets us yield our structures of defense. We are taken back to the crucifixion to see and hear that grace is for us!

As those fishermen were fed, so they were returned to the sweep of his mission on that Galilean shore. It served again to show how incongruous they were and would be. And we as God's own are fed to know that we are a part of his enterprise that goes back into the insanity of the day with a message that creates sanity. Grace and peace are yours, not through control, but through Christ our Lord.

We will feel the pressure to endorse the insanity. We will be called upon to swell the ranks, to give the impression of safety to all. But we have been fed by him who has restored us to himself. And we have been fed to live in a world that can find peace only in his grace.

DAVID C. PRINZ
First Lutheran Church of the Redeemer
Vallejo, California

FOURTH SUNDAY OF EASTER

Keeping Us in Suspense
John 10:22-30

"How long will you keep us in suspense?" This question, put to Jesus by the Jews in the text for today, is a question that persists in our day. Both Jew and Gentile ask it. Jesus still seems to keep us in suspense. We still wonder who he is and what he has in mind for us and our world.

Why Suspense?

Jesus seems surprised that his listeners are in doubt or have uncertainty about him. "I've told you who I am," he says. And even if they could not understand his words, they had only to look at his deeds to know who he was. "The works that I do in my Father's name, they bear witness to me," he insists.

But there is a deeper and more profound reason for their lack of understanding. And Jesus is quick to point to it. They do not know him nor do they understand his mission because they do not believe. Not once, but twice he says, "You do not believe." They are in suspense and confusion, not because he has spoken to them in veiled words and not because he has hidden his purpose behind confusing actions, but simply because they do not believe. We sometimes say, "Your actions speak so loudly, I cannot hear a word you say." In the case of Jesus both actions and words gave a clear message. The problem was not with him, but with them.

A Pattern Seen Everywhere

This text from John is a microcosm—a small illustration—of what can be seen from one end of the Bible to the other. We often say that Judaism and Christianity are "religions of revelation." That is to say, they are religions based on the conviction that God always takes the initiative, that God *reveals* himself to us.

In creation, in the flood, in the call to Abraham, in the exodus from Egypt, through the prophets, in the return from Exile, in one Old Testament event after another it is the same pattern—they did not climb up to find God; he came down in the events of Israel's history to reveal himself to them.

Then comes the event of events, the revelation of revelations—the incarnation of Jesus Christ. In his birth, his life, his sufferings and death, his resurrection—in each of these and in all of them together God is revealed to us through his Son.

But, contrary to what we might expect, they do not know him. As John says in the opening chapter of his Gospel, "He came to his own home, and his own people received him not."

Do We Know Him?

It is easy for us to be judgmental. We wonder how they could have missed all of the signs. "If I had been there I certainly would have realized he was the Messiah. I would have accepted him as the One promised through the prophets of the Old Testament. I would have been one of his most ardent followers."

Are you sure about that? You and I have the advantage of knowing the whole story—not just the beginning, as is the case with the Jews in our text for today. We can put all of it—his life, death, and resurrection—into perspective. Most of us have come out of family backgrounds where the story of our faith has been known to us from early childhood. And yet, our devotion to Christ is hardly much more intense than that of the people in our story. We live and act like those who scarcely know about Jesus Christ.

Endless Reformation

Someone has observed that the whole history of God's activity in the world has been the history of God's attempt to reform his own people. In spite of their obvious advantage, it seems that his own people are constantly in need of repentance. They keep wandering off into the far country, forgetting that there is no place like the home their Father provides for them.

None of us is an exception, including me. My office as bishop does not protect me from error, doubt, ignorance, envy, fear, belligerence, and all of the sins that keep me from knowing Jesus Christ. Like others, I have had to face the discouraging prospect that my faith is weak and often faltering. My best resolves go unmet. I am ashamed of my failure to acknowledge him more forthrightly as my Lord. In spite of his works in me and around me, I fail to see him again and again.

My personal experience is not unusual. You see it in yourself, too. We seem trapped by our doubt, our unbelief, our insensitivity to his word and his work.

What is our hope? It is only in our certainty that God saves us *in spite of* who we are—not *because of* who we are. He keeps coming and coming, always wanting us to be renewed in our relationship with him.

A Seeking Shepherd

It is for this reason that the image of the shepherd in our text is appropriate. The phrases of grace tumble one over another: "I know them"; "I give them eternal life"; "They shall never perish"; "No one shall snatch them out of my hand."

He cannot, of course, be a shepherd to those who will not follow him. They remain those "other sheep" he wants to have in his fold. But for the sheep of his fold, for those who stumble and fall and fail—but believe— for them there is assurance that he will not forget them. If they find them-

131

selves "in suspense" like unbelievers it will only be because they have resisted his word and act.

Whose Fault?

This brings us back to where we started. If God seems remote and even absent, who is to blame? It may be that there are times when he tests us or keeps us "in suspense" for a time. But more often than not it is our own fault, the result of our own resistance or neglect.

Pastors often counsel with people who are bitter against God for one thing or another. It may be due to the loss of a friend or loved one, a disappointment in employment, a debilitating physical illness, a handicap, a broken relationship of love or trust. Whatever the situation, we are tempted to react with anger against him. We wonder, like Job, why he doesn't order his world in such a way that we are spared these griefs and sorrows.

We discover, however, that time heals, that grace prevails, and that perspective is recaptured. His purpose is hidden for a time, but only for a time. We learn, too, that in the worst of circumstances, there is more than enough grace to see us through.

A Testimony of Faith

A woman in her 50s was stricken with multiple sclerosis. She is confined to her home. Her husband suffers from cancer. He is able to continue his work, but there is no energy left for other activities.

One could expect bitterness and anger. Instead, there is that remarkable and rare spirit of gratitude that one stumbles onto as an unexpected surprise. "I was so fortunate," she says. "I didn't get multiple sclerosis until I was 40 years old. Most people get it when they're much younger. I was able to keep working until I was 45. And most important of all, my husband has stuck with me through all of these troubled years."

I am ashamed as I hear her story. "Could I go through so much personal tragedy and still witness to the grace of God?" I ask myself. "With every apparent reason to be angry, would I be able to see some reason to be grateful?"

The answer, again, lies at the heart of our text. God keeps coming and coming and coming. He does not want us to be kept "in suspense." He wants us to open our eyes, to believe, to trust. When we do, we will see that the shepherd is there, that he knows us, that we can hear his voice if we listen for it.

I have been fascinated by the accounts of the resurrection of our Lord. In each appearance we observe that he is only known to eyes of faith and hearts of trust as he reveals himself. On the road to Emmaus, for example, his companions do not recognize him until they enter their house, sit down at table and break bread. Luke says, "Their eyes were opened and they recognized him."

On the shore of Galilee the disciples see him but do not know him until he speaks to them. Only then does Peter exclaim, "It is the Lord."

So it is for us. He takes the initiative. He comes. He reveals himself. In faith we respond. In trust we recognize him. In hope we expect him to come to us again.

HERBERT W. CHILSTROM, Bishop
Minnesota Synod—LCA
Minneapolis, Minnesota

How to Glorify God
John 13:31-35

Glory! It's an old fashioned word. Most of us don't use it much any more—except in church. Here, every Sunday we respond when the minister says, "Glory be to God on high." And of course, every time we pray the Lord's Prayer we say, "For thine is the kingdom and the power and the *glory.*"

Does the word have any meaning to us when we use it in these ways? Or is it just one of those ritual words we repeat without thinking?

What does glory mean? What pictures go through your mind when I say the word?

Maybe you see something shining: a brilliant light, like the sun. Or perhaps you think of the glories of nature or a glorious sunset: something of striking beauty. Jesus spoke of Solomon in all his glory, suggesting splendor, wealth, richness, and authority. Perhaps you remember some glorious occasion: a great celebration, a moment of overflowing joy, or a momentous achievement.

Glory may suggest to us power, or perfection, or some great and extra-ordinary distinction. Our national flag is called Old Glory, recalling heroic exploits and calling forth honor and reverence. When something is glorious it is good; it is great; it is much admired and highly desirable. It is worth shouting about—or to use church language, it is worthy of praise.

133

God Is Glorious

All of these qualities are associated with God. He is most glorious of all. He has all good qualities to perfection. So to acknowledge that God has glory, as we do in the Lord's Prayer, is certainly proper.

But we are also told to glorify him. From Psalms to Revelation, the Bible urges us to give glory to God. The letter to the Ephesians says that we have been appointed to live for the praise of God's glory; our purpose in life is to glorify God.

How can we do this? We can scarcely add to the qualities that make God glorious any more than we can increase the brilliance of the sun or improve the beauty of a rose.

For us to glorify God, therefore, must mean that we recognize his glorious nature. But there is a further dimension to it. Not only do we personally acknowledge the glory of God, but in glorifying God we also call the attention of others to his glory. Psalm 19 says, "The heavens declare the glory of God." We too are to demonstrate or declare the glory of God, so that other people will be led to acknowledge it.

We are to reflect his glory, as the face of Moses did when he came from the presence of God. The Israelites understood at least something of the glory of God as they were blinded by its reflection from Moses' face.

How can we help others recognize the glory of God? We can learn from Jesus. For he came to this world to glorify God. How? In his high priestly prayer, Jesus said, "I glorified thee on earth, having accomplished the work which thou gavest me to do." Today's text says that God was glorified when he, that is, Jesus himself was glorified.

What was the work he came to do? To die for our sins. When was he glorified? When he was crucified.

That doesn't sound right, does it; it doesn't seem to fit. Even though you may like to sing "my glory all the cross," did you think of death or crucifixion when we were calling up images of glory a moment ago? But look at what Jesus says.

Glory Means the Cross

"Now is the Son of man glorified," he said. What was the occasion? Jesus had just sent Judas away to carry out his intention of betrayal. Shortly before this he had said, "The hour has come for the Son of man to be glorified." What hour was he talking about? It was clearly the time of his death, for he went on to say, "Unless a grain of wheat falls into the earth and dies it remains alone, but if it dies, it bears much fruit." The book of Revelation repeatedly associates the death of Jesus with glory. "Worthy is the Lamb who was slain to receive . . . glory," the heavenly beings sing.

Jesus glorified God by his death. By his life and resurrection, too, of course. But there could be no resurrection without his death. By dying Jesus called attention to the glory of God. He showed what kind of a God we have: a God who loves the world enough to send his Son as a sacrifice for sin. That's love which truly deserves to be called glorious.

In Christ's loving self-sacrifice, everyone can see demonstrated the glory of God. Thus by his death Jesus glorified God.

We too are to glorify God. How? We cannot do it in the same way as Jesus. "Where I am going you cannot come," he told his disciples. Does this mean they could not follow him in death? They didn't—but they could have. More likely it meant they couldn't follow him when he went to his Father after his resurrection. But perhaps it also means they couldn't follow him by giving glory to God through dying as Jesus could.

The death of Jesus was unique. Only his death could accomplish the salvation God wants all to have. Nor can our death, though it might in some cases glorify God, have the results of his. Only the death of Jesus glorifies God by demonstrating so fully the glorious love of God.

A New Command

But as Jesus glorified God in his obedience which led to death, so we can glorify God by our obedience. Christ gave us a command in connection with his comment on how he glorified God: "A new commandment I give to you, that you love one another."

This command may bother some of us. The church teaches that we are free from the law because of what Christ has done. We are not saved by keeping commandments, but by the love of God, extended even to us lawbreakers. Christ is not a lawgiver, we insist, but a loving Savior who by his grace forgives us who are unable to keep his law. How can we reconcile our belief in the grace of God with this command from Jesus himself?

Note that he calls it a new command. It was not new in content. The Jews had always had the command to love their neighbor. But it is new in purpose. The old command said: This is the way to remain God's covenant people—obey the law. "Do this and live." The new command has nothing to do with life or becoming a child of God. Christ has forgiven us and given us life before we even thought of obeying him. The new command does not tell us, "Do this if you want to be saved," but rather, "Do this if you want to glorify God."

It is thus not a command to qualify us for the kingdom. It is a command to us as members of God's family. Only here does Jesus address his disciples as "little children." He is speaking to them as part of the family, not as people who are seeking admission. He is not telling them how to become members, but how they are to act as family members.

As parents we give instructions to our children. If they don't obey we are sad, but we don't throw them out of the family. Obedience doesn't make us members of a family; birth does. Likewise we become members of God's family not by obeying his commands but by receiving the new birth he gives us. Our obedience is how we glorify God. If your intention is to glorify God who has made you a member of his household, here's how: obey the command of love.

New in Extent

The command is new not only in its purpose, but also in its manner or extent. Jesus said, "Love as I have loved you." That's new. The old command said, "Love your neighbor as yourself." The new command says, "Love your neighbor more than yourself"—as Jesus did. Love, even if it means your own death.

In fact, then, we are called on, as Jesus was, to give ourselves in death if we want to glorify God. Just as the glory of a flower appears only after the death of a seed, so we are able to glorify God only after giving up our own will to him. Only as we put to death what Paul calls our flesh—our selfish desires that seek our own glory and comfort—can we do God's will.

We glorify God by loving one another—by giving up our selfish desires for the benefit of others. So John calls on us to "lay down our lives for the brethren" (1 John 3:15). Peter says we should use the gifts God has given us in service to others. Why? In order "that in everything God may be glorified."

Our obedience to this command to love one another will glorify God because such an attitude, such actions are unusual. It is not common in this world for people to give up their own comfort for the benefit of others. This unusual behavior marks us as disciples of a glorious God.

Why do we act this way? Because God has loved us so much that we are motivated to reflect his love to others. Because God has given us his Spirit, who enables us to carry out his commands. Not perfectly, to be sure; only in Christ are we perfect. But with the power of the Spirit in us are we able to love one another. Then people will see our good works and give glory to our Father in heaven. And this is our intention as members of his household.

136

Shared Glory

This is not the end of the glory story. This glorious God, whom we in gratitude wish to glorify, shares his glory with us. Just as Jesus shares glory with the Father he has glorified, so we too will receive glory from God. Paul says, "When Christ appears, you will also appear with him in glory." Peter adds, "When the chief Shepherd is manifested you will obtain the unfading crown of glory."

Glory is a word worth keeping in our vocabularies; it has important meanings. It reminds us of our glorious God who has done so much for us; who continues to act in love on our behalf; who will continue to keep us in his family until we finally share his glory in person.

Truly he is a glorious God, worthy of praise, worth calling attention to. As we receive his glorious gifts we may use them in loving service to others, so that people may see our good works and give glory to our Father in heaven.

ROLF E. AASENG
Mapumulo, Natal
South Africa

Legacy
John 14:23-29

If you visit any church college campus, you need be there only a few moments before you will notice a building or tennis courts or some other facility named after a particular person. No doubt that facility is named after a person who has contributed generously towards its construction. It is a legacy left by the person or family. And such legacies form a major part of these college building programs; most church and other private colleges would not be able to exist without such legacies.

Normal human beings want to leave something worthwhile as they depart from this world. In reality only a small fraction of people in any one generation will leave anything that will long be remembered even by a small community, much less by the world.

Take music, for instance. Of all the musicians in the world—both performers and composers—only a minute fraction of them are well known. Only a small number of them will leave a lasting impression on the world of music. Bach, Mozart, Beethoven and other greats have left legacies that

137

are likely to remain indefinitely. But most of the millions of music students throughout the world will not attain the heights of music proficiency and performance to leave any musical legacy to future generations.

The same is true with writers. Oh my, wouldn't most writers like to have their works read for untold generations to come, even as Shakespeare, Tennyson, Emerson, and others are read by all school children and scholars. And preachers! How *we* would love to have all our old sermons "discovered" after our death, and have these rich gold mines made available to the impoverished world.

Alas and alack. Most sermons simply aren't interesting to read, and our messages are generally applicable only to a specific time and situation. That's neither bad nor good—it's normal. And I'm afraid that even those who have managed somehow to get a few sermons published will have to be reconciled to the fact that such volumes will soon languish forgotten on bookshelves, the legacy consisting of an anonymous code number in the Library of Congress files. (Sigh.)

Still the desire is there to leave a legacy. What, then, can we leave? It's difficult to leave much in material goods because most of us don't have much even at the end of our lives. But the desire is strong and the heart yearns for us to *leave* something! Something which will remind future generations "this is what he contributed to the world."

Of course, there are the few exceptional and wealthy people who will contribute enough to build a library or endow a professorship or build a chapel—providing it is named after them! Such legacies are good and constructive and beneficial to future generations.

Jesus Left None of These

Jesus left none of the above kind of legacies. He had no material goods and even his clothes were gambled for while he was still dying. He left no endowed professional chairs, no libraries, no rare book collections. So far as we know, Jesus played no musical instruments nor composed any music, hence no legacies in that field. We know of no written treatises or other documents left by Jesus. In fact, Jesus appears to have had nothing to leave as a legacy—certainly not in the way the world generally describes a legacy.

Yet his legacy to humankind overshadows and dwarfs all the combined legacies of humankind. Indeed most of the great music written by humans has been written because of Jesus' legacy. And the greatest art and awesome cathedrals were inspired by that same legacy, left by someone who seemingly had nothing to leave.

I see in our Gospel text for this Sunday at least three benefits Jesus left to all of us. He left the legacy of love, the legacy of the Spirit, and the legacy of peace. They are intangible and different from those things normally left behind by people. But they are more lasting and beneficial than libraries or music or art or any of the other great contributions left to us by our forbears.

Jesus Knew What He Would Leave

A major difference between the legacy we might leave and the legacy Jesus left is that he knew precisely what he would leave to humankind. There was no doubt or uncertainty in Jesus' mind as to what he would leave, even as there was no doubt about the course of his life or the pursuit of his Father's designated mission for him.

Jesus knew what he would leave. "This is why I came," he said to his followers. To him it seemed so simple and fundamental that he should know not only the course of his life, but the result of it.

We, on the other hand, aren't so certain—either what we are doing here or what we will leave when we're through. We don't even know for sure if we'll leave our good name intact. And if we do possess a few material goods, will they be worth anything after we depart? No matter how much we have done, no matter what influence we have had, will those who come after us remember us or even have the slightest flicker of recognition as they see our brittle and fading photographs in the ancient and yellowing pages of a long forgotten photo album?

If we can't leave a library building on a college campus or an endowed professor's chair; if we can't leave musical compositions or performances stamped on record albums, will our only legacy be a silent stone in a cemetery that has no resemblance to our life?

Jesus' Legacy Reflected His Life

The legacy Jesus left for us is many-fold; our Gospel text shows three, maybe four, of those folds. The important feature of his legacy is that it is a reflection of his life and ministry. Jesus left us the legacy of love, of the Spirit, and of peace.

In one sense the legacy of love was one of the few things that could be left by one as materially poor as Jesus. Normally a legacy will cost the donor something in terms of physical assets. But the legacy of love costs nothing in those terms. The legacy of love cost him his life.

That legacy stands forever, not as a mute marble memorial in a cemetery nor as a statue in a city park, but as a living active force. Jesus left for us the love of the Father, the forgiving creative love that would stand forever in a world of hatred. It is a legacy which sets the high standards and describes the godly nature of our relationships with our fellow human beings. Such is the legacy which Jesus left us that it continues from one generation to the next as a perpetual endowment which is never depleted.

The legacy of love often stands alone in the desolate battlefields of hatred and stubbornly proclaims that loving our neighbor—and our enemy —is the only way. The creativity of this legacy rises above all the monuments and all the creative arts that have been left to our world by all the great people who have passed this way.

The Mysterious Legacy of the Spirit

Perhaps the most mystery-shrouded aspect of Jesus' legacy to us is the sending of the Spirit. The Spirit, who comes mysteriously and mystically to shore up our sagging wills; who enlightens befuddled minds with the light of truth; who strengthens weak hearts and shattered spirits.

But how can we describe this gift to those who come after us? We can't see the gift, we can't feel or touch it in a physical way; how do we even know it has been given to us? The legacy of the Spirit who—much as the wind—blows and moves stealthily and unpredictably through the maze of our human scene. The Spirit, speaking through the cries of the oppressed and poor, showing up where and when we least expect him! Or her. What a legacy! We sometimes don't know whether to laugh or cry at this legacy. Or maybe to give thanks.

Jesus says the gift of the Sprit will teach us all things. That sounds pretty good, doesn't it? *All* things? I, who nearly flunked chemistry, will be taught all things?! Yes, what a legacy!

A legacy of teaching. Teaching us how to live as disciples. Teaching us how to *be* the people of God in a world and society where this is unpopular if not downright impossible. Teaching us to live as disciples in spite of the crushing fear that captures our minds and paralyzes our wills. Teaching us to step out in front and *be* what we can be in Christ.

My Parting Gift to You . . .

Jesus tells his disciples, "Peace I leave with you; my peace I give to you; not as the world gives do I give to you" (John 14:27). How forlorn a promise that must have seemed to the disciples as they huddled in fear for their very lives. In a world where image was wrapped in violence and physical power, the peace Jesus offered must have seemed the far-off product of a daydream.

How many men and women of good will have made similar promises of peace? How many of our own country's leaders have envisioned themselves as peacemakers in this troubled century?

"Make the world safe for democracy" they said at the time of World War I. And "Peace in our time" was one of the expressed hopes at the time of World War II. And "V for Victory!" And "Roll back Communism." Etc.

Thus have we hung our hopeful banners of peace from the rafters of our shaky houses built on sand. We have too often left only a tattered and fading memory instead of a promised peace.

"Let not your hearts be troubled, neither let them be afraid," Jesus told his disciples when he promised them peace (John 14:27b). And we know that to understand that promise and to absorb it into our lives, we must understand that it is God's own special peace, not as the world promises nor as the world gives. It is a legacy, that parting gift of peace, that will shine through all the murky troubles and disputes swirling about us in our small or larger worlds.

Thus the poor wandering Jew of Nazareth left his legacy to humankind. Dying on a cross he proclaimed it by pleading with his Father to "forgive them, for they know not what they do." Meeting for one of the last times with his rag tag band of disciples he promised the legacy of the Spirit, "whom the Father will send in my name." And rising from the sealed tomb he announced it, "My peace I give to you." For all people in all times he left it: the legacy.

MERLE G. FRANKE
First English Lutheran Church
Austin, Texas

THE ASCENSION OF OUR LORD

Welcome Home
Luke 24:44-53

On January 20, 1981, following 444 days of captivity in Iran, the 52 American hostages were released. For all who had prayerfully awaited that moment it was a resurrection experience. A country that had long been torn by dissension was spontaneously united. Young, old, rich, poor, black and white rejoiced as one. Yellow ribbons were everywhere. Old Glory was unfurled with pride and dignity. Horns blared. Churches rejoiced in thanksgiving and praise. The White House hosted a reception in their honor.

141

Yet as exciting as those first few days of freedom were, the highpoint was yet to come. Soon television and newspapers began to show the hostages returning to their communities, to their wives and children. Now they were truly home!

We at Wartburg experienced it ourselves. It was an unforgettable moment when President Vogel said to one of "our family," alumna Kathryn Koob, "Welcome home Kate!" The packed gymnasium erupted in spontaneous applause, applause that could not be stopped. With lumps in our throats, knots in our stomachs and tears in our eyes we rose to greet her. It was really true! She was here! She was home!

What does all this have to do with our celebration of Ascension Day? Well, if one could compare the days of captivity inflicted upon the hostages with the ordeal of the cross, and their initial release with the first hope and experience of the Resurrected One, then the actual return home would be analogous to the ascension! The drama of salvation was now complete. As in the incarnation, God had assumed our place, so now in the Ascension of the Son of Man, we are elevated to the place of God.

Thus as we gather to celebrate the Ascension, we mark the consummation of the entire drama of God's salvation. The Ascension is God's declaration to his own Son, "Welcome home!" The Ascension is a foretaste of our final destiny. The Ascension is a call to witness in the world the Good News of God's act of salvation in Jesus Christ, an act now completed.

The Context of the Day

The Early Church Fathers held Ascension Day in high esteem. It was for them the crown of Christian celebrations. As St. Augustine so eloquently expressed it: "This is that festival which confirms the grace of all the festivals together, without which the profitableness of every festival would have perished. For unless the Saviour had ascended into heaven, His Nativity would have come to nothing ... and His Passion would have borne no fruit for us, and His most holy Resurrection would have been useless." (Cited in J. G. Davies, *He Ascended Into Heaven*. London: Lutterworth, 1958, p. 170.)

This is a rather astonishing assertion for us to hear, for clearly times have changed. Today the Ascension of Our Lord is a festival that hardly rates a second glance on the church calendar, let alone in the secular world. Somehow we have lost its meaning.

In some ways Ascension Day is a victim of our times. In an age of space shuttles and satellites, if our central image of the Ascension is Jesus going up into space, this very image creates great problems for us. On the positive side, perhaps this seeming conflict makes us dig deeper and search harder for the central meaning of this day. Ascension Day must signify more than Jesus' escape from this planet, his defying of gravity, and cannot simply be explained away as a wishful fantasy of the early disciples. As St. Augustine suggests, this day can only be appreciated within the greater context of the entire Christ event. It must be viewed as an intimate part of the Gospel itself. Apart from this total context it makes no sense whatsoever, and without this final consummation, we are left hanging on the various resurrection appearances.

The Meaning of the Day

Ascension Day serves as a validation of the life and ministry of Jesus. Already in the Old Testament those who found special favor with God were "taken up" into the heavens to be with him. This was true, for example, of both Enoch (Gen. 5:24) and Elijah (2 Kings 2). Thus the Ascension of the Risen Christ to the Father confirms that indeed, his mission is fulfilled and that he has met with the favor of the Father. The blessing of his baptism, "Thou art my beloved Son, with thee I am well pleased" (Luke 3:22), is now repeated, this time in action rather than words.

Thus the presence of the cloud which "took him out of their sight" (Acts 1:9) has nothing to do with the atmospheric conditions of the day. This cloud is no ordinary cloud; it is the Divine Presence in all its holiness. It is the same cloud which led the Israelites in the wilderness, covered Mt. Sinai and the Mount of Transfiguration. Being taken up by the cloud therefore represents less change of place (going up into the sky) and more a change of presence. Through the Ascension the Risen Christ merges again with the eternal, transcendent Godhead and the mystery of the Trinity is again completed. He who had "humbled himself and became obedient unto death" is now the exalted Lord of all.

Ascension Day adds significantly to our understanding of the resurrection. The resurrection of Jesus demonstrated the power of God over the foes of evil and death. Jesus' ascension to the Father exalts him as victorious Lord of both life and death. His union with the Father likewise points the way to our own future reunion. As victorious Lord it is he who reconciles us to the Father, who intercedes for us, bestows his grace upon us, and opens to us the door to the future.

The Ascension is yet another confirmation that Jesus is the Messiah, the Christ, the Anointed King. His ascension fulfills the Old Testament images of the Son of Man, the mysterious, eschatological figure who, according to Daniel, would come upon the clouds of heaven and reign as triumphant Lord of all. Listen to the words of Daniel in light of this day:

143

> ... there came one like a son of man,
> and he came to the Ancient of Days [the eternal Father]
> and was presented before him.
> And to him was given dominion
> and glory and kingdom,
> that all peoples, nations, and languages
> should serve him;
> his dominion is an everlasting dominion,
> which shall not pass away,
> and his kingdom one
> that shall not be destroyed. (Dan. 7:13-14)

Clearly the Ascension fulfills this Old Testament image. He who was crucified, dead, and buried is now the risen, ascended Lord of the nations. The early Christians confessed that "Jesus is Lord." The Ascension points to his lordship not only over suffering and death, but also over the "principalities and powers" that threaten to destroy both the present and the future. Thus the future is ours, regardless of a failing economy, the threat of a nuclear holocaust, personal or communal disaster. The Ascension is an assurance of our future destiny.

The Human Verdict, "Guilty"—God's Verdict—"Glory"

But, you may be saying to yourself, it's one thing for Christ to ascend; it is quite something else to think of myself in these terms. After all, He is the Son of God, while I'm only human.

But that is precisely what has changed—our very concept of what it means to be human. Apart from the glorified Christ, our humanity is absolutely vulnerable. All our feeble efforts at goodness, all our unfulfilled dreams and promises, all our perishable possessions and transient relationships ultimately give us only limited comfort and security. Anyone who has ever stared into the dark abyss of a grave and placed a loved one there, must cry out with Job, "Where then is my hope?" (Job 17:15). Deep within ourselves we know our own brokenness and sin. We are all too aware of our failure and frailty. Aware of our own mortality, we also know that there is no power within us that would enable us to transcend our broken condition and hope for more than a return to the grave.

Yet it is precisely here that the glorified Christ meets us. It is here that the power of grace is most clearly revealed. In the Incarnation of Jesus God came to join us, to take upon himself our very nature, and in so doing to transform that nature, redefining it for once and for all. Thus the final destiny of humankind is not guilt but glory. Our very concept of humanity has been transformed.

This truth is central to our understanding of the Gospel. Contemporary attempts to reduce Jesus to a good person, a fine teacher, a dedicated, loyal son of the earth, or whatever, also reduce the power of the Gospel which has been entrusted to us. Christianity is more than a code of ethics, more than a key to earthly wealth and happiness, more than a collection of outmoded myths. The ascended, glorified Christ points us beyond our narrow, everyday world. This Jesus is no do-gooder guru dispensing the latest do-it-yourself formula for life. This Jesus is Lord—Lord of earth and heaven, Lord of death and life!

Forward Not Backward

As a child I often wished one could go back in time, back to the days when Jesus actually walked on earth. Then, I reasoned, we could all know exactly what he did, said, and willed for us to do. For a time scholars attempted to do just that—to go back and trace the path of the historical Jesus in an attempt to remove the mystery from the life and person of Jesus.

The Ascension points us in the opposite direction. The key to a living understanding of Christianity will never be found in its past. Neither historical proof nor human knowledge will open the door to the power of the Christian life. The key to Christianity will only be found in confronting the mystery and power of the risen, transcendent Christ. It is this Christ who leads us into the future, who calls us to faith and community, who challenges us to life lived in the Gospel.

So much of our life is joyless because it is lived either in regretting our past or in worrying about our future. But note the sudden change of mood seen in the disciples in our text. Their outlook of bleak despair and terror for their very lives is transformed to a spirit of freedom, courage and joy! One might have expected that Jesus' departure from them might have served to heighten their already overwhelming fears, for now they are alone again, their dreams of an earthly messianic kingdom altered. Instead we read that, "They returned to Jerusalem with great joy." The very disciples who only days before had cowered behind closed doors "were continually in the temple blessing God."

What had happened? The terror of their uncertain future had been removed, their preoccupation with self and safety overcome. For the first time in their lives they were truly free—free from the guilt of the past, free from the insecurity of the present, free from the threatening uncertainty of the future.

145

You Are Witnesses

"You are witnesses of these things," Jesus said. And from that time on the disciples were! While the power of their witnessing is traditionally traced to Pentecost and the gift of the Spirit, the command to witness is given at the Ascension. Here too the vision of their future is opened and their freedom in the Gospel confirmed.

The Greek word for "witness" is literally our English word for "martyr." The martyr is one who witnesses to his/her faith through death. But Robert Neale, in his book *Art of Dying,* points out that for the martyr the act of dying is actually insignificant. The martyr lives and dies for a cause. It is the cause that matters in the martyr's life, and because the martyr witnesses to this cause with his/her whole life, death actually loses its power and significance. "Whether one lives or dies," to quote the Apostle Paul, is not even important. What is important is the fact that "we are the Lord's." It is to this faith that the disciples were called. It is to this faith that we are called, called to be witnesses, martyrs for God.

It is so easy for us to miss the challenge and power of the Christian life. It is tempting to follow Christ for our own sake—so we can find personal happiness, success or peace, so we can "get to heaven." If we succumb to these temptations, the cause for which we live once again becomes ourselves! The challenge of Christianity is to transcend ourselves. We are called to be witnesses, martyrs who live in the freedom and reckless abandon of Christian love.

Understood in this light, "Are you saved?" may in fact be the wrong question. Just as appropriate is the concern, "Are you spending . . . spending your self," your life as a witness to the love which Jesus demonstrated in his own life, death, resurrection, and ascension.

As members of his body on earth, his holy church, we are now the witnesses to his love in the world. The ascended Christ has gone to prepare a place for us, and in going has entrusted us to this place! This world and this life are the present arena for the Gospel. It is here that we are to witness, and it is here that we are freed to do so. We are no longer slaves or hostages to sin. Through our baptism we have been made children, heirs of the future to which the Ascended One points. Let us witness boldly, for one day the Father will also say to us, "Well done, good and faithful servant . . . welcome home!"

LARRY A. TRACHTE
Wartburg College
Waverly, Iowa

One and One Is One
John 17:20-26

It's unsettling to the Christian that two such significant events in our life with Christ as his Ascension and Pentecost should flash across the calendar and then disappear with such speed. Ascension Day was last Thursday. Pentecost is next Sunday. Each deserves the same attention as a Christmas or an Easter! Ascension marks a kind of end to one phase in God's plan of salvation. Pentecost is the surprising beginning of a second. Our text helps us remember these two events and build a useful platform from which to see and understand them—as well as Christmas and Easter and other great Christian events. The text is the final few sentences of the prayer that brought to an end Christ's last longer speech to his disciples. These words come as close as any to being the Lord's last will and testament. It's amazing how he could pack so much content into so few sentences! If we had the time, the intelligence or a brighter Christian understanding we could draw from this section of Scripture more content than would seem possible. Rather than do everything, let's lift out one key thought and reflect on it. May the Holy Spirit shine upon us with a light divine as we consider and seek insight into a puzzling point of Jesus' prayer: *One and One is One.*

One and One Is One

Jesus said, praying to the Father: "I want them to be one as we are one . . ." We are one? Two one? That's not possible. It doesn't make sense.

One of the fascinating things about Christians is that we think if we say something out loud that we understand it. For instance, we have invented the word trinity and have written a very long creed trying to explain what it means but after all these words do we understand it? We say, "God created the heavens and the earth" and, "We are saved by grace through faith." But is the saying the same as understanding? You know the answer.

With God it is different. He understands what he says. But not so with us. What God announces is automatically beyond the full comprehension of our minds. Doesn't he say so? "For my thoughts are not your thoughts, neither are your ways my ways, says the Lord" (Isa. 55:8). His explanations and statements of clarification are beyond our understanding. One such example of incomprehensibility, wonder and beauty is the unity of the Father and Son.

The Father and the Son are united. They are united in every way. They are united in will, in power, in loving intent for mankind, in commitment to salvation, in a mercy that endures forever. That's what Jesus is stating in his prayer. He says, ". . . as thou, Father, art in me, and I in thee . . . ." Do you want to know more about the Father? Look to the Son. This is a case of "like Father, like Son" carried to the ultimate: like son, like father. It's a perfect oneness. To know and see the one is to know and see the other. That's a divine fact.

A practical application of that fact lay in the Son's promises. Because they are united, Christ's promises are the Father's, too. At the Ascension he said, ". . . you shall receive power when the Holy Spirit has come upon you . . ." (Acts 1:8). Remember some of the other things, too? ". . . I am with you always, to the close of the age . . ." (Matt. 28:18) and ". . . I go to prepare a place for you . . ." (John 14:2). These are not comforting assurances of a Christ who is set to escape this world and live on somewhere else detached from humanity and humanity's history. Those promises are the clear expression of the united will of the Father and the Son. Their will is one. Theirs is a perfect and unchanging unity. That's why there have been no "new" revelations since Calvary—or any need. Why should there be? What concern in human history was not dealt with, and resolved, by Calvary's beginning and end? His atoning sacrifice, together with all the other events of his life, is the ultimate and completed expression of the united intent of the Godhead. One and One is One.

Those last few sentences flowed out so easily! They sound so good they must be fiction or a fairy tale. People have called them that. But they aren't. Those words are his own words spoken for all to hear. In our baptism our full family relationship was established. Since then, by many means, we are drawn into the Father's intent and empowered to speak all that he has given us to speak. More than that, we must! We can say no more than he tells us. But, for sure, we dare say no less.

As good as this has sounded I haven't told the whole story yet. There's more in the text that needs to be shared. To help me to share with you the further meaning of this text, close your eyes and picture Christ's cross —empty. First focus on the vertical beam leading up out of the ground. That's like the first one-and-one we spoke of between the Father and the Son. Now think about the second beam—the horizontal one. That's like *our* oneness with them. From their vertical relationship the Father and the Son reach out to you and me. But that's not the final visualization I want you to make. Imagine that the horizontal beam is growing and extending. Let it stretch further and further and as it stretches further curve the tips toward each other until finally they touch and form a giant circle. That picture represents the third understanding of unity in Christ's final prayer: All the "another ones" (that's you and me) are to reach out and connect with still other ones, too! Isn't that what he's saying: "I do not pray for these only, *but also for those who believe in me through their word,* that they may all be one . . ." (John 17:20-21).

All Another Ones and Every Other Another One Are One, Too

Now that sounds complicated. But what's complicated about, "one and one is one"? It's not the words. They are simple enough. It's the concept. Our self-centered sense of the reasonable is offended. One and one isn't one. One and one is two.

Maybe in our minds it is, but the miracle of the divine is that his expanding oneness keeps absorbing more and more of the "other ones" of the world into himself, making all of us one. His way of achieving this gigantic and incredibly beautiful oneness is through "linking" from person to person *through us.* We are his linkers. We connect others into one gigantic linked chain. We are his way—his only known way—for making international and eternal unity a reality. Using us he achieves his purpose. Did you hear him in his prayer? Did you hear him say that he prays ". . . for those who believe in me through *their* word . . ." (John 17:20)? We are the "their".

The Great Commission (. . . of course you know about that), the words of Christ on the way to the Ascension (. . . you can read about those in Acts 1 . . .), this prayer and whole mood of Scripture force us to the realization that there are many more people whom Jesus wants. *We are his way of reaching for them.* We don't really need another evangelism plan, no matter how well reasoned and complete it may be. We don't require further institutional commitments to world outreach. We need a down-to-earth acknowledgment of the transparently simple and intentional place for us outlined in Christ's last words. And we need a Spirit-given willingness to do what he says.

The only way I know such a commitment will ever be made is through the work of the heretofore unmentioned third divine partner linked so inextricably to the first two: the Holy Spirit. By his power people are called to faith and action. He does this through baptism and the shared Word. It first takes place here among us. Before it will happen anywhere else it must happen in our one-to-one relationship. This parish is the beginning point for this blessing and his first move is toward *you.*

149

One and Another One Is One

From this point on things are going to seem a little cloudier if that's possible. We will slide past Christ's absolute statements into the realm of what some hear as divine wishful thinking. Jesus prayed in that final series of sentences, ". . . that they may also be in us . . ." (John 17:21). That "they" are his disciples and us—I mean you and me. He not only sees and claims a unity with the Father but he also includes his followers in it.

Turn back to the record of Easter evening in John 20. Did not Jesus say, ". . . as my Father sent me, so send I you . . ." (John 20:21)? His plan for his life is our plan. His growing is our growing. His Father is our Father. When Jesus taught us to pray we were told to address the Lord of history, the ruler of heaven and earth as "our Father" (Matt. 6:9). He *is* our Father. Now, united with the Father and the Son, the stage is set for our continuing work as God's family. We, like Jesus the firstborn, must ". . . be in our Father's house . . ." (Luke 2:49) and, while there, be about their Father's business. And such a business!

To a world of sinful people, who bear the burden of their guilt for real and imagined transgressions, we have the exclusive international franchise on forgiveness: "If you forgive the sins of any, they are forgiven . . ." (John 20:33). Just as emphatically we are charged with judging society, measuring things moral and immoral against the standard of his Word and with finally reaching a conclusion of right and wrong. ". . . if you retain the sins of any, they are retained" (John 20:23). The only reason that we can function in the forgiving and the retaining realm is that we are united in him and speak with his authority. The church is a family-owned business. We are members of that family, made so by our very special adoption (Gal. 4:4) and can lay a legitimate claim to the eternal family inheritance set aside for us by our Father's will (Eph. 1:11-14).

I have intentionally skipped one of the more common applications of this text. Some people use it almost exclusively as a plea for denominational unity and for organizational mergers. There's no question that Christ's prayer argues against unreasonable sectarianism and institutional exclusivism, but it's hard to imagine that Jesus in his last moments was making a pitch for one international church or one world wide mission board or one universal hymnbook. Those are interesting yet important dreams of lesser men. Whatever their eternal worth they follow far behind the commitment to unity. First our hearts must be set to the oneness which he wants for us with him and then with the connected oneness that we are to effect with others. Then we can worry about reorganizing the church into something that looks more like his body. But first things first!

But What Can We Do Right Now?

We shouldn't leave our time of worshipping without specific action. May I suggest three? First, determine to read our text every morning this week. On Wednesday set aside a slightly longer devotional moment to read the entire chapter in which the text is found. Second, pray for unity in our own congregation and a deeper sense of oneness among those who call this place their parish home. Third, choose somebody to link into his unity by giving them a call or making a personal contact. Become one with someone else. Do it because he is one with you. In this one glowing moment, one (that's you) and one (your linked friend) become one with the oneness of the Father and Son. Don't worry about the arithmetic. It doesn't have to make sense. It just works. In God's plan one and one is one.

CHARLES S. MUELLER
Trinity Lutheran Church
Roselle, Illinois

THE DAY OF PENTECOST

The Holy Spirit and Hospitality
John 15:26-27; 16:4b-11

You have probably heard of the Holy Spirit as prodder of prophets. You may also have heard of the Holy Spirit as gift-giver and sanctifier of people. You have also likely heard of the Holy Spirit as comforter. In the Gospel of John (chapters 15 and 16) the Holy Spirit is called a Counselor.

The departing Lord promised, "But when the Counselor comes . . . he will bear witness to me; and you also are witnesses. . . ." (John 15:26-27). A good counselor does many important things. I'd like to focus on just one of those things—hospitality.

Hospitality—Space for Strangers

Henri Nouwen in his book *Reaching Out,* defines hospitality as "providing space for strangers." He says that the word hospitality has lost its meaning in our society. "Hospitality is one of the richest biblical terms that can deepen and broaden our insight in our relationships to our fellow human beings." Space is what people need. Space is what a good counselor helps people discover.

151

Since 1960 when I became a pastor, I have counseled many people from many walks of life on many agendas. I started as a twenty-four-year-old telling people too much. Then for awhile, I just listened—the Rogerian style they call it. I know God helped people in spite of my fumbling efforts. What recently occurred to me is that whenever people were helped, it was because they departed feeling that they had more space.

Walls crowd in on us. Exits seem few. The closed-in feeling is what depression really means. The Holy Spirit as counselor provides space—space for the lonely and the strangers to make friends.

Nouwen says, "Hospitality . . . means primarily creating free space where the stranger can enter and become a friend instead of our enemy." He goes on to show that the purpose of a good parent is to provide hospitality for a child and the purpose of a good teacher is to provide hospitality for his or her students. Children and students are not properties, but guests. They are not submissive little people whom we must teach, but temporary dwellers who will grow with guidance and hospitality. They are strangers who can become friends by their growth (and ours). It suddenly dawned on me recently at Bible Study that one of the gifts of the Holy Spirit is to provide space for people. Is space needed? Yes, I believe it is.

An enormous resistance to learning in homes, schools, and churches would be overcome if hospitality—providing space—could be seen as the real agenda for all places of learning. For example, the church is not an institution forcing us to follow its rules, but a community wherein hospitality can be experienced, a place where strangers can really be friends, by the power of the Holy Spirit. As space is provided, hosts and guests in home, school, church or wherever, discover their own gifts and one another's gifts. Communication barriers begin to drop in this atmosphere.

For example, on the day of Pentecost—originally an Old Testament agricultural festival—Parthians, Medes, and Elamites were in Jerusalem. They spoke different languages. They did not understand one another until the Holy Spirit, the great host, came upon them. Then they each heard the good news of Christ in their own language. One of the oldest of all human problems is the communication problem. This problem was evident at the tower of Babel through human pride. This problem is evident today with all its complexity and divisiveness. At Pentecost the Holy Spirit provided space to Parthians, Medes, and Elamites. They heard God and therefore they began to hear one another. They were crowded into the tiny little world of their own culture and language. They were members of the largest family in the world, the Christian church, the hallmark of which is "they understood one another." Is that needed today?

In the movie "Cool Hand Luke," Paul Newman speaks a classic line for all of modern life: "We have a communication problem here," he says. Today, a loud "Amen" might be heard from

• Husbands and wives,
• Parents and children,
• Republicans and Democrats,
• Employers and employees,
• People of different colors and races,
• Jews and Arabs in the Middle East,
• Protestants and Catholics in Ireland and elsewhere.

We have a communication problem here.

We see things too narrowly—squeezed into a dark, truncated space that doesn't have room for a neighbor who is different, who speaks a different language, who lives in a different world. That's our problem, isn't it? We see things through the myopic glasses of "my little world," with me standing right in the middle and everything else radiating around "me."

The gift of the Holy Spirit is the gift of providing space by bringing us closer to God, providing a healing community, thus leading us out of a distorted individualism and isolation. The Holy Spirit provides hospitality —space for strangers to become friends.

The hospitality of the Holy Spirit provides relief from the communications problem; this hospitality also provides relief from the two-headed monster "Guilt-Fear," which inhibited the early Christians right after the death of Christ and continues to inhibit people today.

Hospitality—Space for You and Me

The apostles had deserted their Lord in time of need. Peter, as predicted, had denied his Lord three times, the last time with a curse. Guilt pervaded the motley little group of ex-tax-collectors and fisherman called the apostles. And fear.

In the twentieth chapter of the Gospel of John wherein we read of Jesus giving the Holy Spirit to the apostles on Easter evening, the opening sentence is revealing: "On the evening of the first day of the week, when the disciples were together, with the doors locked for fear of the Jews [the Jewish authorities] Jesus came and stood among them . . ." (John 20:19). Jesus said, "Peace be with you." Then he said, "Receive the Holy Spirit. If you forgive anyone his sins, they are forgiven . . ." (John 20:23).

The apostles whose sins were scarlet because of their betrayal and whose fears were so inhibiting that they were paralyzed, became the most excited little group of world-changers ever known. In the history of the world, we have never known any more unlikely group to "turn the whole world upside down" (as their enemies said of them in the book of Acts) than the apostles. Yet, they did just that.

With all its human limits, Christianity has, nevertheless, spread to every land and been translated into thousands of languages as it moved in and changed the lives of countless millions of people over the face of the earth. How did all this happen? A gigantic human effort on the part of a well organized minority with brilliant leaders? Hardly. The Holy Spirit did it through people who were previously paralyzed by guilt and fear. The Holy Spirit is the great host who provided hospitality space, by freeing people from fear. Jesus said, "Fear not, for I am with you." Then he fulfilled his promise by being present with his people in the form of the Holy Spirit, whom Paul calls "the living Christ." Fear is cast out, space is given.

The Holy Spirit is the great host who provides space from guilt too. Guilt immobilizes. Freedom from guilt means that a great distance is put between us and our sins. Today when many people think of sin as an outdated concept, when masks of self esteem are for sale everywhere, there is a thin veneer of human assuredness, underneath which people are crying for freedom from fear and guilt. The Holy Spirit, the host who gives space, is relevant to our real problems today. The Holy Spirit reconciles us to God and to one another by providing space. "As far as the east is from the west, so far have I cast away your sins," says the Lord.

That, my friends, is very good news. The great host of God, the Holy Spirit, is freeing people from guilt and fear today. That, my friends, is the best news of all. The Holy Spirit provides space—space for you and me.

In that space we are free for what God wants us to do. "I can't do anything," many say. Wrong. You can do anything God calls you to do. God frees you—providing space for you to be yourself—and sends you to work the good he wants you to do.

What was the problem at the tower of Babel? Pride! People doing their thing in their way. Result: confusion and isolation. What happened at Pentecost? The Holy Spirit descended on people who were confused— speaking many languages. Result: understanding and communication. The Holy Spirit provided the space for strangers to become friends.

A good counselor helps people come to terms with guilt—fear—resentment—and alienation.

The Holy Spirit—the hospitality giver—does just that; then invites us to pass it on. "You are my witnesses. . . ."

R. J. Lavin
Our Saviour's Lutheran Church
Tucson, Arizona

154

Can We Really Know the Truth?
John 16:12-15

The Deep Search for Truth

There is a deep urge in every one of us to discover something new. No matter how much we know, we want to learn more. Like wanderers in the wilderness of ignorance, we long to discover one day the promised land of truth. Our life is a voyage bent on discovering things we have never known before. So it was with Christopher Columbus. The old ditty tells us, Columbus sailed the ocean blue, and discovered America in 1492. That's the way we learned it; we thought it was absolutely true. Now our children tell us that's not the way it was at all. A poster I saw in the 1960s read: "INDIANS DISCOVERED AMERICA!" Columbus had no inkling of what he was actually doing. He was in search of a shorter route to Asia when he landed on an island, and ever since that time the islands off our southeastern coast are misleadingly called the West Indies. Columbus died in the belief that he had found only a new way to the old world.

But the spirit of discovery lives on. There's a bit of Christopher Columbus in each one of us. Maybe that's partly what we mean by saying we are created in "the image of God." We are built with an urge to learn the truth, to discover something new—*terra incognita*. We are human, that means finite and limited, confined to the boundaries of space and time, and yet we are driven by a deep inner impulse to strive for what is absolutely beyond us. Why is it we can't be satisfied to live within the limits of life we know now? We seem to be always striving and stretching, always trying to burst the boundaries, to explore the frontiers and discover new worlds.

The eighteenth century German philosopher, Gotthold Ephraim Lessing, put it so well. If God were holding all the truth that exists in his right hand, and in his left hand he held the restless urge to find the truth, even if it meant you could never reach it, and then God said to you, "Choose!" what would you choose? Lessing said, "I would humbly fall upon God's left hand and say, 'Father, give me this. Pure truth is surely for thee alone.'" Lessing put his finger on that part of the human spirit that refuses to have its wings clipped and its feet tethered. Isn't this what St. Augustine meant when he said, "Man's heart is restless until it finds its rest in thee, O Lord."

There's a deep search for truth—for God—throbbing in the human heart. In the book of Job, Zopher the Naamathite poses this question: "Can you find out the deep things of God? Can you find out the limit of the Almighty? It is higher than heaven—what can you do? Deeper than Sheol —what can you know?" People all over the world are striving for the truth, but they don't necessarily call it "God." They are simply searching for truth.

When I was at Harvard University, I was impressed with the sign *Veritas*—the Latin word for truth—inscribed everywhere, on bulletins and buildings. That was the educational ideal, and yet I knew that only a minority of these students searching for truth would profess to be searching for God. Perhaps many would even call themselves atheists. To me as a Christian it didn't matter. If they were searching for truth with deep passion and love, they were in some way searching for "God," even though they did not know his name.

We Christians can confess that Christ is *the* truth, but this does not mean we want to disregard or deny the quest for truth wherever it takes place. We believe that whenever people find a bit of truth, they are at least touching the hem of God's truth. We believe the Spirit is leading people into all the truth there is, whether the small truths of physics and chemistry, the bigger truths of history and philosophy, or the still larger truths of religion and revelation. For all truth is of God, and the Spirit is in charge of every human quest for the truth.

The Arrival of Truth

We have this promise that when the Spirit of truth comes, he will guide us into all truth. All truth? All the truth there is to know of biology? All there is to learn about astronomy? Everything about history and psychology and medicine and computers? Like most people in our privileged culture, I have gone to school a major part of my life, and yet I don't claim to know more than a minor portion of all truth. And being a Christian hasn't provided any shortcuts. The newspapers are now reporting court battles over "Creation Science." Groups of fundamentalist Christians are trying to enact into law teaching the Bible as a textbook on science, giving direct scientific knowledge on how the world began. Do we really want to say as Christians that the Spirit cracks open the Bible as a book full of creation science, giving us all the truth and nothing but the truth about how the world began? That is not what the Spirit of truth is doing in the world. "He will take what is mine," Jesus says, "and declare it to you." Not as a substitute for the many truths of science and philosophy, not as a shortcut to knowledge we can learn by research and reason in this world, but as the way to the truth of life eternal the Spirit is at work to guide us into all the truth that counts, decisively about your life and its final meaning and goal.

How do you come to know this truth? It comes as a surprise, not as a reward for hard work. It comes as a gift, perhaps when you least expect it. The truth comes; it is something you can meet; rather, he is someone who has come to meet you and takes you by surprise. A little farm boy in South Africa found a shiny pebble and played with it as a toy. It turned out to be a diamond and led to further discovery of diamond fields. Just a pebble, but it contained the promise of vast treasures. Columbus set out to find Old China, but he found a new land, a new world. We too have set some goals and have worked hard to meet them. Perhaps it was to get a college degree, land a good job, gain a promotion, run for office, win a prize, finish a book, or any of a thousand other things, but the joy of achieving does not last. The glamor of the moment vanishes, and history does not remember our great deeds.

This is the great secret of Christian experience. While we are on our way, pursuing our goals most earnestly, believing that when we attain them, then we'll be happy and feel fulfilled, we are stopped in our tracks by meeting someone who reveals to us "the pearl of great price," the ultimate meaning of truth, an absolute Goal that goes infinitely beyond all our rather measly goals. We learn that the truth of life is not in what we discover, but in being discovered; not in what we achieve, but in what God has already done for us. We may spend a lifetime looking for God, until that day we wake up to the great truth that he has already found us. "While we were yet sinners, Christ died for the ungodly."

The Name of Truth

What do we really know about truth? There is the truth of a proposition. Two plus two equals four. That's a true proposition. Two parts of hydrogen to one part of oxygen makes water. That's also a true proposition. But there is the deeper truth of personal encounter. Jesus said, "I am the way, and the truth, and the life; no one comes to the Father but by me." That is truth that lies in a name.

You never know a person, not really, until you know the person's name. There's magic in a name. If you meet some very special person, and you're bowled over, the first thing you ask is: "What's your name?"

In our restless search for God, we never really come to know him until we come to know him by name. We want to know him on a first-name basis. This is what Martin Buber called an "I-Thou relationship." Many people are searching for "God," but God is for them, in the words of John Updike, an "oblong blur." The Bible has given us a personal revelation of God. We can call him by name. Jesus talked to God as "Abba," and that means "Daddy" or "Papa." And so we salute him in the prayer he taught us to pray, "Our Father."

Because of the intimate relationship between Jesus and the Father, we have an expanded list of names of God. We have been taught to speak of Jesus as the Son of God, because he reveals the true nature of the one whom he called his Father. Like Father like Son! So the Father is God, and the Son is God, and so is the Spirit who proceeds from the Father and the Son. These three: Father, Son, and Holy Spirit, One God to be worshiped and adored. This day in the church year, the first Sunday after Pentecost, we celebrate the Holy Trinity. The struggle continues in the church to understand the nature of the truth that has arrived in Jesus Christ. The classic conflict between a unitarian and a trinitarian interpretation of truth is still going on in modern Christianity. There are still theologians who think; If God be One, he cannot be Three! Some call it a mystery, a paradox, even a dialectical truth; others call it absurd, a contradiction, even a nonsensical statement.

We learn from Scripture, and with the chorus of confessors in the one, holy, catholic church we believe and teach the truth that God is one, and that this one God is Father, Son, and Spirit. It is a mystery; it cannot fully be grasped by reason. But only as Triune can we most adequately speak of the true God who has arrived in Jesus Christ for our salvation and the redemption of the world. This knowledge of the Trinity is bound to our confession of Jesus as our Lord and Savior. Jesus declares, "What is the Father's belongs to me, and what is mine, that the Spirit of truth will give you. I am the Truth." Here we have the three persons of the Trinity. Here we have the heartbeat of the Christian faith. This is the mighty meaning of the Gospel. The Spirit of Truth who comes glorifies the Father in the Son.

CARL E. BRAATEN
Lutheran School of Theology
Chicago, Illinois

Right Vision
Luke 7:1-10

The Eyes of a Realist

Our text for this morning is from Luke 7, the first ten verses: the story of the centurion who looked to Jesus for the healing of his slave. As I read through that text, another picture of healing came to mind . . . one from hundreds of years before, recorded in the fifth chapter of 2 Kings: the healing of Naaman. Surely, the fact that I had, just a few weeks before, read with my youngest son the story of "Seven Baths for Naaman" had something to do with the immediate connection; but there was more that bound the two together and kept nagging at me.

Naaman, you remember, was from Syria . . . a country north of the land of Israel; a country whose people did not believe in the God of Israel; and (not unlike today) a country that found itself frequently at war with Israel. It was in that arena, you may recall, that a young Israeli girl was brought as a servant into Naaman's house; a young girl who, wanting to help Naaman who was a leper, told Naaman's wife of a man in her homeland whom she believed could heal Naaman. And Naaman, after obtaining his king's permission to seek out this man, set out with his chariots and fine horses laden with bags of silver and gold and ten fine garments, all to buy his healing in the land of Israel.

Well, there was a short interlude of Naaman bringing the greeting from his king, the king of Syria, to the king of Israel, demanding that the king of Israel see to the healing. Of course, to the king of Israel, this could be an opportunity for the king of Syria to wage war once again. But Elijah the prophet heard of the note sent from king to king, and asked for Naaman to be sent to him instead.

But then . . . how the bargaining ensued! . . . as poor, frustrated Naaman (who had brought all this wealth with him; who was ready to meet man-to-man and to bargain man-to-man . . . with all his chariots and fine horses . . . his bags of silver and gold, and piles of fine clothing that he had brought with him) . . . poor Naaman was greeted, not by *the* man, but . . . by a servant who did not even invite him inside, but relayed Elijah's message: "My boss says you ought to wash in the River Jordan." And you may recall Naaman's remarkably reserved reaction: "There are better rivers back home! Why should I wash in this one?—one of the least of all the rivers! Why am I not seen personally? Why does this man treat me so?"

159

Then, fortuantely, entered the wisdom of Naaman's own servants, who ask: "Why not take the bath? Why not give it a try? You can't lose anything!" So Naaman bathed seven times in the River Jordan. And when he came up . . . after the seventh time . . . he was healed. He then went back to Elijah's house with great praise for the God of Israel, as Elijah (refusing the gifts that Naaman offered) pointed away from himself and toward his God . . . with Naaman saying: "I know that your God is the true God." And Naaman rode home with his chariots and his horses, with his silver and his gold, his rich clothing, *and* the gift of health and the knowledge of God.

What's the connection between Naaman and this centurion in Luke 7? Well, the connection for me is simple and powerful. When Naaman came to be healed, he came loaded for bear . . . with all those fine chariots and horses, those bags of silver and gold, those mounds of rich clothing. He also came with the eyes of a realist. He came to make a deal. He came to pay for his healing, convinced that the healing that was there was not a gift, but something that he deserved, as long as he was ready to pay the price. He came boldly before the king of Israel with those eyes. He rode up boldly to Elijah's house with those eyes. He responded boldly to the servant's directive from Elijah to wash in the River Jordan—with those eyes. Naaman came clearly with the eyes of a realist: with arrogance and with pride.

But the centurion in Luke 7 did not seek the healing of his slave at the hand of this Jesus with eyes such as Naaman's: the eyes of a realist. Consider his position. Not only was he a soldier of the Roman Empire, but he was honored even among those soldiers. And yet, he was willing to risk it all in his approach to the elders of the Jews. Even if he was in the habit of speaking to them (indicated by his hand in the building of their synagogue); and even if his confidence in their God was present before this event—still, if this was not an initial risk, it was a least a continuing risk; putting his station in this town and his stature in the eyes of his peers on the line. In fact, he was putting his love for his servant before his own well-being and his conviction that Jesus was the man to see before all reason. And . . . look at his reaction as Jesus approaches his home! He sends his friends out, and has them tell Jesus not to come in because he was not worthy to have Jesus come into his home; and ends with the topper of "I say 'jump,' and men jump. How much more will *your* word do its work!" No, the centurion did not approach with the eyes of a realist like Naaman. Indeed, for all the love (if he really had it for his servant) . . . had he approached as a realist, he would have waited for (even demanded) the touch and the hand, the actions and the physical magic of Jesus (as Naaman had expected of Elijah—to "come out to me, and stand, and call on the name of the Lord his God, and wave his hand over the place, and cure the leper").

No, this business of sending servants out to say, "Don't come any closer, because my house isn't worthy for you to set your foot into"—or—"Say the word, and let my servant be healed"—this is not the act of a realist. No . . . these are different eyes.

The Eyes of Faith

I have a sign that's been hanging in my office for some time. I don't remember where I first saw it. It's a scoreboard, and it has on it the teams "Realists" and "Idealists." In the first inning, the Realists have one or two points, and the Idealists have none. The second inning, the same. The third, the same; the fourth, the fifth, the sixth—all the same . . . all the way through the ninth inning. All along (each inning), the Realists have been marking up the points, and the Idealists have been marking up no points at all. And then at the end, the TOTAL reads: Realists, 0; Idealists, 1.

That was the connection that I saw between the healing of this centurion's slave and the healing of Naaman. Naaman came with the eyes of a realist, but the centurion came with the eyes of faith. And to have such eyes . . . is a marvelous gift.

I know that church-year-wise we are quite a few months from it (forward *or* backward); and yet, to call your attention to how powerful a gift those eyes of faith are, . . . I'd like to remind you of that gift to Mary, the mother of Jesus.

I remember reading something that Luther, as he pondered the event of the Annunciation, had written concerning the faith of Mary. I read it about four years ago now, but it has stuck with me . . . and I share it with you. Luther said that there were three great miracles involved in the Annunciation: first, the miracle that God should become a man; second, the miracle that a baby should be born to a virgin; and third, that Mary believed it. But Luther said, "The third miracle is not the least of the three."

That God should become a man, or that he should so see to it that a virgin could give birth to a baby—these things are "natural" events in the hands of God. But for Mary to believe it—a young woman about to be married, having the hopes and the dreams of youth and blissful tomorrows before her shattered with a word—for Mary to believe it . . . that gift of faith is the greatest gift of all.

And here we see that gift again in the eyes of this centurion . . . now risking all for the sake of a slave; now risking all, with the eyes of a faith that knew where healing was to be found. Here we see it again in the eyes

161

of this centurion: "Lord, do not trouble yourself; for I am not worthy to have you come under my roof. Therefore, I do not presume to come to you. But you say the word, and let my servant be healed." The eyes of this centurion are the eyes of faith.

And what about us? Well, we all, like Naaman, or like the centurion's slave, need help. We need healing. We need strength. We need deliverance. Deliverance . . . from the pressures of the world that would "conform" us (as Paul warns in Romans); from the vision of arrogance that we are warned of in the first chapter of 1 John (the deceiving of ourselves with the truth not in us); from the brokenness in our spiritual relationship to our Father; and from the tragic/"natural" result of that unnatural (broken) relationship.

But what is our approach to our own need for healing (as we pray our intercessory prayers, and bring before our Lord our petitions) for the deliverance for ourselves or others? Our approach ought to be with the eyes of faith taking our cue from that old hymn-line: "Nothing in my hands I bring, simply to thy cross I cling." Our approach ought to look nothing like Naaman's (stockpiles gathered to bargain). And yet we say, "I'll pay!" In fact, we often demand it!

Eyes That "Work"

Yes . . . "I'll pay!" And, in all fairness, we've been raised to believe it's the only way to operate. If someone promises us something, or gives us something, or offers us something . . . our response is, "How much? What does it cost? What do I have to do for it? Where's the catch?"

But either way we look at it, we've still got to refer to that hymn-line . . . yet . . . for a moment: What have we to offer? Even if God worked that way, what have we to offer? What kind of a caravan could we set up that would be worth the gift? What stockpile could we "own" that could buy the gift of wholistic healing that God has for us? What kind of caravan, when Scripture makes clear that even our best deeds are (before God) like dirty rags . . . and "None is righteous"—and—"All have sinned and fallen short of the glory of God"? What could we bring? Even if God did work that way . . . ?

No . . . Nothing . . . And he doesn't work that way; but, in fact, *longs* for the *eyes of faith* to possess his love; longs for those eyes to be the vehicle for his love-acts. In fact, he calls for and demands those eyes.

That is why the "push" on Naaman (to wash seven times in the muddy river; seven times in the junky-Jordan). That is why the "push" so often in Scripture and in daily life (like the woman, you remember, who came to Jesus, wanting a healing, and who got in return: "Woman, what have

162

I got to do with you? I came only for the house of Israel. I did not come for dogs like you." You remember that "push"? What for? . . . So that her eyes of faith would be opened—all the way; so that her wide-eyed eyes of faith could be seen by all those around her; so that they could hear her "eyes of faith" as her voice said, "Yes, Lord, but even the dogs get the scraps from the master's table").

God longs for those eyes of faith, that his love might be perceived; longs for those eyes of faith just as the centurion had; eyes filled with a confidence in spite of risk; eyes that expect miracles; eyes that make for a readiness rather than surprise; eyes so sure in whose hand the future lies, that the beholder is able to walk, rather than stumble into . . . to face, rather than cower from the future. God longs for the eyes of faith from his people like this centurion; for those eyes are the vehicle of his love-acts.

WILLIAM C. LARSON
Dobbs Ferry Lutheran Church
Dobbs Ferry, New York

THIRD SUNDAY AFTER PENTECOST

Word of Life
Luke 7:11-17

The Old Testament Lesson and the Gospel confront us with death—with a vengeance! The women whose only sons have died are widows. So, they have had a particularly traumatic experience of death. They have lost the important men in their lives and, in their times and places, that would involve a great loss not only of meaning but of power. It could mean almost total helplessness.

Our Story, Too

That's not the kind of thing we like to think about, but it is right that we are confronted by it, because it is true to life. It is true to our life. The widows' story is our story. Though at first we might well feel that we have little in common with them, when we stop to think about it we realize that they and we have everything in common. We, also, will be helpless in the face of death. That is the ultimate fact of our life too.

I'd love to ignore that . . . and so would you! We'll deny it whenever we can. Even in the church—perhaps especially in the church—we're

163

tempted to premature celebration; to going around the cross to dwell exclusively on resurrection; to jumping immediately to the conclusion of our texts, the restoration of the sons to their mothers, without ever taking seriously the deaths and the loss, the weakness and the despair.

But all of that is part of the story. It's our part. It's the only part that is ours. It is the story of our life. To deny that is to deny our life. Any hope that depends on such denial is an illusion. The emphasis in our time on death and dying has served us well to the extent that it has led us, through denial, back to reality.

Yet acceptance alone is not an adequate response to death. Death is a scandal, an obscenity, "the last enemy." Resignation will not change that and mere acceptance can become a kind of denial. Better then, by far, to "rage against the dying of the light," as Dylan Thomas put it.

The Death of the World

Even when they have accepted death, people have avoided real confrontation with it by attributing a kind of immortality to the world. That idea has sometimes given us the feeling that we can triumph over death by leaving something that will live on. It's false, of course. We all know very well that the world itself will not go on forever. But we have been able to put that "vast death of the solar system" so far in the future that we could still comfort ourselves with the fiction of its immortality. That option is all but gone.

Today the events and conditions of our time confront us with the death of our world . . . not as something unimaginably distant and remote and, so, unreal, but as something very conceivable, possible, imminent, that threatens all that we are and have, everything we hope for, and does it *now,* where we live! These events and conditions have made themselves known, to some degree, to almost everyone. The proliferation of nuclear arms. The depletion of natural resources, including even water and the land. Exploding populations. Shortages of food and hunger all over the world. The pollution of the environment. Economic maladjustment almost everywhere. To these can be added what may be the greatest danger of all: the apparent indifference of so many, and the unwillingness to do anything about such problems.

Once again we are strongly tempted to ignore and to deny. One reason for that is certainly what we call sin, the blindness to anything else of the one "curved in" upon self. But another is our feeling of powerlessness, like that of the widows. Yet another, paradoxically, is our seemingly incurable optimism, our naive assumption that things will work out. (They always have!) That form of denial, too, has invaded our churches, where we have sometimes come to speak of Christain hope in terms of positive thinking (and the denial of everything negative).

The Life in Awareness

But denial doesn't make it here, either, for the same reason: it is a denial of our life. There is no real hope for the world, any more than there is for us, in fantasy and illusion. There is more meaning—more life—in reality, at its most forbidding. There seems, in fact, to be a kind of life (and, therefore, hope) in the *awareness* of reality, including threatening reality, including death. The very confrontation which reveals our powerlessness and can make life seem senseless can also (again, paradoxically!) shock and waken us to a new vitality, releasing energies we didn't know we had, making us aware of much we had never suspected was there. Elie Wiesel has said of life in the Nazi concentration camp at Auschwitz, "You should know that no one is as grateful as a person who was there. We died more than once. But now, every hour is an hour of grace. Every smile, every word, is something we didn't expect." When we deeply know how fragile our life and our world are, and how transitory, we may appreciate and enjoy them more!

But, again, acceptance is not an adequate response. Here, too, that can become a denial of the meaning of death, at least for others. Really to confront it we must see it as enemy, something to be resisted, fought! We have no more right simply to allow the world to degencrate, thereby hastening its demise, because we know it is not eternal, than we have to neglect and abuse our bodies because we know they are not immortal!

But here again we are soon maddeningly aware of our powerlessness, and we must quickly admit that the hope that would make that struggle meaningful is not to be found in our lives or in our world. That is not part of our story.

The Rest of the Story

We desperately need to hear another story! A story other than our own. A story like that which Paul preached, which "is not man's gospel"; which comes "through a revelation." We need to hear the rest of the story of the widows, the part that is not their story. We need to hear the part about Elijah and the part about Jesus . . . which is the story of a Word of Life. "Now I know," said the widow to Elijah, "that the word of the Lord in your mouth is truth." "A great prophet has arisen among us," was the people's reaction to Jesus . . . a prophet being one who brings "the word of the Lord." We, too, must hear that Word, that Word of life, that Word that creates and renews life, that Word that became flesh to give to all who receive him the power to become children of God. We need to hear that Word which is the plot of the one true story.

That can give meaning to our story, to your life and mine. To every part of our lives, including our death! As we hear it and "keep it in good and honest hearts," it becomes that "imperishable seed" by which we are "born anew to a living hope." And death is no longer just the end of the old but the beginning of the new. It becomes the culmination of a process by which we enter into life. And it (or something like it) becomes a *way* of life: "as dying, and behold we live!" It becomes a way of participating in the humbling and emptying of self and the service and obedience of the Word-become-flesh. Our dying can be made the ultimate earthly participation in the story of Christ, our being crucified with him, so that, in some wild sense, "it is no longer I who live, but Christ who lives within me."

Our death becomes but the last stage in a dying to a separate, independent, self-sufficient existence (which is the real death) and a coming alive to trust in the Lord of Life and love like his for others (which is the real life). "He who hears my word," said Jesus, "and believes him who sent me . . . has passed from death to life." "We know that we have passed out of death into life, because we love the brethren." By the power of the Word of Life, our death becomes the final phase and the completion of a dying to sin that frees us to be alive to righteousness and to walk in newness of life.

In that newness, we will respect our bodies: "flesh" shared by the Living Word; "members of Christ"; places where God still chooses to dwell in our world. And we will love the world because he loves it and have some freedom—like Elijah, even like Jesus—to put our bodies on the line for the despairing and the powerless . . . for the world itself. We can live with hope and joy (though dying people in a dying world) not because of any confidence in our own ability to save the world, or anyone it it, but because of the knowledge given to us, too, that "God has visited his people" with the Word of Life . . . and "our times are in his hands."

We can pray the ancient prayer of the day:

O God, the strength of those who hope in you: Be present and hear our prayers; and, because in the weakness of our mortal nature we can do nothing good without you, give us the help of your grace, so that in keeping your commandments we may please you in will and deed; through your Son, Jesus Christ, our Lord. Amen.

LOWELL O. LARSON
Vinje Lutheran Church
Willmar, Minnesota

The Sinner's Risk of Love
Luke 7:36-50

If deemed appropriate, this Gospel can be read from the center of the church and the sermon begun either there, or further to the rear, with the speaker coming to the front as he describes the woman approaching Jesus. This light dramatization may help set the mood for the application of this lesson.

You have heard this Gospel before, and perhaps you have also been invited to relate it to today's life by imagining that it happened at a dinner party in your own home with Jesus as the honored guest. We don't even have to stretch our imaginations that far. When we gathered together this morning, we began our service with the invocation. An invocation is a public declaration inviting and acknowledging the presence of the Lord in our midst. The Lord is here. He is present in the feast we share.

Since the moment of the invocation we have gone through forms of confession and praise. Now you have settled back to hear him speak through the Gospel. He is here. We need only imagine him as being *visibly* present, standing at the pulpit. That's not too hard, is it?

But now imagine a woman standing in the back. She didn't come in with the rest of the crowd, taking a bulletin from the usher, reverently bowing her head in prayer, and perhaps even crossing herself. No, she did not enter boldly, but slipped in late, as unobtrusively as possible. She doesn't belong in the church crowd at all, and her appearance proves it. Some may even know where she generally hangs out, and it sure isn't here! But she has heard of Jesus and the news that his words are meant for her. She has been told that she can find him *here*. She is terrified at the thought of what may happen to her. Will she be stopped? Laughed at? Even publicly scorned by Jesus? It wouldn't surprise her. She has known such humiliation before.

The Woman's Risk

But she must do what she must do. She walks down the aisle, moving more swiftly with each step until at last she is running to Jesus. She awkwardly starts to minister to Jesus, then breaks down completely,

167

weeping profusely. She falls at his feet. Then, having nothing else to use, she begins to wipe his tear-soaked feet with her hair.

And what about the pastor, the official host of this gathering? Sitting in his chair next to the pulpit, he cranes his neck to see what is happening. He can't believe his eyes! Frantic thoughts begin to race through his mind. What are any visitors going to think of this? They are going to think that this is what Lutherans do all the time! Perhaps they will never come back. They might even think that this girl is a member. And some of the regulars, the pillars of the church—what abotu them? They are going to say that if this is what the *Lutheran Book of Worship* calls for, then they are through for good. Oh, he's going to hear from the church council about this one, that's for sure! Doesn't Jesus realize what is going on? Two ushers have moved quietly down the side aisle. They are ready for action. If only Jesus would give them the nod!

Then Jesus turns to the pastor. "I have something to ask of you and everyone else here."

"What is it?"

"Two men without a dime in the bank had mortgages on their homes with the same money lender. One was one month behind in his payments. The other one was a whole year behind in his payments and was ready to be foreclosed. Then the mortgage holder told them both he would cancel out what they owed. Tell me, which one of them will love him more?"

"I imagine," the pastor said, "the one who was going to be foreclosed."

"Of course," Jesus said, "And I am sure that everyone here agrees with you. But now look again at this woman and compare her actions to how you and your whole congregation have behaved toward me this morning. You have been more or less polite, but you haven't really rejoiced in your hearts because I have come here to be with you. You sang 'Amazing Grace,' but none of you looked very amazed. You are not really that happy about my being here, and you know it!"

Then he points to the woman. "But this woman! What love! She can't do enough to show me honor. I tell you, the great love she has shown proves that her sins, which are many, have been forgiven. But whoever has been forgiven little, loves little" (TEV).

The Risk of Exposure

It scares me to death to think that there might be some who think that the lesson here is that if you have been a prostitute (as this woman most likely was), or a habitual drunk, or a junkie, or an unscrupulous business operator, or a con man, then you really need forgiveness and if you get it, well, you certainly do have something to be thankful for! Nor was Jesus saying, "I'm giving her forgiveness because she has been slobbering all over me."

No, Jesus' point is that you must know how much you have been forgiven before you can love him as you ought. His point has to do with becoming a Christian according to his terms. He is teaching that the first thing you have to do, as this woman did, is to take the risk of acknowledging the greatness of your sin. He is challenging Simon, and you, and me, and anybody else who might be ranked with the "ins" instead of the "outs," to take the risk of loving him for what he alone can do. It is the risk of admitting that it is not your goodness, your support of services in a lovely church building, your having your children baptized, your going to Communion or anything else you would put in the category of "respectable good deeds"—that nothing of this sort is going to bring you one inch closer to being in the kingdom of God. Only the forgiveness of your sins can do that.

The risk you are being called to take is that of a heart-wrenching moment of honest confession in which you say that you know that something is radically wrong with you, too. The sinner's risk of love is to confess that the myth of the happy sinner is just that: a myth. It is to admit that happiness does not come through sin, and it does not come through looking down on others whom we think are less worthy than we. It comes only through casting ourselves totally on the mercy of God. It is the risk of coming face to face with Jesus and hearing him say, "Friend, don't try to fool me. I know you for what you are, and I am not impressed." And then you say, "Yes, Lord. You are right. I need your mercy."

You are being confronted by Jesus in this lesson and you are being asked: Do you think of yourself as someone who ought to be dissolved in tears at the thought that, instead of pushing you away, Jesus willingly opens wide his hands and his arms to you? If you don't think of yourself in such terms, what should I say to you? I can say, "Well, congratulations! It's nice to know that there are such good people in this world who do not need the miracle of God's grace." Or perhaps it would be more appropriate to say, "My deepest sympathy. I am sorry that you still do not see those things in your life which should cause you to fall weeping at the feet of your Lord and Savior, throwing yourself on the mercy of God."

The Risk of the Cross

This is strong language in a world that is accustomed to talking about how we ought to feel good about ourselves. I don't want to be wholly negative, either. I will seek to put it in a more positive way. I will define the meaning of this risk-taking by speaking for myself. I feel good about myself because of what Christ has done for me on Calvary. But for those words to mean anything to you, I must confess that I need God's forgiveness terribly. If you knew me as I know myself, you would be terribly disappointed in me; for I know how disappointed I am in myself.

There is a risk in such an admission. People don't like to think of being disappointed in their pastor, but I have to take that risk if I would be serious and on the level in what I say about becoming a Christian according to Christ's terms. I do gladly confess to you that there are not enough tears that I could shed to match the love he first showed me on Calvary. I confess to you that to partake of his body and blood in the Lord's Supper is a moment of delight to me because it assures me that he has forgiven me so much. What more joyous moment can there be than to remember that he gave his life for me, that he shed his blood for me? We love him much because he has forgiven us much.

The Risk of Change

The risk of love goes on. It is significant to me that Jesus did not spend time preaching a sermon to Simon. His sermon to Simon consisted of his final words to the woman: "Your *faith* has saved you. Go in peace." He let Simon figure out the rest. And what might have happened next has always fascinated me. When I was scarcely past twenty I wrote a short story about Simon, picturing him at last coming to terms with God that night on a darkened hillside. Such a scene is not completely farfetched, for it is my private theory that some of these events which Luke had carefully researched and could report in such detail, including even the name of the Pharisee, were possible because these people had become a part of the new Christian community and had told of their meeting with Christ which had changed their lives.

Such a change was not impossible for Simon, not any more than for us when we are touched by the love of Christ for sinners. As we are touched by that love we are led to realize that the risk of a sinner's love consists not only in admitting what the mercy of God must do for us, but in asking now for the Holy Spirit's power to go to work in our lives. The sinner's risk of love leads you to ask: What should I be doing for Christ that I am not doing now? What should be radically changed in the way I am conducting my affairs or living with my family?

As an example of this risk of love, think of Simon and this woman meeting the next day on one of the streets in their little village. If Jesus had got through to him, would Simon cross over to the other side, or would he speak to her? Would she drop her eyes in continued shame, or would she hold her head up high as a forgiven member of the kingdom of God? It is proper to ask such questions because Jesus doesn't just leave us sitting forever frozen in solemn assembly. He sends us back into the streets as forgiven sinners who meet other forgiven sinners. There his love leads us to forgive as we have been forgiven, to accept others as we have been accepted by him, to deal with one another as God deals with us.

This is the risk of a sinner's love. It is to openly and enthusiastically love Jesus because we know there is so much in us that he has forgiven. It is to dare to ask, touched by his love so wide and so deep, "Lord, in my attitudes and in my relationships with others, work with your power within me so that I might be changed!"

VERNON R. SCHREIBER
Resurrection Lutheran Church
Yardley, Pennsylvania

FIFTH SUNDAY AFTER PENTECOST

The Gospel of Promise
Luke 9:18-24

Payoff or Cost?

To live, we have to die. As Luther urges: "I say die . . . taste death as though it were present." There is no way of escape or shortcut. Instant victory over evil is an illusion. God's "Yes" to all his promises in Jesus Christ in no way disqualifies the "No" of human life. For even that "Yes" is forged in the fire of the crucifixion itself. The cross is hardly a divine tool placed in our hands for a snap-of-the-fingers solution to human pain and perplexity. The cross of the crucified Christ was an engagement *with* evil. "If any man will come after me," says the Crucified One, "let him deny himself and take up his cross daily and follow me." The cross-taker engages every bit of the same evil. We *have* to die to live.

But countless speakers appear on the religious stage voicing their celebrated elimination of the negatives, the evils, and the contradictions that beset all of us. The Christian gospel now rests in the framework of a payoff. False comfort always sells, whether it is the counterfeit promise of a physical shrine or the easy peace of mind of a shrink. Packaged with appeal and peddled with sentiment, the gospel becomes a list of favors— answers to whatever we find questionable, palliatives for whatever we consider burdensome, payoffs for whatever we deem necessary. The opti-

171

mism merchants convert the gospel into a verdict we can render against evil or natural aches and pains—*as we see fit*. They grant us permission to handle the gospel as protection against life and experience. In turn, moreover, we readily arrange the gospel to follow the lines of *our* desires and to do *our work*. Absent, of course, is the perspective of the "cost" of the gospel, "whoever loses his life for my sake, he will save it."

This payoff syndrome attracts those of "pseudo-innocence" (Rollo May), those who shield deep sickness and disturbance with sweet goodness and simple solutions. No longer is God the end of faith, rather, one's own welfare and state of bliss becomes ultimate. So we witness cozy words offered to the suffering from those who have never truly suffered themselves; we hear pious platitudes on how to flee the wilderness from someone who has never been there. These tiny imaginations shrink the cosmic scope of evil and the great cost of love. Instead of taking up a cross, we are encouraged to cash it in. In place of self-denial, we are instructed to become absorbed with cures for our problems. The payoff gospel makes human existence manageable or solvable. But darkness can be more dangerously present in these facile answers than in the problems they are supposed to solve. For we do not find life by holding onto it, administering it, or resolving it. We *have* to die to live.

The Dying to Be Truly Born

William James notes in *The Varieties of Religious Experience* a summary of the Lutheran tradition—"salvation through self-despair." He explains: "something must give way, a native hardness must break down and liquefy. . . ." Certainly this is a stark contrast to religion-as-solution in which something must be added or gained, especially in a quick and easy payoff for our desires and experiences. We have to die both to "the desires of the flesh" (Gal. 5:16) and "the works of the flesh" (Gal. 5:19). We must bury, therefore, the self turned in on itself. We must "die" to a self infatuated with control for personal benefit. Indeed the self desiring to exist apart from suffering and contradiction must break down. There is a necessary kind of destruction of the self pretending to overwhelm the negative by shouting positives or payoffs. Before the cross can be taken up, self-denial must precede it.

Who can save a child from undue fear without taking time to know the child? Who can hear the story of loneliness apart from the risk of hearing the same loneliness in his own heart? Who can draw attention to a friend's self-centered behavior without the risk of losing the friendship? Some "dying" is involved with anything worthwhile. A parent takes a chance when investing time and affection for the enhancement of a child's growth.

172

Small or great gifts never command an automatic response or equal action. If saving our soul (or "own skins" and "face") rises to prominence, we can risk nothing. To deny ourselves, there has to be a self to deny, neither protected by "pseudo-innocence" nor instant solutions. What is to be denied is the self in all its illusions and evils. We *die* to live, not *lie* to live. A self utterly anxious about itself takes up nothing but its own anxiety, certainly not the cross which embraces the problems and pains of others. A preoccupied self is a shaky self, possessed of its own weight.

But God will teach the self the *need* for denial which precedes the *gift* of new life. Salvation is a promise, a free offering. It is truly "out of our hands." Payoffs are *handled* transactions. To know God, to trust him, and to follow his chosen, beloved Son can only be received as gift. The cost to ourselves, then, is every attempt or achievement to have God in hand. To take up a cross is to let go, to open up, and to live on razor's edge. The wilderness is the time of emptying; the winter is occasion for purifying. In dying we are born. Rollo May observes the death and resurrection motif, the losing and finding, in this manner:

> In Europe at Easter time, people turn out *en masse* for the sacrament of Good Friday, since they want to make sure Jesus is dead. The celebration of his death is a necessary precursor to any rising from the tomb. The renewal requires the death beforehand. That Christ has risen has meaning only if he has been really dead. In America, there is scant attendence on Good Friday, but the churches are filled to capacity on Easter. This is indicative of our lack of belief in tragedy in this country. It is a demonstration of our endeavor to overlook the death that must occur before the resurrection, the suffering that precedes joy, the tragedy that precedes achievement, the conflict that precedes creativity (*Freedom and Destiny*, p. 240).

And it is a demonstration of our endeavor to have "abundant life" according to the tastes of American prosperity and dreams, notably the ever-present quick and easy gospel that "pays off."

The Promise of Life

The Christian life is waged between the old self with its tastes for direct and immediate results and the new person in Christ waiting for grace to dawn. But the cost is not a blank check. The cost is backed up with promissory notes: "my yoke is easy," and "he who follows me will not walk in darkness, but will have the light of life."

God invites us to lose ourselves but not senselessly. The invitation issues from one who cares and is faithful to his caring. It is always a losing for the sake of him who cares for us. Care, originally a word meaning to mourn and to share in pain, is God's own participation with us in the denying, the following, and the losing. Instead of concerning ourselves with the gospel as cure or payoff, we trust the gospel as God's grandiose and gracious expression of care for us. The immense mystery of our salvation is that God came to us in Jesus Christ. He lost himself ("emptied himself") and found us. He came to share our pains in care, not blot them out with rapid-fire cures.

Interestingly enough, the words of Jesus did not come out like this: "If anyone would come after me, let them take good stock of themselves and take my cures upon themselves and find my payoffs."

The crucified one is the embodiment and the model of the cost of life. And so he bought us not with gold or silver, but with his own blood, his own life. He was the first one to lose his life and find it. And there was a cost, for surely there is a cost for anything worthwhile. You and I are worth all the caring. The cost of self-denial and taking up a cross is the cost of love. He who loves us, gives himself for us. He has invited us to journey the same path of care he himself paced off beforehand. But the path is strewn with impediments and haunts: followers who lose courage, opponents who weary with jealousy and strife, people who demand payoffs. But he invites us to travel this road in *his name*. He is present among the tracks and footprints, caring for us even as we care for others.

We *have* to die to live. But the dying is for the sake of the crucified who never disappoints and always keeps his promise. If you are looking for instant solutions and easy payoffs, you're on the wrong path. But along the way, there will be promises kept and blessings given in the long haul. For God wants us to trust him, not control and use him. And he can be trusted even while your hands are carrying the crosses of life and experience.

> He gives power to the faint,
> and to him who has no might he increases strength . . .
> they who wait for the Lord shall renew their strength,
> they shall mount up with wings like eagles,
> they shall run and not be weary,
> they shall walk and not faint
> (Isaiah 40:29, 31).

When all is said and done, it is either *that promise* or the false comfort of some payoff. The gospel is promise. The other invitations to protection, escape, and solutions are suspect. The gospel promise comes as a gift and surprise of God's own will and with divine timing. It is a promise of *strength* to those who *wait* for the Lord. He invites us to follow and promises that we "shall run and not be weary" and "shall walk and not faint."

No shortcuts. No clear-cut answers. No razzle-dazzle cures. No immediate payoffs. The invitation to follow is the call to trust the redeeming hands of the crucified. And those hands can be trusted, the hands of the dead and risen Lord.

Peter L. Steinke
Lutheran Social Service of Texas
Dallas, Texas

SIXTH SUNDAY AFTER PENTECOST

Dangerously Faithful
Luke 9:51-62

We know that our Lord wants us to follow him faithfully and joyfully. All of our thinking, acting, and feeling is to be lived under his gracious persuasion. But what does it mean to belong to him and obey him? What of this day-to-day business of life-styles and relationships? Following Jesus, we say, does not demand of us any one set of rules for behavior. That is Christian freedom, we insist. But consider this: our problem today is not so much with freedom as with faithfulness.

Is it enough to say, "You follow Jesus in your way and I will follow him in mine"? T. S. Eliot said of his poetry, "It means what it means, and whatever else you think it means." What with our penchant for self-deception, it would be better if we would first learn the meaning of commitment from him who said, "Follow me." Our faithfulness to Jesus should be shaped by his faithfulness to us.

A Different People

In his book, *Christian Counter-Culture,* John R. Stott says, "No comment could be more harmful to the Christian than the words, 'But you are no different from anybody else'" (p. 17). Followers of Jesus Christ, he says, must be different from anybody else—different from both the nominal church and the secular world; an alternative society; a counterculture.

In a marriage counseling session the question of church life was being discussed. A young woman said, "I'm sort of a Christian, like most people." It didn't seem to hurt her at all to be the same as others instead of different. Well, how do you feel about being sort-of-a-Christian? Would it bother you to hear you are no different from anybody else?

There is a man in the national news who is appearing as a different kind of Christian. I first knew him as a high school chemistry teacher in my hometown. Now he is an archbishop who has decided to withhold one-half of his personal income tax as a protest against America's continuing involvement in the race for nuclear arms supremacy. Of course, he is being both praised and blamed. Some letters in the newspaper were supportive: "courageous decision"; "his patriotism is most heartening." Others were puzzled and resentful: "he should stick to saving souls"; "he doesn't speak for me."

Make Peace, Not War

Archbishop Hunthausen doesn't speak for me, either, but I believe we ought to listen to what he is saying. Surely, the nuclear weapons chase is a serious moral issue. Nobody denies that anymore. What more and more of us are sensing is that we must become personally active in prayer and discussion about the problems of nuclear war preparedness and the holo-caust it may lead to. Instead of pointing angry fingers at each other, let us reason and pray together about what we can individually do to help make peace happen on earth.

Certainly we want a world in which nuclear arms are reduced and hopefully eliminated. God bless our president for making that offer to the Soviet Union this past week. There are many approaches to working for peace and doing it in an unwarlike spirit. Some of us may choose peaceful civil disobedience to a law as an obligation to conscience and be willing to go to jail for it.

I'm not sure I agree with what the archbishop is doing, but I do grant that his protest is an expression of his walk with the Lord. That I admire. Perhaps I admire it because there may not be much in my own walk with Christ that stands out as being different from anybody else. And I'm not satisfied with being sort-of-a-Christian. Neither are you. Truly, these are times that summon us to faithfulness.

Chaos or New Creation?

We believe this is God's world, don't we? He made it; he redeemed it from the forces of evil; he rules over it as a loving Savior. The gifts of his kingdom are extended to everyone everywhere; it doesn't matter who you are or what you were in the past. Now, the Gospel says, you are God's creation, made in his image, sustained by his providence, and upheld by his love. Jesus Christ died for you and was raised for you. By grace through faith you can receive resurrection to a new life of forgiveness of sins, the gift of the Holy Spirit, hope in the coming kingdom of God, membership in the Body of Christ, and the calling and equipment to serve God in the world.

That is almighty God's offer to our broken, bleeding world. Claim the new life! Receive peace and power! For every person there is a new identity in Jesus Christ. Neighbors and nations can be saved from destructive selfishness and live in caring community. The Holy Spirit has been poured out on all flesh as a preview of coming attractions, the consummation of all things in Christ.

All of this sounds so good, you say. We hear about these things in church, but when we walk out that door, it's not the same. The conditions of human life in the world seem to belie the Gospel. Nations angrily aim their missiles at each other, like boys daring each other to fight. Family life is falling apart. The hungry multitude, the restless unemployed, the victims of repression—all these and more cry to heaven. And we're supposed to do something about it?

Yes, in our words and deeds, in suffering and joy, we are to proclaim the Lordship of Jesus Christ, to follow him. Sometimes we will feel very alone, sometimes misunderstood. We may be hurt by others, even our friends. And where are we going to find the courage and wisdom to make concrete decisions on complex issues? In the Gospel, of course. So often we attempt to live our lives without the example and teaching of our Lord. "To whom shall we go," said the disciples, "you have the words of eternal life." Before we shape our commitment to Christ, we should consider his commitment to us.

The Final Ascent

In our text St. Luke is describing a crucial turning point in the life and mission of Jesus. "As the time approached when Jesus was to be taken up to heaven, he set his face resolutely towards Jerusalem" (NEB). It is clear to Jesus the moment for his final ascent is at hand.

Jim Whitaker knew not everyone on the expedition team could make the final assault on K-2, the world's second highest peak, on the Pakistan-China border. He must make the choice; he was the leader. As it happened, he chose four men, himself not among them, to be the first Americans to make that heroic trek to the summit.

Jesus must go for it himself, alone. His jaw is jutted; his gaze is fixed; his purpose is sure. "He resolutely set his face. . . ." The bell has rung for the final round. He must go to the Holy City to finish the fight, to give the heavenly Father his last full measure of devotion.

Vision and Victim

Perhaps it hit him fully only a few days before on Mt. Hermon. You recall the transfiguration story. Peter, James, and John go along on a hiking retreat with Jesus. So many people had crowded into his heart of love that there was scarcely room for any more. He needed to get away to rest and pray. It doesn't surprise us that his disciples soon dozed off to sleep. Most nights I go to sleep during my prayers. But when the three awoke they immediately saw the Master's face had changed and his clothes were like shimmering rhinestones. It was a holy moment. The 15th century hymn says—

> O wondrous type, O vision fair
> Of glory that the church shall share,
> Which Christ upon the mountain shows,
> Where brighter than the sun he glows!

Might it have been in that moment of deep, spiritual communion, of wonderful power flooding from heaven, that Jesus decided for the final ascent? We know Moses and Elijah were present, discussing it with him. Had they come to reinforce his commitment to the cross? It appears so. And the voice of his Father confirmed it: "This is my son, my chosen."

So Jesus was firmly, even fiercely committed to the new exodus, a journey which led to Calvary's mournful hill. There he would deliver all people from enslavement to sin's allure, to death and the devil.

A Radical Redeemer

If we follow Jesus in the story we will hear him saying more radical things about himself and his commitment. "I have come to set fire on the earth, and how I wish it were already kindled! I have a baptism to undergo, and how hampered I am until the ordeal is over" (Luke 12:49-55). We notice that Jesus walks ahead of his disciples instead of alongside them. Indeed, there is tension between them. He is totally absorbed in his passion. All he thinks about is accepting the sacrifice of redeeming love.

Every step of the way Jesus must fend off the temptation to be a militant Messiah, running roughshod over his opposition. God will bring salvation to the world through One who has no weapons of war; One who has no strength; One who is despised and rejected by everyone. Oh, he has a secret weapon all right; it is love! He will not crush anyone with it, but will himself be crushed. He, the innocent One, will take on himself the wrongs of others, and yield up his life that they may be spared.

178

Vision and Victor

Jesus also said it was necessary for him to suffer these things in order for him to enter his glory (Luke 24:26ff). So the words from Luke, "As the time approached for him to be taken up into heaven, he set his face. . . ." He is going home. Praise God, he is returning to his heavenly Father. The defeated One is the victorious One. He overcomes the opposition not with swords loud clashing but with deeds of love and mercy. And because of him the earth shall one day be full of the knowledge of the Lord, as the waters cover the sea. One day, faithful sisters and brothers, he will return in glory as King and Prince to rule over us forever, in love, joy and peace. This is Christ's commitment to us. It is his example to all who would walk in his steps daily.

Our Commitment to Christ

There was a resistance fighter in Norway in 1940 who was facing the invasion of his country. The tyranny had come in. It looked hopeless for a long time ahead. What should he do? Come to terms with the tyrant? That's what some were doing. Or join the underground and risk his life? In that moment he wrote these words: "This is not a time for me to desert my faith. It is not a time to turn to new images of belief. This is a time for me to be dangerously faithful." It is a word for us today; that our faith ought to shine. It ought to shine so that all people who are in darkness may see it.

A marching band of a small college wanted to play for homecoming and impress the crowd. But they didn't have a big enough band. So they recruited some students who would march along even though they couldn't play. They could carry tubas. And they looked very impressive; great big shining horns. As they came marching down the street, a little boy who was watching it all very intently said to his mother, "Mamma, there's nothing coming out of those big things." I wonder if sometimes people say this about the church. There's nothing very much coming out of it.

Dangerously Faithful

Maybe this is the day for us to begin at the beginning. If this universe is not glued together in Jesus Christ, as Paul says it is in Colossians, then let's put all our confidence in a nuclear arms standoff, because that is the only hope we have to live out our years. But if the potent, righteous and sole lordship over this world is with Jesus Christ, if all things do cohere in him, it's about time we take seriously what discipleship means, and what kind of servants we must become. Either God's purpose is going to

179

be fulfilled in the future—I don't think it's going to be very soon—or it isn't. But if it is, let's show our world what we believe with all our hearts and minds. Do we believe only sort-of? Can we not believe enough to be different? Or even to be dangerously faithful?

Is faithfulness too heavy for you? Are you thinking, "I'm not the stuff from which modern-day disciples are made"? Then remember this: Jesus is the Savior of the world; we don't have to be. The future doesn't depend upon us, but upon him. He goes before us in love, saying "Follow me." He comes to us in the Eucharist, his wine in our veins, reviving us on the way.

JACK F. HUSTAD
First Lutheran Church of Richmond Beach
Seattle, Washington

Fear Turned into Joy
Luke 10:1-12, 16 (17-20)

What's the most exciting and the happiest place in your town? Some answers we could anticipate to the question would be: the theater, country club, stock exchange, football stadium, bowling alley, music hall, shopping center, or the finest restaurant in town. Do you suppose any person would answer, "My church is the center of more joy and excitement than any other place in our town."

The church has the possibility of being just such an exciting, happy place. I make this statement on the basis of the words from our text, "The seventy returned with joy and said, 'Lord even the demons submit to your name.'" These disciples, who had gathered for a report meeting, were filled with joy. They had seen how God could use them to bless other people. That same joy is found in the congregation when Christian people see first hand how God can use them in ministering to the needs of others.

Prior to leaving on their mission, they were 70 frightened people standing before Jesus. They were being commissioned to spread out in the surrounding towns and minister to people in Christ's name. Jesus was not sending them out to make a few social calls to people who would wine and dine them. He was sending them out as "lambs in the midst of wolves." He told the disciples that in some towns they would be rejected by certain people. He made it clear that not all people would have the welcome mat out to receive them. But then there was a word of challenge. "The harvest is plentiful. There are people whose hearts long to hear the message you have for them. Find them and minister to their needs."

Surely the seventy went forth with fear and trembling. They did not know what specific problems they would encounter. Perhaps their fear was more of the unknown than actually being anxious about how they would handle certain irate people.

Those same fears of the unknown torment us today. Many preachers enter their pulpits fearfully asking, "How will the message be received by the congregation? Is it God's Word that I preach to the people, or is it some personal conviction of my own that has little biblical support? Will my words be used by the Holy Spirit to help some person who comes with his or her hurts?"

The conscientious Sunday school teacher expresses fear when he or she struggles with the question, "How am I going to reach that kid who drives me out of my mind, but who is so precious to the Lord?"

The personal evangelist is a bit anxious as he shares his faith in Christ with a friend. "Will he think that I am invading his privacy? Will he label me a religious fanatic? Will he no longer consider me a friend?"

The good neighbor is dubious about getting too involved with that lonely person. "What if she becomes a nuisance and invades my privacy so that I have to give up some of my spare time for her?"

If our Christianity does not cause us to have some fears, it is questionable if we are letting God use us to bless other people. Sharing our faith with other people can be frightening.

So with a pulse rate of 120 and legs that are shaking, the seventy left on their journey with the light of the Gospel to share with those who sat in darkness.

On the journey, their fears were turned into joy. They saw the power of the word they carried with them. People's lives were changed; their bodies were healed; their spirits were set free.

These same miracles happen today. It is amazing how the Holy Spirit can use our feeble efforts and our stammering speech to reach people with the great message of God's love in Christ. The evidence of the power of God's Word in the lives of people is all around us. People are set free from their guilt. Their values are changed. They find new joy in living for others rather than being concerned only about their own person. It is these evidences of an almighty, loving, merciful God moving in and through the church that makes it an exciting happy place. The difficult times, the frightening moments are soon forgotten.

I always enjoy watching the baseball team that has just won the World

Series. The television cameras take us into the locker room. There is a spirit of victory and a lot of joy. The game is won. Before the game those same players had strained looks on their faces. They were tense. The frightening thought flashed through their minds, "Might we lose this game?" But now that the game is won and their team is the victor, it is time to celebrate. Fear has turned into joy.

There was some of that same jubilation when the seventy disciples returned home. "Lord, even the demons submit to us in your name," they said. They saw things happen which they could hardly believe. Only the good experiences seemed to count. They thought little about the difficult times they might have experienced.

Many of us know the joy that was in those disciples' hearts, for we have had the same experiences.

In our congregation we have an evangelism training program that sends people into homes in our community. When the teams report back to the church following the visitation, there is usually a great spirit. Some of these evangelism teams have had the opportunity to share the Gospel with those they visited. In some cases, these people who were visited have taken the first step back into a more meaningful relationship with Christ. Each Sunday morning there are many people in our congregation who have found new life in Christ through the ministry of the laity. This brings joy to the congregation. Suddenly the ministry of the church becomes exciting. Great things are happening in many congregations, and there is joy in seeing how God is using his Church to touch lives with the Good News of Christ.

It is also interesting to note that Jesus confirmed the joy of the seventy. He warned the disciples not to let their success turn into pride. He wanted them always to remember that they were carriers of the word and it was the Spirit of God who had brought about the miracles they had witnessed. However, Jesus was anxious to rejoice with them and he reminded these disciples that their names were written in heaven.

I am convinced that this story of the seventy was recorded in Scripture to bring a word of encouragement to discouraged churches. The Lord uses the example of "the seventy" to challenge us to move out into our world with the Gospel. There are many in our communities who need just what we have to give them.

How easy it is for us to get so busy around the church with many mundane activities. Then the Spirit of God begins to push us to get on with our Father's business to share the story of Jesus Christ with those who are not saved. First, there is the excuse, "I am not adequate to talk to anybody about Christ." Then someone says that this type of ministry is foreign to our Lutheran understanding of witnessing. We begin to nitpick about how the witnessing should be done. We comb the presentation of the Gospel for theological errors. The results are pathetic. Many do not hear the good news of God's love in Christ, and we, the followers of Christ, cheat ourselves out of the excitement and joy that can be ours in carrying the good news.

The church is not a place of doom and gloom when it is doing the work Christ has told us to do. A seven hundred score at the bowling alley, a delightful evening at the restaurant, a thrilling performance at music hall, a moving play at the theater or a great report at the stock exchange make these places centers of excitement and joy. And they are. But, the joy found in these establishments does not compare to the joy experienced at the church when the members return weekly from their mission and tell what the Lord has done through them. Lives have been changed. Healing has taken place. A soul rests in Christ. To witness such miracles performed by God's power through us is exciting.

HOMER LARSEN
Nazareth Lutheran Church
Cedar Falls, Iowa

EIGHTH SUNDAY AFTER PENTECOST

Eternal Life Comes through Participation, Not Affirmation
Luke 10:25-37

Almost to a person the commentators and sermonizers who have taken the parable of the Good Samaritan as their text have focused their attention on the second question asked by the lawyer. Almost without fail the theologians of high and low degree have dealt with "And who is my neighbor?" Most everyone has sprung from the stance into a vigorous description of all the persons and predicaments to which we are to go with self-sacrificing love.

That broken and bare and bleeding victim is everyman, everyman in need. He is the sagging single for whom separation is a problem. He is the anxious analyst whose firm is faltering. He is the perplexed parent whose children are plagued by thirty-year puberty. He is the hospitalized person who is hurting to get well and the bereaved person who is aching for loneliness to pass and the street person who eats from garbage cans and sleeps in cardboard boxes. He is everyone in need to whom our love should drive us.

Usually the parable of the Good Samaritan has been viewed as an answer to "Who is my neighbor?" But there is a prior question. The lawyer has something more important than that on his mind. He first asks, "What shall I do to inherit eternal life?" His primary interest is, "How shall I be saved?" Now when the attorney talks about eternal life he uses the Greek word *aionios*. *Aionios,* eternal, does not mean a never-ending succession of minutes or hours. *Aionios* doesn't mean a quantity of time that is without beginning or ending. The lawyer is not asking how he can have immortality. He is not interested in how he can escape death, annihilation, extinction and live for as long as there is time. He is not interested in a quantity of existence at all. Rather, when the attorney uses *aionios* to describe the life he wants, he is using eternal in a qualitative sense. He is looking for the good life, the meaningful life, the satisfying life, the life for which he was called into being, the life that is a right relationship with God and all of his creation. It seems to me that when the lawyer of our text says, "What shall I do to inherit eternal life," he is asking how he can have a relationship with God that will transcend and transform every temporal transaction and enable him always and in everything to be God's person.

That is not a once-asked question. Ceaselessly it reverberates through the halls of this world's institutions and echoes through the valleys of its open spaces. Everywhere it is being asked. "What shall I do to inherit eternal life," asks the penitent person who has been driven to private confession by a burden of guilt that is too great to bear. "What shall I do to inherit eternal life," asks the wealthy worldling who has tried everything from a Carribean cruise to a Rolls Royce, everything from a gift to the soup kitchen to his name on a college dormitory. "What shall I do to inherit a relationship with God that will make my total existence meaningful," asks each one of us who are faced with the same maddening and mundane motions day in and day out. "What can I do that will impose some significance on me?" That is the first question of the lawyer in our text. It is the first question in most of our minds and on many of our lips. And I am convinced that the parable of the good Samaritan answers it. From that story told by the Savior we learn that eternal life comes through participation, not affirmation.

What the Lawyer Thought

The first fact that seems to jump out at us from the text is that the lawyer thought that eternal life comes through affirmation. The attorney appears to be something of an academian who is looking for a principle to which he can give assent. The lawyer seems to be a logician who wants some provable postulate behind which he can throw his weight and into which he can sink his intellectual teeth and through the affirmation of which he can be counted as one of God's boys. That is why he comes to Christ and calls him Teacher. He wants to argue out of the new authority, if indeed he is that at all, a new statement of what it takes to have the good life.

When our Lord refuses to be theoretical and etherial, when Christ refuses to offer a dictum through which the attorney might be granted paradise, when Christ gets practical and points to the phylacteries and asks what is written in the Law the attorney squirms into defensive definition and discussion. When our Lord mentions the necessity of being a neighbor, the practical practice of love, the adept and evasive tactician says, "Let's define our terms. Who is my neighbor? Let's talk further about your answer. Define for me your concept of neighbor. Who is my neighbor?" The attorney was not looking for some earthy love that could be put into practice. He was looking for some lofty law in which one could get lost. He was looking for some statement that could be restated six hundred and thirteen times, perpetually refined, discussed, continually affirmed and never fulfilled.

You and I know that old trick. We have been pulling it since our parents called bedtime and we asked about everything under God's blue heaven to put off having to give us to the close of the day. To our inquiries about abundant life Christ responds, "What is written in the Law?" We know what the Law says but that which it does say is so damningly difficult to do that we avoid the action with affirmation. "What does 'all your heart and all your soul and all your strength' mean," we ask. "What do you mean by love? Are you talking about *eros* or *agape* or *storge* or *philia*? And who is my neighbor? Define him! Describe her! Answer me so that I can affirm your position and be saved." Sometimes, I am afraid, we are like the lawyer in that we think eternal life comes through affirmation.

What the Samaritan Taught

However, the Samaritan taught that eternal life comes through participation. This is the second fact that springs from our Scripture.

A word of caution certainly is in order. All conscientious readers of the parable of the Good Samaritan must recognize a participation principle. A large part of the primary point is involvement in the meeting of the need of a neighbor. But that is a far, far cry from works righteousness. Taking the total teaching of the Master into account we can safely say

185

that he never would attach saving merit to stopping for a stranger, even if he were bleeding and dying. He never would suggest that rebellion and ruined relationship between God and man could be overcome by pouring on an ointment of oil and wine. He never would pose the proposition that we could be helped along toward what we were meant to be, that we could be given such a new nature that we would be like a new Adam through putting a poor victim on our means of transportation and lodging him in our room and covering his future expenses.

No, our Lord is not teaching works righteousness. But he is proposing a participation principle. By taking the initiative and coming over to the victim of society the Samaritan is making himself prone to the God of initiative who comes to the victims of sin. By intervening in the plight of the pulverized person the Samaritan was making himself vulnerable to the God of intervention who messes around in the lives of plighted people. By complying with the second law that is like unto the first law the Samaritan lays himself open to the God of the Law, to the Lawgiver. And of course by doing love with his whole heart, soul, and mind, the Samaritan is setting himself up for kinship with the God who is love. Here in the Samaritan's experience is the suggestion that participation is the way-paver. Participation is the pathfinder. Participation is the means by which we come into contact with the Source of eternal life. The proper person of the parable is a paradigm for each one of us because he shows us what we can do to foster eternal life's coming into our experience.

Life Comes Through Christ's Samaritan-Like Participation

Of course eternal life comes through Christ's Samaritan-like participation. That is the third point made quite clear by our text. During my twenty years in the gospel ministry I must have read the parable of the Good Samaritan hundreds of times. Over and over again I have researched it and taught it and preached it. I have read innumerable commentators concerning it. And yet it was not until preparation was being made for this sermon that I caught a glimpse of the similarities between the Samaritan and the Savior. Just as the Samaritan was hated because he was descended from Jews who deviated from the norm and intermarried with Samaritans when most of Israel was taken into Babylonian captivity. Just as the Samaritan was hated for straying from the conservative and orthodox, so Jesus was hated for his blasphemous teachings. Not only did he supplant the Law with love but also eventually he got around to admitting that he was the Son of God. Just as the Samaritan came to the victim freely and without invitation, just as he reversed the roles of the priest and Levite without any coercion or restraints, just as he took it upon himself to get down into the ditch with the life-drained man, so Jesus emptied himself; so Jesus gave up the safety of the throne of the universe and took it upon himself to descend into the ditch and don our dirt and die our death. Just as the Samaritan did all that he knew to produce healing, just as he stirred up a poultice of the antiseptics he had, just as he moved the man in his room and bore the burden of his further recuperation, so Jesus did all in his power to restore our health. In the Jordan he was baptized into our condition. In the wilderness he wrestled with our temptation. In Gethsemane he grappled with our guilt. On Golgotha he died our death so that an Easter and Pentecost might make us whole again. Just as the Samaritan came to one who did not want him, just as the Samaritan came to a man who hated him and probably did not want to associate with him, so also Jesus Christ comes to those who would rather be restored by some other redeemer. Can there be any doubt? I think not! It is Christ's participation, Christ's Samaritan-like participation through which eternal life comes.

Eternal Life Comes Through Our Victim-Like Participation

And yet there is a fourth important point made by our text. It is that eternal life comes through our victim-like participation. Though it may not have been written into the story obviously a very important question was asked the victim of the robbery. It was, "Are you willing to accept help from a totally strange and unexpected source? Are you in such need that you will receive and respond to the Samaritan?" Remember, the man in the ditch probably was a Jew. He would have hated and despised the Samaritan. He would have been repulsed by one for whom Jewishness was not the most important aspect of being. Normally he would not have wanted contact with a heretic whose life followed a path deviating from the known and accepted design. Of course the salvation of the sufferer depended on his acceptance of and participation in the salvation offered by the Samaritan. His deliverance depended on his submissive surrender to the Samaritan because he was all that was available, the only one who could do the job.

Here is the final and perhaps the most powerful stroke of the storyteller. Christ is telling ancient Jewish and contemporary hearers something very important. He is saying that we can't be choosy about who rescues us. We can't let consternation clog us. Because he comes as a carpenter instead of a coronated Son of David. We can't let perturbation prevent us because he rides into Jerusalem on a donkey instead of a stallion. We can't let our extended hands be drawn back because he dies on a cross instead of creating a new world by his word. We who are down here in the ditches of doubt, despair, depression, and darkness can't say, "You pass by on the other side too. You go the way of the priest and Levite because you are neither what I expected nor what I require!" No! That doesn't bring eternal life. It is our participation, our victim-like participation, our letting ourselves be picked up and taken home by God's kind of Man that brings eternal life.

The first question asked by the lawyer is important too. In fact, it is on our lips most often. "Teacher, what shall I do to inherit eternal life?" "How can I be in the proper relationship with God?" The story-teller answers that eternal life comes through participation, not affirmation. Eternal life comes through our participation in paving the way for Christ, through Christ's participation in our plight and through our participation in his means of saving us. It isn't the affirmation of some law but the participation of Rescuer and rescued that brings eternal life.

RALPH WALLACE
St. Paul's Lutheran Church
Columbia, South Carolina

NINTH SUNDAY AFTER PENTECOST

Mary or Martha: The Problem of Priorities
Luke 10:38-42

I've known some Marthas in my life who give new meaning to the women they resemble in Luke's text for today. Women and men of great faith and initiative who carry out the practical tasks of daily life within the community of faith with unwavering dedication.

I'm thinking of the man in one congregation who took personal responsibility for the condition of the furnace in the church. He checked it several times each week during the coldest months of the year, sometimes making the two-mile trip from his home to the church in the evening to be sure it hadn't stopped and caused pipes to freeze and other equipment to be damaged by the sub-zero weather. The furnace was his special project and he cared for it very well, reporting on its condition and its maintenance needs regularly, talking often to other church leaders about the importance of keeping it in top shape, worrying about the cost of fuel and the congregation's ability to pay for it. He was a "Martha", a practical, sensible servant of the church who valued the daily operation of the furnace and, consequently, the daily operation of church offices and programs above all else.

Other "Marthas" are gifted cooks and servers who conscientiously provide food and refreshment for every gathering of the faithful—from lavish and luscious smorgasbords and potlucks to welcome and ever-ready coffee and treats. Some of these Marthas are careful caretakers of church buildings and office duties—from pew polishing to lawn care, newsletter colating to phone call reminders. Countless are the prayers of gratitude and thanksgiving I have sent heavenward for these stalwart Marthas, these soldiers of the kingdom who work so tirelessly at keeping the ship of faith, Christ's church, afloat from day to day, from season to season, and from occasion to occasion. Their number is legion; their mission is in the here and now of today; their accomplishments are visible though not always acknowledged.

I feel a oneness with the Marthas of the church. I share some of their moments of great satisfaction when jobs are completed, when the furnace runs smoothly or the fuel bill is paid, when things are in order and go according to plan, when everyone pitches in and a task is undertaken that needs doing for the congregation to enjoy its premises or its programs more readily. A room repainted, a new rug installed, a good turnout at a potluck promised, a bargain on remodeling seized.

Perhaps you identify with Martha, too, or even with all the Marthas of today's church, and in our identification we may occasionally wish that all of God's children were of our same ilk, were Marthas, especially as we cast a judgmental and sisterly eye toward the Marys in our lives. The Marys are the women and men with whom Marthas somewhat grudgingly share partnership in the Gospel, membership in Christ's church. The Marys are those who are less concerned with the financial cost—gain or loss—of a ministry than with the call to be the body of Christ to the larger community.

I'm thinking of the woman in one congregation who had a finely developed sense of what was most important in life. She was the one you could depend on to have read the texts prior to Sunday worship. She was the one who sought out new faces at services to welcome them to her church home, to put them at ease with her relaxed and warm greetings. Even more important, she noticed who wasn't there—at worship, at Bible study, at circle—and found time to call or drop a card to or stop by to see a number of them, to show her concern, to listen to theirs, to be with them in whatever the circumstance. She was a Mary, a woman with her priorities in order as a Christian, a woman who brought Christ's presence to others through her natural and genuine style.

Marys are like that, the faithful few who turn out for every Bible study, every class, every opportunity to learn and to share their faith. Other Marys I've known are talented befrienders—they are there when times are hard; they are beside us in hospitals and homes, at funerals and at divorces, in times of quiet loneliness and times of inner struggle. Countless are the prayers of gratitude and thanksgiving I've sent heavenward for these perceptive and loving Marys. Countless, too, are the times one of us may have said to one of these Marys in our lives: "You don't have to stay. You must have other things to do." Only to hear with great relief the response: "You are more important than anything else right now. . . . I'm staying."

There are times when I feel a oneness with the Marys of the church. I share some of their moments of exhilaration when the message of the Gospel comes clearly and powerfully into focus and I feel my understandings growing and deepening: when I take time to seek out the new face, to call the absent one, to just listen; when I am humbled and honored to realize I've been the presence of Christ in another's life; when I know the satisfaction of having put priorities together wisely; when the Martha in me has not been overly compulsive and preoccupied with the practical so that she balances the Mary in me who continually seeks to foster a vision of the kingdom coming on earth in my daily life.

A Question of Priorities

The Mary and Martha we meet in Luke's Gospel as they interact with Jesus are not strangers to us, they are of us and we of them. Perhaps more keenly than with any other character we meet in all the Gospels, we identify most strongly with these two sisters in faith. They dramatize the question that comes to every Christian life. A question of priorities, a struggle with which responsibility takes precedence when we walk with our Lord to Jerusalem and the cross.

The context of Luke's story of Mary and Martha's encounter with Jesus must keep its central place in our study of them, and more important, in our identification with them. Apart from the lessons to be learned from the scenario in their Bethany home as Mary and Martha welcome Jesus and his disciples and act out the differing styles, we must be clear about the circumstances surrounding Jesus' visit with them. It is no idling away of a free afternoon, no casual dropping over to share food and talk of the joys and troubles of the ministry. Rather, there is an urgency to this visit, a purposefulness to the stopping by as though it were planned as one of the essential stops on a long trip—an experience that builds toward some other destination, a respite en route to a greater goal.

Jesus, on his way to Jerusalem, stops at Bethany at Mary and Martha's home as a natural, logical resting place. Jesus, on his way to Jerusalem, stops at Bethany to visit Mary and Martha, his faithful and devoted followers, sharing his radical message of new life with them again . . . for the last time. Jesus, on his way to Jerusalem and the cross, does not have time for daily practicalities such as who's helping prepare food and who isn't. His time is better spent talking, telling the miraculous story of God's redeeming love for his people as it is being shown in his very life and impending death. This visit carries that sense of urgency and purpose that characterizes all of his encounters in these closing days. It is the kingdom of God that heralds; the message of forgiveness and hope and of new life which he preaches and which his believers hear with a new significance as they walk with him to Jerusalem.

Sensing the Context

If we are to hear that message today with new significance, if we are to open ourselves again to Jesus' powerful words of forgiveness and hope, if we are to be the redeemed people God calls us to be through Jesus Christ, if we are to live as Christian people of the cross—then we hear Luke's story of Mary and Martha in its urgent, pressing-toward-the-kingdom context as response to our daily struggle with priorities in Christian life and as response to that question of balancing our Marys and Marthas as we walk with our Lord to Jerusalem.

Luke's Mary intuitively knew that context, her priorities were in order as she listened to and learned from her Lord. She clearly saw the opportunity for a cherished visit with Jesus and seized it, made the most of the little time she had with him, even savored it. Every other typical duty of a hostess entertaining guests, every other priority fell by the wayside while she basked in Jesus' presence, rightly making him her sole priority.

Luke's story of Mary and Martha and their priorities in serving and being served by Jesus their Lord provides us with an analogy for our own lives. We may identify with Mary or with Martha, perhaps a bit of each. It's a matter of context that is most important, however, in their lives and in our own. You and I surely don't want to be downstairs checking the furnace when our Lord comes to visit, when the kingdom is at hand, anymore than Martha wanted to be out in the kitchen when Mary sat with Jesus. We do want the Mary in us to dominate; we do want those instincts and perceptions of what ought to be important, of what is high priority to take precedence in our lives of faith and servitude that others may know of the kingdom of our Lord through the witness we offer.

We do want to be aware of our context, clearly focused on that vision of the kingdom he promised coming even now; we do want to be capable of following the Holy Spirit's guidance that we, like Mary, seize the moments of learning, of growing, of sharing, of befriending and in so doing that we demonstrate Christ to the world and hear him say of us: "You have chosen the right thing, and it will not be taken away from you."

ANDREA F. DeGROOT-NESDAHL
Minot, North Dakota

God, Our Best Friend
Luke 11:1-13

(This introductory material could be printed in the service folder or used before the Entrance Hymn to set the scene for the dialogue in the sermon. It could, of course, instead serve as an introduction which is spoken before the sermon dialogue begins.)

Discussion about the preferred form of our Lord's Prayer is not new to us. For years there was a difference between those who said "trespasses" and those who said "debts." Another difference—Protestants and Roman Catholics said "Amen" at different times, either before or after "thine is the kingdom and the power and the glory for ever and ever." It was certainly believed by both groups but it was said only by the Protestant branches of the church. And today, even though a common translation was prepared by an international consultation on the English texts of the liturgy, the preference for the "old" form, with "thy's" and "thine's" has been so strong that new hymnals have printed both forms.

How much discussion there must have been in the early church about which form to use. Count the petitions in the version Luke records in today's Gospel. The longer form to which we are accustomed is that given by Matthew. Some suggest that it was because Christians prayed in that longer form in the early liturgies that it was written down with the added phrases in Matthew's Gospel.

If we could listen in on a discussion by those early Christians, we might well learn something about the Lord's Prayer, and perhaps even more usefully, learn something about our own praying.

In our praying as in all else that we do we who have "received Christ Jesus the Lord" ought "to live in him, rooted and built up in him," as the Second Lesson urges. Surely the fact that God has "made us alive together with Christ," his beloved Son, makes it possible for us to "approach God boldly and confidently in prayer even as beloved children approach their dear father" (Luther: Small Catechism on "The Lord's Prayer"). God

192

would have his faithful today be even more confident in their praying than was Abraham, the "father of the faithful," in the account of the First Lesson.

In the sermon today we will imagine a group of first century Christians sitting around a table in a cafe after the early morning eucharist. We will hear them discussing the service and in particular the way the presiding minister spoke the words which "our Lord taught us to pray."

God, Our Best Friend

The form is to help us in our function

THOMAS: Did you hear the way the pastor prayed the prayer Jesus gave us?

AMOS: He does it a bit differently each Lord's Day.

THOMAS: But he really shouldn't, should he? You were there, weren't you, Joseph, the day the Lord Jesus gave the prayer? Didn't someone ask him, "Lord, teach us to pray," and didn't he then say, "When you pray, say—" and then he told them the words to say.

JOSEPH: That's true. Of course—

THOMAS: Of course. And the words? What were the words?

JOSEPH: He said, "Father, hallowed be thy name. Thy kingdom come. Give us each day our daily bread; and forgive us our sins, for we ourselves forgive every one who is indebted to us; and lead us not into temptation." But, of course—

THOMAS: Right. Those were his very words. All I'm saying is that those are the words we should use, the words the pastor should use, not add extra words, not change the words.

JOSEPH: Not add words?—like adding "Amen," for instance?

THOMAS: Well, that's all right. That gives us all a chance to agree, to to make the prayer our own, too. "Amen"—that's one of his favorite words, too, our Lord's. Remember he would say, "Amen, Amen, I say to you"? "Verily, verily," that's what "Amen" means, and I feel good about adding that to the Lord's Prayer. That's our chance to say, "It shall be so."

JOSEPH: Well, what else did the pastor add?

193

THOMAS: He didn't just say, "Father." He added "who art in heaven." And then after "Hallowed be thy name" and "Thy kingdom come," he added, "Thy will be done on earth as it is in heaven." And after "Lead us not into temptation" he added, "But deliver us from evil."

AMOS: Something was different about the forgiveness petition too— "forgive us our sins *for* we ourselves forgive every one who is indebted to us."

THOMAS: And he said, "Give us *each day* our daily bread." That's not much of a change; but it's the principle of the thing. He shouldn't change the words that way.

JOSEPH: I had rather hoped you would have recognized from "Amen" on how much you sound like people who "strain at a gnat but swallow a camel." The real principle of the thing is that Jesus didn't intend to give us a set of magical phrases we were to repeat. He gave us "a way" to pray.

AMOS: That's just what I've been trying to tell you, Thomas. When we pray all together the way we do at Eucharist, we need all the help we can get to think what we are saying and to include all the meanings the words he gave us carry.

THOMAS: Yes, but . . .

AMOS: Both of us are proofs of that. Instead of praying we were counting the lines and criticizing the phrases. What the changes should have done was to help us pray the real meaning of the petitions.

THOMAS: Well, all right . . .

To know God as our best friend

THOMAS: But still—how about those phrases he added? How about that "who art in heaven" bit? God's our friend. Why try to make him some other-worldly, far-removed celestial being? It makes it sound as if we somehow don't deserve to think of God as our friend.

JOSEPH: Oh, Thomas, Thomas. How quickly we forget. No . . . let me talk now. It sounds to me as if you are already taking for granted that you can now address God with such an intimate name. If only I could help you realize the thrill we felt when

194

we first heard our Lord say to us, "When you pray, say, 'Father'!" Remember Abraham—only a few were so blessed by God to be able to talk face to face with him. But he couldn't call God, "Father." Before the destruction of Sodom and Gomorrah, when he prayed God to save the cities if even ten righteous people were found there, remember how he said to God, "Behold, I have taken upon myself to speak to the Lord, I who am but dust and ashes"—remember? That's the closest we could deserve ever to get to God.

But now Jesus told us to call him "Father"! That's the word you called your earthly father when you were a child, isn't it?

AMOS: That was true in our house. We said, "Abba, Father!"

JOSEPH: We could scarcely believe our ears! That's what we talked about the most among ourselves as soon as Jesus had given us the way to pray. I remember people were saying, "Father? Call him Father—like 'Papa,' like 'Daddy'? We can call him that?" And, of course, Jesus knew what we were saying, how we were amazed.

And he said, " 'Father,' of course, say 'Father.' He is your friend, isn't he? Your best Friend."

"If you say, so, Lord . . ." I can't remember for sure, Thomas, but I think it was your namesake disciple, Thomas, who said that. His tone showed how dubious he was, how we were all shaking our heads at the very idea.

Someone else added, "But we don't even get that informal with you—we call you 'Lord.' " And Jesus then said something which later he repeated in the upper room, the night he was betrayed. We understood it only a little better then. He said, "You are my friends if you do what I command you. No longer do I call you servants, for the servant does not know what his master is doing; but I have called you friends, for all that I have heard from my Father I have made known to you. You did not choose me, but I chose you and appointed you that you should go and bear fruit and that your fruit should abide; so that whatever you ask the Father in my name, he may give it to you" (John 15:14-16). All that is clear to us now, but when our Lord first told us we could call God "Father" it was almost unbelievable.

AMOS: All this happened, this talking about whether God is a Friend to us, right after he told you the words of the prayer?

To know him as the friend who keeps on giving

JOSEPH: Yes, and then he went on to tell us the story—you know it—about the man who had an unexpected guest and didn't even have enough bread to give him a late night snack. He went to a friend's house, remember, and said, "Friend, lend me three loaves." But his friend had gone to bed . . . just a one-room house with the children on their sleeping pads on the floor and the door barred. He didn't want to get up and disturb everyone, and unbolt the door and have it all to do over again. So he said, "Don't bother me." But the man kept knocking and asking over and over again until finally the friend relented and gave him the three loaves he needed. And Jesus' point, of course, was that if the kinds of friends we have here on earth will be ready to help us—even though sometimes we have to knock and knock, ask and ask—how much more can we expect our best friend, God himself, to answer us!

THOMAS: In a way that's my point. If God is our good friend, why not relax and just accept the good things he gives us? The way I learned it we were supposed to pray, "Give us each day our daily bread." The pastor changed that to "Give us *this day* our daily bread." If you say "this day," you'd have to pray the prayer every day to make sure you would have bread for every day.

JOSEPH: That's not such a bad idea, is it? I mean, to pray our Lord's prayer every day?

THOMAS: No, of course not. But it's the principle of the thing. Anyway, Jesus made the point that if we can count on our earthly friends, we can surely count on God our best friend.

AMOS: Thomas has a point. God gives bread even to the wicked, just as he makes the sun shine on the evil and the good. Why keep asking every day for what you already know you're going to get?

JOSEPH: That, it seems to me, is what the pastor's phrase is to help us remember—that God is a giver who keeps on giving and giving. If we remind ourselves of that, we'll remind ourselves not to take his gifts for granted, but to be thankful!

To know him as the friend who forgives us so that we will forgive his friends

THOMAS: I think I'm being persuaded.

How about that other addition? Instead of "Forgive us our sins, for we ourselves forgive everyone who is indebted to us," the minister said today, "Forgive us our debts as we also have forgiven our debtors." The change from "sins" to "debts"— that just harmonizes the phrases; but "as we also have forgiven"—that really puts the pressure on. That means if we haven't forgiven, God shouldn't bother to forgive us.

JOSEPH: As I remember, it was the Lord who first added that pressure. Remember how he once said, "For if you forgive others their trespasses, your heavenly Father also will forgive you; but if you do not forgive others their trespasses, neither will your Father forgive your trespasses" (Matt. 6:14-15).

AMOS: Does that mean our Father will only forgive us if we forgive others?

JOSEPH: I think of it differently. If we do not forgive other people—who are, after all, his *other* friends—that is one of our sins. And as we are made aware of how often we fail to forgive his other friends, we remember really to *mean* it when we ask, "Forgive us *our* sins." Beyond that, it helps us go and be reconciled, really to forgive his other friends.

To know him as friend who tests but helps us stand fast

THOMAS: I think I can make the case for the other change this morning. After "And lead us not into temptation," the pastor added, "But deliver us from evil." It really is a way to help us think through what we are asking. We would all prefer not to be "brought to the test." We'd all prefer to be saved from the time of trial. But we need to remember that when God permits tests to come upon us, he is dealing with us as with his children. It's like disciplining our children. What we actually want, then, is to be helped by the testing, not hurt by it. So in the liturgy the pastor added what we were really all praying, "Deliver us from evil."

JOSEPH: The greatest evil we could fall into when we are tested is to be

197

angry with God for permitting such tests to strike us, or to doubt that he cares.

Amos: That's what the Evil One would like to see happen.

Thomas: And so when we pray "Deliver us" we are asking to be freed from all the Evil One tries to do to us—really to deliver us from all this evil world.

To know him as friend in whose power we are confident

Amos: Add it all up—praying to God as our best friend helps us more and more to know him as our best friend.

Joseph: And so Jesus urged us, "Ask and it will be given you; seek, and you will find; knock and it will be opened to you." And he promised, "For every one who asks receives, and he who seeks finds, and to him who knocks it will be opened." All of that, you see, helped us to realize he really meant it when he told us to call God "Father," when we prayed.

Thomas: Why add "who art in heaven" then? No one has really answered that for me.

Joseph: You're the reason, if I may say so, Thomas, or rather one of the reasons. *We* are other reasons. Already you seemed so ready to take it for granted that God is your friend it almost suggested that you think you deserve his friendship. Perhaps we all need to be reminded that our best friend is indeed the celestial, other-worldly God, even while he is our friend.

Amos: And perhaps we often need to be reminded as well that there is nothing he cannot do for us, this friend who is in heaven.

Thomas: And that there's nothing we would want to happen here on earth which would be less than what God wants.

Amos: That's reason enough for the other extra line, "Thy will be done on earth as it is in heaven."

Joseph: Surely we want what he wants. If our earthly fathers would not give us a serpent instead of a fish, or a scorpion instead of an egg when we are hungry, surely the will of our Father in heaven will be good for us.

Amos: And he's proved that with his best gift since Jesus—the gift he keeps giving us over and over—the Holy Spirit!

THOMAS: This has helped me more than I can say. I've even got a suggestion for one more change in the way we use our Lord's Prayer. I would like a pause after we say "Our Father in heaven."

JOSEPH: Why that?

THOMAS: Because I would like to remind myself—I'd almost like to pretend—that the Father speaks, in the silence—and what he says is, "Yes, Thomas?"

AMOS: And Amos!

JOSEPH: And Joseph!

GEORGE W. HOYER
Christ Seminary—Seminex
St. Louis, Missouri

ELEVENTH SUNDAY AFTER PENTECOST

Travel Lightly
Luke 12:13-21

A few years ago, our family celebrated an anniversary by taking a trip to Scandinavia and Germany. Instead of using suitcases to carry our clothes and possessions, we used backpacks. This made it possible for us to have our hands free to help each other. It also meant that we had to make plans to travel lightly.

I have found that this is also a good way to travel through life. It doesn't mean that we have no possessions at all. It does allow us, however, to be free to enjoy life and be able to help others in need. It's easy for the best of people to worry too much about the wrong things and to forget what is really necessary.

The Feuding Brothers

Jesus told a story about two brothers who couldn't agree about their inheritance. The one brother asked Jesus for help, saying: "Teacher, bid my brother divide the inheritance with me." Unfortunately, stories of this kind are often repeated in our time. And it tears up our hearts to see how families can be divided forever because of such disputes. The very thought of such a thing happening can give nightmares to parents today. We never do find out the details of this story, but it must have been a troublesome event and it needed help.

Good parents like to plan ahead so that they can give their children an inheritance, a last will and testament. Jesus did this for the church too. In Holy Communion, we celebrate his gift to us. Not all parents are able to leave an inheritance that can be measured materially. Bad times, disaster, unfortunate investments, and missed opportunities sometimes prevent any legacy at all.

When this brother asked Jesus to act as a judge in the inheritance dispute, it seemed like a wise choice. Who could have arbitrated with greater justice? Still, there was something wrong. Jesus could tell that the brother did not have kind and unselfish reasons. So he answered:

> Take heed and beware of all covetousness:
> For a man's life does not consist in the abundance
> of his possessions.

If we take these words seriously, they can change our whole point of view about wealth. Maybe we should put up a sign, saying, "Coveting is harmful to health!" It is much better to travel lightly.

The Dilemma of the Wealthy Farmer

Jesus told the worried brother a story to help him see things better. Our Lord thought of himself as a friend rather than a judge. He showed intense honesty as a friend. He told the story of the wealthy farmer whose problem was that he had more than his soul could absorb. This man probably worked very hard for long hours, managed things well and took good care of his possessions. He may have also denied himself vacations to insure his prosperity. We like success stories like these. It suggest that if we work hard, we might be successful too.

But something went wrong. He forgot the meaning of life. He confused ownership with stewardship. When he thought that he had finally made it, he lost it all. It's a comfortable feeling to have enough money to pay the bills, to buy presents and to make investments. It got to be more for this man, however. In a careless moment, his heart mused:

> Soul, you have ample goods laid up for many years;
> take your ease, eat, drink, be merry."

It sounded like the perfect retirement program. It turned out to be the ultimate tragedy. He was so well off that he didn't feel the need for God any more on a daily basis, much less his neighbors.

You have got to admire people who do so well. But we also need to ask, "What is success?" God spoke the last word in this story:

> Fool! This night your soul is required of you;
> and the things you have prepared,
> whose will they be?

That is a point well taken. A few years ago, the tomb of Philip of Macedon was found. This is in the northern part of modern Greece. It was the custom in those days to kill the slaves who buried the rich and their treasures. This was to prevent grave robberies. It worked so well for Philip that his tomb was concealed for almost 2400 years. Even his son, Alexander the Great, does not appear to have known where it was. Philip's immense wealth turned out to be a curse, both to himself and to his servants.

The Vikings would plunder the monasteries of Ireland and England to seize the treasures hidden there. People would put their valuables in the holy places, much like banks today, for safekeeping. When the Viking kings died, they were buried in their ships, completely outfitted with supplies and servants for the long journey through the dark seas of death. It was no fun for the servants or favorite wife. They would be buried alive or killed, if unwilling to join in the journey. The ships were dug deep into the clay and have been remarkably preserved to this day. Later, pirates would search for burial mounds as the ground settled. In this manner, however, many Viking kings thought that they could "take it with them." Their accumulated wealth ultimately benefited no one and became a curse. It would have been much better to have shared the wealth and to have travelled lightly.

How Should We Regard the World?

Is the world and its possessions our friend or foe? The writer of Ecclesiastes spoke of it both ways. He said:

> There is nothing better for a man than that he should eat and drink, and find enjoyment in his toil. This . . . is from the hand of God. (Eccles. 2:24)

At the same time he could say:

> I hated all my toil in which I had toiled under the sun, seeing that I must leave it to the man who will come after me; and who knows whether he will be a wise man or a fool?" (Eccles. 2:18-19)

St. John wrote:

Do not love the world or the things in the world. If any one loves the world, love for the Father is not in him. For all that is in the world, the lust of the flesh and the lust of the eyes and the pride of life, is not of the Father but is of the world. And the world passes away, and the lust of it; but he who does the will of God abides for ever. (1 John 2:15-17)

What is wrong with the world anyway? We sing, "This is my Father's world." In our baptismal creed, we confess: "I believe in God the Father, almighty, creator of heaven and earth." Would it be safer for us to renounce ownership of property and become desert hermits? No, the world and the things in it are not evil in themselves. The problem lies in us. The power of darkness within us is our enemy. It prevents us from clearly seeing the ownership of God and his goodness in letting us live in the world. Darkness makes us afraid so that we don't love God and our neighbors as we ought. We need Christ to give us light and to help us travel lightly.

The Inheritance Waiting for Us

God has another inheritance for us. Paul writes of it like this:

If then you have been raised with Christ, seek the things that are above, where Christ is, seated at the right hand of God. Set your minds on things that are above, not on things that are on earth. For you have died, and your life is hid with Christ in God. (Col. 3:1-3)

Peter described this inheritance as "imperishable, undefiled and unfading, kept in heaven for you" (1 Peter 1:4).

We celebrate this inheritance in baptism. It is worth infinitely more than the world's wheat, gold, steel, or oil resources. This is why there is a heavy responsibility in receiving the gift of baptism. It is not to be accepted thoughtlessly. It is a way that we become "rich toward God." Whatever excuses the successful farmer may have used, he found himself without the riches which are imperishable. He was outside the kingdom. The words of Jesus describing his tragic life's ending are also somber words for us: "So is he who lays up treasure for himself, and is not rich toward God."

We are reminded of the words of Jesus: "What shall a man give in return for his life?" (Matt. 16:26). The prosperous farmer might have had it both ways if he had not forgotten the true riches of God's kingdom. The Lord says also to us:

Do not seek what you are to eat and what you are to drink, nor be of anxious mind. For all the nations of the world seek these things; and your Father knows that you need them. Instead, seek his kingdom, and these things shall be yours as well. (Luke 12:29-31)

Blessings On Your Journey

We have seen what pain has come into the world through coveting another's wealth or worrying too much about our own. It's a heartbreaking experience to see otherwise decent children come to hate each other because of inheritance disputes. If parents could see into the future, they might decide to distribute their earthly belongings in some other way. Parents want their children to love each other more than anything else. God is like that too. It must break his heart too when the blessings he gives us become the occasion of jealousy.

Whether you have much or little, there is real value to traveling lightly. It is not just the energy it takes to worry about so many things. It is that the kingdom of our Lord has better riches for us. We confess these true riches in the creed: "I believe in the forgiveness of sins, the resurrection of the body and the life everlasting." That's better than owning Wall Street.

Travel lightly. It's more fun and safer too. Discover the difference between the worries of ownership and the joys of stewardship. It's the difference between being free or a slave. Blessings on your journey.

ARLAND O. FISKE
Bethany Lutheran Church
Minot, North Dakota

TWELFTH SUNDAY AFTER PENTECOST

Called to Faithful Waiting
Luke 12:32-40

The word Armageddon appears only once in the Bible. It is found in the Book of Revelation, 16:16. The word Armageddon is a combination of two Hebrew words, Har- meaning "Mountain," and Megiddon- the name of a place (whose exact location remains unknown). The context in Revelation indicates that Armageddon is where the "Kings of the whole world are gathered together, under the incitement of demonic spirits, for the battle on the great day of God the Almighty."

Now that means in some way that it is the battle at the end of all things. And people who talk about the end of all things like to talk about Armageddon. But Armageddon is not the end of God's world. The end, the New Testament makes very clear, is after Armageddon, after this great battle. That is a subtle but important difference in what our Gospel speaks about today. This text, which throughout church history has often been used for the last Sunday of the church year, is not really about the end of the world and all of the things that are supposed to happen then. It is rather a story about the in-between time. Jesus does not answer the question in this story or elsewhere in the Bible about when he will return again. So our question today is not speculation about the end and when it might come and how we should stay awake. But how do we live in the present that prepares us best to face the future. In the text today we are called to faithful waiting. How do we wait as those who have been called to live confidently, wisely, and expectantly for the return of our Lord?

The Mark of a Waiting Christian Is Faith

The mark of a waiting Christian is faith. We see that facet of the Christian life uplifted in all three lessons for this Sunday. In the Old Testament Lesson, Abram is promised a great reward, but this reward is dependent on his having a son. Despite having no offspring and with no immediate prospects for that wish to be fulfilled, Abram believes the word of God and his faith is reckoned to him as righteousness. It is the champion of faith that the writer to the Hebrews in our Second Lesson describes and praises. It is a faith based on the "assurance of things hoped for, the conviction of things not seen."

So our faith is in God and not in what we do or accumulate. In our society, and even in our congregations, so many of us are treating life as if we are about to be overcome by the events around us. We are anxious because it looks like we might lose what we have so carefully and painstakingly accumulated. What I mean is that we spend a good portion of our lives working diligently to acquire those things that make life meaningful and good—friends, a wife or a husband, a home, children, a job, material comforts, money, and security. And we are afraid that we might lose them. If our energies are centered in only preserving these things, as good as they might be, what does this say about our faith? Have we made our possessions a more important treasure than our faith in God? Jesus teaches us again in this lesson that where our priorities are, there will be our hearts, and we will follow our hearts.

So, waiting Christian, be marked by faith! Do not be afraid. You can trust God. It is his good pleasure to give you the kingdom. He will give your more security than you can possibly provide for yourself.

The Mark of a Waiting Christian Is Service

To illustrate what he means about this kind of waiting faith, Jesus tells a story about servants and a master. It is in his faithfulness to service that a waiting servant is prepared and ready for the return of the master. It is in service where our treasure lies and where our hearts should be also. In fact, when the master returns he reverses his role and serves those who have been faithfully waiting. It is an act of love. Love is the greatest treasure!

So we too are to "gird our loins" and "burn our lamps." We are called to service. We are to do something while we are waiting for the Lord to return. Something useful. The late Albert Schweitzer spoke to a graduating class in an English boys' school in 1935. He told this group of boys: "I do not know what your destiny will be. Some of you will perhaps occupy remarkable positions. Some of you will become famous by your pens, or as artists. But I know one thing: The only ones among you who will be really happy are those who have sought and found how to serve."

So where shall we serve? A congregation is a place to serve. Sister Mary Corita once said, "Accept an assignment, then you won't feel responsible for everything." In this congregation we have people who teach, sing, pray, and reach out to others through our ministry. Be a part of that service. Give of yourself with your time and your talents. Support the mission of your church with your gifts of money.

Often I have heard visitors to our congregation comment that our congregation appears to be alive and alert. A congregation that is committed to service will be a lively place and prepared for our Lord's return. In our lesson it would appear that watchfulness is the key element for preparation for the master's return. But watchfulness is only one element of this lesson. Jesus' message was not to press everyone and everything into one mold. The parable does not mean that everyone is to be a doorkeeper or a prophet. It does mean that those looking for the time of the end are to stay watchful and be awake at the right time. It does mean that we are to continue to serve according to our various gifts. If we can think of this in terms of Paul's idea of the body, then we see that the community has members with many different functions. It will be an alive and healthy congregation that serves in many different ways.

The Mark of a Waiting Christian Is Hope

Finally, the one who waits faithfully is marked by hope, a hope based on the return of Jesus Christ, who is the Lord over life and death. That is the certainty of our faith. That is the witness of our service. This hope leads us through our pilgrimage in this life which ends in death. But we know that we belong now and in eternity to the Lord who comes again. This assurance should make us ready, not for an Armageddon, but for something new to break into our lives. The day and hour of his return remain hidden to us. This must not make us tired of hoping. This hope carries us over every difficult time of life and allows us to witness daily to him in word, and daily to serve him in love.

Hope is indeed expressed in the way we live. In his book, *The Meaning of Hope,* C. F. D. Moule writes that "Christian hope must take concrete shape in Christian action. Christian hope is simply false to itself if it does not express itself at every stage in political and social action." That statement picks up the close relationship between hope and love.

As we wait, we are called to responsibility, to love one another. For this reason Christian hope is more than just words, it is to be found in an attitude, a life-style. It must be something personal, vital, that you have made your own in the face of suffering and adversity, or for that matter when things are going well. For me, Christian hope is something that gives me a positive attitude toward the future despite unhappiness with myself and what I am, despite tragedy, disappointments, sadness, and unexplainable accidents that may happen to me or others, because I feel a part of something that is moving toward a goal.

Reinhold Niebuhr once wrote: "The Kingdom of God does not come in history, but at the end of history." What that means is that there will always be evil, death, the power of sin and the devil to overcome, so long as man still lives in history.

But the biblical message, in Jesus Christ, is that God is a gracious God, and therefore the future is open, we can hope.

The Son of man is indeed coming at an unexpected hour. We do not know when he will return. But we can be ready. We can be prepared. We can continue to live with faith, assured that he will uphold us; we can continue to serve knowing that our love will be a blessing; and we can continue to hope, because God will keep his promises.

CHARLES H. MAAHS
Atonement Lutheran Church
Overland Park, Kansas

The Jesus of Fire and Division
Luke 12:49-53

I came to cast fire upon the earth; . . . do you think I have come to give peace on earth? No, I tell you, but rather division; for henceforth in one house there will be five divided, three against two and two against three. . . .

PASTOR: The gospel of the Lord.

CONGREGATION: Praise be to you, O Christ.

Did you catch the irony of our Gospel response today? The Gospel quoted Jesus saying: "I have come to bring fire and division on the earth." I called that the "good news from God." The congregation responded, saying, "Praise be to you, O Christ." How can we call such a message of fire and division "good news"? Anyone who has experienced the agony of family division and disrupted relationships can hardly call that good news. How can we praise Jesus for such a message?

Jesus the Fire-Eater!

Fire! Jesus came to cast fire on the earth and to create division that splits families and divides people. Jesus, the fire-eater, sets forth a red-hot message to bring division and pain. His word is like a hammer which breaks rocks in pieces and challenges the very bedrock of society.

John, who baptized with water, predicted that Jesus would baptize with the Holy Spirit and with fire. Jesus said, "I have not come to bring peace, but a sword." What do we make of such rhetoric? How does this message and picture of Jesus reconcile with the sweet little Jesus picture, the gentle baby of Bethlehem, or the quiet Christ who stood mute before Pontius Pilate?

The Fire of the Spirit

The Christmas hymn proclaims "The little Lord Jesus lay down his sweet head." But the little Lord Jesus grew up and was baptized by the Holy Spirit of God and he cast fire upon the earth. His head no longer rests easy on the pillow of earth. Jesus antagonized the authorities at Nazareth; they sought to stone him. He challenged the religious fraternities of Jerusalem and they put him to death. Fire!

He brought fire upon the earth and the fire that Jesus brought was the fire of the Holy Spirit cast upon the earth to bring forth the kingdom. That fire invaded the hearts and lives of his followers. The Spirit rested upon their heads "like tongues of fire" on Pentecost day. Those few followers of Jesus "turned the world upside down" in a single generation. Fire! Yes, the fire of the Holy Spirit burned in them and changed the world.

What is the nature of this fire of Jesus and the Holy Spirit he brings? Opportunists in every generation seek to co-opt his fire for their own purposes. Jesus came as no moralist trying to reform the social conditions of his day. He came as no revolutionary to overthrow the political systems of his time. He came as no religious purist to refine the worship of God. No, he came to kindle the fire of the kingdom of God in the world. The Gospel of Thomas records in Logion 82, "He that is near me, is near fire; and he that is far from me is far from the Kingdom." These words attributed to Jesus imply that to be near him is to be near the fire and in the kingdom. When Jesus says he will "cast fire upon the earth," it is a figure that he will inaugurate the kingdom with the very Spirit of God.

What Is This Kingdom?

His kingdom is a new way of life, a new peace, a new relationship to God, a new rule of God in the hearts and lives of everyone. But the coming of that new kingdom demands an end to the old. The fire of Jesus separated the true from the false; his fire called for a division between faith and unfaith, good and evil, new and old, easy and hard. The coming of that kingdom drives a double-edged sword into the world. His coming brings peace on earth and also division. The Gospel brings comfort and fire. The baby Jesus allowed Simeon to depart in peace, but was a sword which would pierce the soul of Mary. Jesus Christ is a "child set for the rising and fall of many in Israel, and for a sign that is spoken against." The coming of Jesus Christ calls for division and decision.

Jesus is like a surgeon who cuts away at the cancer of a patient to eradicate the disease in order that wholeness and healing may rule. His surgical blade cuts at our own hearts to divide and conquer them. Whenever we would hold on to the old and simply attempt to mend our diseased lives with a new patch of cloth, we will fail. When we attempt to put the new wine of Christ into the old wineskins of our brokenness, we will lose everything. Jesus calls us to make decision about ourselves. He comes to cast the fire of the Holy Spirit in our lives and divide us for his conquering.

A Choice Demanded

When the sons of Zebadee asked Jesus for a special place in his kingdom, he asked them: "Are you able to be baptized with the baptism with which I am baptized? And, are you able to drink the cup that I shall drink?" Following Jesus necessitates giving up your selfish ways. Jesus' baptism is his death and martyrdom and he implies that to follow him is not to blaze a trail to success, pleasure, affluence, and popularity, but to drink a bitter cup of suffering and death with him. Jesus asked us, "Will you accept my way?" Implicit in that very question is the assumption that our way is contrary to his way. The fire of his spirit refines and divides in order to produce purity of heart.

A Disturbing Lord

It is a delusion to think that following Jesus will only bring serenity of life and peace of mind. No, following Jesus will bring warfare, constant skirmishes and disturbance of conscience over agonizing decisions. Christ calls us to be uncomfortable with our moral compromises, to be wrenched by our neighbor's need and to show compassion to the helpless. Jesus is a disturbing Lord as well as a comforting one. He comes to disturb the comfortable and comfort those who are disturbed. For the most part, Americans of our generation are the comfortable of the earth and the good news of the Gospel comes to cause us discomfort and disruption to our way of life. Jesus does not call us to self-torture or masochistic behavior, but he does make demands on us and challenges our self-centered world that is at ease with itself with the shattering hammer of his word. Commitment to Christ may split families. Enthusiasm for the kingdom of God may divide nations and friends. Parents and children may be divided over the claim of Jesus Christ on their lives. The stakes are great. Jesus comes as the great divider. He comes to divide and conquer. He comes to drive away the chaff from the wheat, and to cast out our demons so that we may be filled with the spirit of God.

The Fire Purifies

Fire is used in the smelting process to refine precious metals to their purest quality. But the same fire destroys the impurities that would blemish the precious metal. The Gospel of Jesus Christ is such a fire to refine our faith and destroy impurity. Jesus Christ invades our lives and exposes the privacy of our hidden self. There is a disturbing scandal in this message of Jesus who brings fire and division. The scandal is that the holiness of God is demonstrated in the sphere of the secular world. Jesus entered into the secular world of home, family, ethics, and business, the world of politics and history, and precisely there the Gospel is manifest. Paul is right on target (1 Cor. 6:19), "Do you not know that your body is a temple of the Holy Spirit? . . . so glorify God in your body." Ultimately, the Gospel and our faith comes down to what we do with our bodies, our life, and our world.

Ernst Kasemann, in his book, *Jesus Means Freedom* (p. 87) says, the church "has managed to reduce Jesus' red hot message, which promises to kindle fire throughout the world, to room temperature." We have tried to domesticate the Gospel and tame the Holy Spirit of God by reducing it to pabulum. Someone asked me recently, "What does it cost to belong to your church?" I had to answer, "Very little." What does Jesus ask of us and what is the cost of serving the kingdom of God? The writer of Hebrews used the metaphor of a long distance runner in saying: "We must lay aside every weight and sin which clings so closely and run with perseverance the race that is set before us." Discipline is called for and the race is grueling, hard and long. It demands perseverance and is painful. There can be no ease in Zion or relaxation in the house of the Lord, because Jesus calls us with his fire and he comes to divide in order to conquer.

What must this Jesus of fire and division have to say to us today? Jesus calls us to take an enthusiastic stand on our belief in Christ as the Lord of Life. He calls us to act out our belief and let the power of the Holy Spirit guide us permitting the radical message of hope to spill forth into the world. "Christianity cannot entirely do without enthusiasm," wrote Kasemann (ibid., p. 51). The church has lost its fire and the Gospel has been domesticated so that it means virtually nothing and asks nothing of us.

Rekindle the Fire

This word of fire and division means for Christians today that we show concern for our brothers and sisters in Poland whom we have never met. It means that Christians grieve over the victims of air crashes and tragedy. It means that Christians anguish over the plight of the poor and seek to adjust their life styles to share generously in alleviating hunger. "As we have done it to the least of these his brothers, so we have done it to and for Christ."

Jesus comes to divide and raise controversy, to split families over the nature and implications of faith in him. The world is divided by Christ as well as united by him. He brings truth to put aside falsehood. He initiates mercy to end cruelty. He proclaims love over hatred. He gives freedom and destroys bondage. He brings forth compassion and ends indifference.

The Fire Is Good News

Jesus said, "I have not come to bring peace, but a sword; to cast fire upon the earth." What is the fire? It is the fire of the spirit of God in our lives and world. Let it burn! Let it bring warmth and light. Let it bring God's peace in a cruel world.

210

"You think that I have come to give peace. No, I tell you, but rather division." Christ's fire and his division is for a purpose. He divides for the sake of justice and righteousness. His kingdom and his Holy Spirit come to put down all other kingdoms and to bring forth life in him.

It does make sense that the words of Jesus: "I came to cast fire upon the earth, and . . . division," are the good news for which we praise Christ, because this fierce fire from the gentle Jesus ignites the world and brings forth the reign of God which is explosive, dangerous and breath-taking. Praise be to you, O Christ!

WARREN A. SORTEBERG
Christ the King Lutheran Church
Denver, Colorado

The Narrow Door
Luke 13:22-30

"Lord, will those who are saved be few?" someone asks Jesus. His answer, as so often, gives the question a new twist. It doesn't help to talk about numbers, or about other people. What needs to be talked about is *you*, whether *you* will be among those saved. "Strive to enter by the narrow door," Jesus says, "for many, I tell you, will seek to enter and will not be able." That is a thought you need to hear and pay attention to—all the more so if you are among those we think of as good church members.

So I invite your attention to Jesus' imagery of "the narrow door." Your reaction will depend very much on your perspective. Once when we were closing out a vacation at somebody's cottage and needed to use up the left-overs, I found a little ground beef and two eggs in the refrigerator and the last of a box of Wheaties in the cupboard. I mixed it all together and fried up five patties for breakfast. "What's this?" the children complained suspiciously. Our son Paul put it into perspective for them. "If you think of it as hamburgers," he said, "you are in trouble. But if you think of it as Wheaties with a little ground meat thrown in, maybe you can make it."

Thus also with "the narrow door." If you think of it as "narrow," you are in trouble. But if you recognize that perhaps you are too "big" and need to become smaller, maybe you can make it!

211

The Door as "Narrow"

A narrow door may be hard to find, harder still to squeeze through. It doesn't make for a very glorious entrance! If "few" are saved, that may be the reason. You may even be offended, and delay coming in at all until the door is shut, as Jesus suggests in his little parable.

So now you stand there knocking from the outside and pleading your case. "Lord, open to us," you say. "I don't know where you come from," he answers, but you say, "Come on, Lord, you must be kidding! Surely you know *me!* I've been a Christian all my life, active and dedicated, baptized and married and buried right from this church. I have even been a Lutheran—and you know that that's the best and safest kind! Surely you know *me!* I ate and drank in your presence, I came to worship and to Holy Communion with some degree of regularity! Why, you even taught in our streets—and I was there, hearing sermons, going to Bible classes. Don't you remember me? Come on, Lord, open up!"

But you argue all this from the *outside!* You have *not gone through* the narrow door when it was open to you! Therefore the voice of judgment comes back to you saying again, "I tell you, I do not know where you come from; depart from me, all you workers of iniquity." And you find yourself weeping in self-pity and anger, and gnashing your teeth against God's injustice to you, his terrible memory, his insult in classifying *you,* of all people, among the "workers of iniquity"!

Frightening, isn't it? Yet Jesus doesn't say this to scare you, or because he wants to exclude you. He wants you rather to *think,* and to understand what is so offensively "narrow" about this "door" of entrance into what he calls "the kingdom of God." For if you are to find this door and go through it, you have to become small! You will have to leave behind all the pride of your own importance, so that God can receive you by his grace alone!

And that is as offensive and difficult for your sinful flesh, as it was for Jesus' own people in his day. Imagine what it was like then, when the story of Jesus had unfolded to the end in his dying and rising again, to hear Jesus say, "I am the door! If anyone enters by me, he will be saved." Or again, "I am the Way and the Truth and the Life! No one comes to the Father but by me!" When you know the pure love by which Jesus the Son of God gave himself into death for your sins, when you understand how he took upon himself the wrath and judgment that should have wiped out the whole world in that dreadful hour—Gentiles, Jews, and disciples alike—then your heart can grasp those words and find peace and rest in the wonder that God so loved you and did not want to destroy and lose you!

But when you have not known Christ as your Savior, then how offensive and arrogant his words sound! The door is too narrow, Jesus claims too much! "Look, God," the Jew would say, "I am a descendant of Abraham. I have been faithful to your Law, I have held myself apart from unclean things! Surely you will recognize me, remember me! Surely I don't have to go through that narrow door, surely I have some claim, some rights!" That is what St. Paul calls the "stumbling-block of the cross" for the Jews, on which he himself had stumbled and fallen.

So also the Greeks with their wisdom are offended at the narrow door. Surely the cross is not for the sins of the whole world! That's too narrow, too intolerant. Every religion claims to be exclusive and right. Surely, God, you would not exclude from your kingdom and banquet the millions of people in other religions. Surely you have many other doors, wide open, by which people can come in!

Your own sinful flesh and wisdom is no different. You make yourself the judge and critic of God. "Come now, God," you say, "the design of your house and kingdom is unacceptable. The door is too narrow. It looks as though you are deliberately trying to exclude the decent people who try to do what's right and make something of themselves, and to give the kingdom to the sinners and the worthless—like a sieve whose mesh is too fine. I just can't go with your crazy idea that 'the last shall be first and the first last.' What's the good of my working hard to make something of myself, and obeying the law, and serving you faithfully—if in the end there is no advantage in it, no credit, no recognition?"

So you are peeved at God. You complain. You tell God off, tell him what kind of God he ought to be—a God who gives credits, a God who will help you build your own little kingdom, who will recognize your superiority.

The Door as Wide

Do you catch the perspective of Jesus and of our text? The problem is not really that the door is too narrow. The problem is that you are too big for it! What Jesus is asking, indeed insisting, is that you give up this pride and boasting of your imagined superiority. Give up the idea that you have a kingdom and a worth of your own making! Start over! Become like a new-born baby again, the very "least" in the kingdom! Only then can you catch the wonder of God's grace and wisdom—and the honor that God should want you and call you to belong!

For the secret of the kingdom of God is that it is founded on grace alone. This is the secret Jesus himself knew and lived by, the secret which, as he says in our text, "Abraham, Isaac, Jacob, and all the prophets" knew and celebrated! You have no rights, no superiority! Everything you have is yours by the undeserved love of God alone! Everything you are, and the whole world in which you live, is yours by his creation and gift. You are only the receiver of what God made and called you to be. When you know that simple truth, then you do not complain against God. Rather, you praise him, give him thanks, and put all his gifts to work to serve him gladly! You do not look for rewards and credits. Rather you trust his promise, that the kingdom is already yours and will be yours—and that no trial or disability or hardship you endure, and no injustice from a sinful world so full of oppressions, can take from you either your honor as a child of God or your hope for the kingdom and life still to come!

This is the secret that becomes so gloriously visible in Jesus himself! He had the fullest of honors from the beginning, of being born and named "the Son of God." Therefore he served his Father joyfully and freely, against all hardship and through all the testings of the devil. Therefore he could love sinners with the Father's own love, and gather the lowest and most lost, and call the proud down to truth and humility. Therefore he was willing to endure sufferings and death rather than surrender a sinful world to wrath and judgment—and to rise from death as the Father had promised, not to accuse and shame us but to gather us into his own victory and joy!

Now that's a whole new world, this banquet of the kingdom to which God invites you and which you share by way of your baptism and at every celebration of the supper of Jesus' own body and blood for the forgiveness of your sins. That's the feast where the patriarchs and all the prophets sit, where Jesus himself sits as the Son by whom you are given the glory of sonship and life forever. But there is no place at this table for the proud, for those who think they are superior, for those who wear garments of their own making and who expect to be admired and applauded. At this feast we celebrate the grace of God alone! And we celebrate first and above all by willingly *receiving* what he gives, without imagining that we can somehow maintain our own pride by paying our own way. Let God be God! Let our Lord Jesus, our Redeemer, be King alone at God's right hand!

So you become very small. Yet the moment you enter in such joyful smallness through the narrow door, in that moment you discover your true honor. God has named you his *child*, his son or daughter in Christ! God has named you his *heir*, and surrounded you with promises to walk with you and be your God, delivering you from every threat of evil, giving you every good and perfect gift. God has set before you an everlasting triumph of life and glory, even against all that looks like death and shame. And

God has called you to *serve him,* to be part of his work in this world. You are his "body" by which he himself can carry on his work in your daily work, his creating in your creativity. You are his eyes and hands to reach out to the people God loves, and to gather sinners whom God wants to gather and not lose—to comfort, to heal, to lift up, to liberate in the joy and freedom of Christ. Your life is crowned with dignity, purpose, hope. You do not stand there on the outside! You come in, and you belong!

Then you discover also the wonder that the "door" that looked to be so narrow is actually the very widest of doors—able to gather into one all the nations of the world, from the least to the greatest, with nobody excluded.

Look around you at the kingdoms of this world. Do you see anything like this elsewhere? By the power of sin and flesh, of pride and despair, every person is driven to establish and preserve his own private little kingdom. You have to prove your worth, establish your rights, defend your integrity, hide your faults, put on a good show, win praise. Or maybe, when you know you have failed, you have to retreat from the world in which you cannot compete, and become a recluse in the safety of a privacy where nobody can see you. That's not liberty! That's bondage to sin, to Satan. You are not ruled by God then in the glory of sonship, but by your own lusts and fears.

Therefore, in such a world, everybody is continually judging everybody else. You find yourself ranking others—superior or inferior. Instinctively you think that white is better than black, that male is better than female, that rich is better than poor, that success is better than failure. You cannot love then, or forgive. You are too busy defending yourself. Can't you see what the insistent love of God is all about? He doesn't want to leave you in that prison and death! Neither can he compromise with it. "Come out of it," Jesus pleads, "Come into my kingdom, through the narrow door. Become small, so that I can make you great and glorious in the kingdom and knowledge and joy of your God."

When that Word gets out to the nations, to the sinners who thought they were worthless and excluded by their guilt, to the prisoners of their own futility—then they will begin to come in with eager joy! "From the east, west, north, and south" they will come, as Jesus says, to "sit at table in the kingdom of God." And the door that seemed so narrow will be wide enough to receive all who come, from the least to the greatest! And the whole world will shine with the glory of the grace of our God, and of his Son, Jesus Christ our Lord! Amen.

PAUL G. BRETSCHER
Immanuel Lutheran Church
Valparaiso, Indiana

The Magic Touch
Luke 14:1,7-14

The text for this Fifteenth Sunday after Pentecost is the well-known parable of the marriage feast. In this parable Jesus gives a rather straightforward speech to the assembled guests that reveals his awareness of the natural antics of people, and it also specifies the unusual style of life he desires in those who follow him. Verses 13 and 14 provide us with a helpful focal point:

> . . . when you give a feast, invite the poor, the maimed, the lame, the blind, and you will be blessed, because they cannot repay you. You will be repaid at the resurrection of the just.

Ever since childhood I have known that to be a follower of Christ does not mean to be a person who has no faults. It means, rather, to be someone who possesses some quality . . . a quality that comes from being part of an organized community, knit together by the Spirit of God, and reaching out with mind and heart in active service for the things of God.

The most convincing proof of our Christian convictions is found in the manner in which we live our faith. One may well be an expert in the art of debate, but all the arguments in the world may never convince another person of what we believe. We might be very persuasive in our case for honesty or virtue. But if we deviate from that in our living in the slightest degree, the argument breaks down. We may have the most eloquent proofs of God and His Son, but if we deny them in our living they lose their power.

It is not unusual for someone to ask: "How do I know that your claim for God is for real? How do I know that he can lift and heal and save?" And it is so easy to respond by saying, "Listen to me." But it is quite something else to be able to say, "Look at me." The truth of the matter is that "actions speak louder than words."

The proof of our faith is not in some mathematical formula or a theological dissertation. It is rather to be found in the texture of our lives. If someone is looking for proof of what we say, they will look for it in our integrity, in our courage, and in our compassion for others. They will not search for it in the logic with which we interpret our creeds, but rather in the sincerity with which we follow Jesus Christ. The persuasiveness of our faith is the result of what is in our hearts, not what is on our lips. God is not found at the conclusion of an argument, but he can be found in the touch of mercy.

Every day you and I touch people with our lives. What do we do to them? What happens to them because of us?

Each time Christ touched someone's life, something happened. There was an obvious consequence. So it is with every one of us. A touch of the heart, and a life is influenced. It shatters the notion that we are isolated creatures, each going our own selfish way. In contrast, we are dynamic organisms that grow with each other, live with each other, depend on one another, plague or bless each other, bedevil or heal one another. We always do something, good or bad.

The proof of our faith lies in the measure with which we allow our hearts to feel for others. Christ is found in the spiritual concern with which our hearts are burdened.

Our Current Situation

In a sense, our days have been hard, and they have made us hard. For most of our life-time, whether we are young or old, you and I have witnessed a constant parade of war and death and destruction. For years we have been reading about such things as crime and confusion and moral irresponsibility. As our civilization becomes more chaotic, you and I seem to become more callous. And maybe that's a necessity. Maybe it's the only defense mechanism we have to employ against the horror stories that have been written in our time.

There is no hope for us in the future unless we can become a compassionate people. There is no escape from our current dilemma until we look again at the Lord himself and see how deeply he was able to feel the agony of another soul. He looked at a city and wept. He looked at the suffering, despondent soul, and responded with loving concern. He opened a blind man's eyes, and he made a leper well.

Our Response

When you and I see the tragedies around us, how do we respond? How can others believe in Jesus when we look at suffering, but do not suffer in response? How can anyone find credibility in our faith when we see hurt and agony, but do nothing about it? How can others trust our words and accept our creeds when we see wrong in every direction, but are so passive in our response?

There is nothing more persuasive than an understanding heart. Without it there is neither love nor forgiveness, no hope, no trust, no help, no guidance, no strength, no redemption.

Oftentimes when we see the signs of rebellion in the lives of our children we are so quick to excuse and quick to condemn. But why? In like manner, when a young student takes a wrong turn on the road of life we are so quick to weep or to even become angry. But why? All too often when someone bruises us with foolish actions and harsh words we are so quick to retaliate, to get even, to complain. But why? And where is the proof of our faith?

The Real Proof

You and I prove our faith when we reveal all of God. Even the disciples found it difficult to see God. He seemed to elude them more often than not. Their minds evidently could not leap that high or reach that far. They were told that God was gracious and forgiving, endless in his power, and plenteous in his mercy. But they could not see him that way until Jesus stepped into the picture and answered their difficulty with these words, "He that has seen me has seen the Father." Then they knew. Then they understood. They looked at him, and they saw all of God.

Our lives are inclined to be so fragmented. And as a result, others are able to see very little of God in any one of us. Oh, they see something. Now and then there are some dim indications of his goodness or his grace. But do they ever have the opportunity to see all of him?

Sometimes they hear us say that God is the designer of the universe ... the One who made us and came to save us. But as they look at us do they also discover that he is a God of compassion? Sometimes they hear us say that God is a God of justice and mercy. But as they look at us do they see those qualities in action?

My internship year was spent in a California home mission church that was barely seven years old. One of my Sunday responsibilities was the High School Bible Class. One Friday morning as I was working on a portable bulletin board in my crowded corner of the assembly hall, two little four-year-old girls came wandering into the building. They walked hand in hand, with eyes as big as saucers.

I greeted them with, "Hi there! What are you doing here this morning?" And one of them answered with excitement, "We've come to see Jesus!" From a squatting position so we could look each other straight in the eye, I asked them, "And where do you think he is?" The response was given in a manner that made me feel as though I ought to know. "He's in our teacher," the little blond explained. "In your teacher?" I questioned. "What do you mean he's in your teacher?" And then came a simple, honest answer that told the whole story in a nutshell. As she kicked her shoe against a chair and swung her little friend's arm very hard these words were spoken, "Our teacher loves us."

That's all it takes! Just a touch . . . of your life and mine. To be one of his followers is not to be a person who has no faults, as much as it is to be someone who possesses some quality . . . the kind of quality that comes from being a part of an organized community, knit together by the Spirit of God, and constantly reaching out with mind and heart and hands in active service for the things of God.

That might well be called "the magic touch." And for that, Jesus said, "you will be blessed."

DAVID L. ANDERSON
Trinity Lutheran Church
Moorhead, Minnesota

SIXTEENTH SUNDAY AFTER PENTECOST

Jesus-in-My-Shoes
Luke 14:25-33

I can't pretend to appreciate that advice Jesus gives about family life in today's Gospel. The way it goes we can't be his disciples without hating our parents and our spouse and our children and our brothers and sisters. What kind of a religion would teach *that* to its followers?

Don't we already have enough hate in families nowadays without baptizing it as somehow beneficial? As it is too many modern gurus have been exploiting those feelings and leading the young away from those who love them. Jesus ought to sit where I sit, listening to people pour their hearts out precisely because of the hatred that characterizes their families.

Or maybe he ought to be in my shoes, me as an old-fashioned family man, and tell me exactly how he proposes that I go about hating those people who are so special in my life. My elderly parents, for example, and me an only child. My wife of more than thirty years, through thick and thin together, so knowing of each other we can all but read each other's mind. My four sturdy sons grown tall beyond their parents, and the wives of the first two whom we keep hoping will soon be making us grandparents.

Just how do I go about hating my family, Jesus?

They are what I am, and back. They define my very existence. Their birthdays and anniversaries punctuate and enliven the seasons, the years. Their ambitions I apprehend for myself. Their names are in my prayers, and though I perhaps may know their every foible and failing, it is for the love of them, really, that I have my being.

So that when that Jesus asks that I forsake them, and even that I hate them, we part company, he and I. Let him try it for himself. Let him be me, and see what it might be like.

In which case, were Jesus to be me, I have to believe that much of what would happen would not be hate, but love. Jesus, surely, would write more often to those far distant, would remember to prepare for birthdays and anniversaries long before my customary last possible minute, would get over and fix his parents' back screen door immediately and not wait for months to get around to it. Jesus, were he me, would help with the dishes with less reluctance, would pick up after himself, would stop tracking sawdust up from the cellar. Jesus, in my shoes, would be less prone to losing temper and patience, more willing to forgive, more tender and thoughtful and kind.

But Jesus, were he me, would still be concerned about the coming of the kingdom as well. So there would be sermons to prepare and services to conduct, meetings to attend and people to see. So that Jesus, in my shoes, just might have my kinds of problems too.

Like when we've planned for a day's outing for weeks ahead, maybe, even, to commemorate a wedding anniversary, and then two days before someone dies and so there's a funeral service cancelling the outing. Or we're figuring out our pledge and wondering how we'll ever get the Sears bill down to nothing. Or I'm run so ragged my wife starts talking again about how I should be getting that physical exam, and someone calls insisting no one else can chair that United Way committee.

So how does it feel, Jesus-in-my-shoes, tugged this way and that, more to do than time or energy to do it in, and all the while knowing the competition for the kingdom isn't so much the world, the flesh and the devil as it is your family? First things first, right? "Those whom God has joined together let no one put asunder"? Or "take up your cross and follow me"? Which shall it be?

Maybe there's something missing from the Gospel according to Luke at this point, because Jesus never gets us off this hook. What we'd like is for him to tell us he doesn't really mean what he's saying, that he was just exaggerating for the sake of having a greater effect. And it could be, I suppose, that such a disclaimer got lost somewhere back in the early days of the church, or even deliberately removed in the interests of keeping up the morale. The earliest Christians, under persecution, frequently found themselves betrayed by their own relatives, so perhaps they needed to have a sense of commitment to their Lord that carried them beyond family ties.

More probably there was no such softening of the idea, and Jesus said it as we heard it, and meant it to be taken seriously.

The two little illustrations he employs underscore the radical nature of his advice. If you want to build a tower, he tells his listeners, you'll first calculate the cost, and if you see you can't afford it, you won't even start. Who wants to be a laughingstock in town for not having enough sense to know what a thing will take?

You want to know what it takes to follow Jesus? Very simply, it takes everything. Everything! Count that cost before you start.

Or a king, going off to war, sees the enemy is twice as strong, and knows there's no chance of victory, so the better part of wisdom is to sue for peace. It's humiliating, of course, and probably there will be losses to be endured, but that's better than a crushing defeat.

And what does it take to follow Jesus? Know that it won't be cheap, and you can't get by with half of what's needed, and that your lackluster, mediocre resolve won't save you when the great battles of life have to be fought.

People should count the cost, Jesus insists. What it takes is a carrying of a cross, a renunciation of business-as-usual, even a turning aside from otherwise honorable responsibilities.

In Africa I stood at the grave of a German missionary at Pare Mountains in Tanzania. An African bishop was my guide, proud to show me the missionary's headstone in an old cemetery. There in that place the man had started a school, a clinic and a church, and there, after a ministry of more than thirty years, he died and was buried, thousands of miles from his native Germany and, one might imagine, all the relatives who had tsked over his abandonment of "civilization" so many years before.

The simple fact is that it has taken that kind of single-minded dedication in every time and in every place. From the chain of martyred apostles down to the latest victim of an oppressive government in our time, the call of Jesus Christ is a call to the cross.

And yes, we'd prefer that it be otherwise, that Jesus be kept in the Sunday mornings of our lives, boxed in on our altars for the "comfort and relief of our consciences," but not out where we make our hard decisions and accommodate to our high-pressure world.

Because in the world the choices are never simple. What's right, what's wrong? Everything is so relative.

And speaking of the relatives, again, those choices get to be pure agony on occasion. That's the crux of the problem, isn't it? This Lord of our lives makes his claim on the whole of our lives, and we begin to see some of the implications of that claim as they influence the way we make our living and the things we do for recreation and the style we've come to prefer for food and drink and clothing and house, and then the squirming starts. It's not for myself, we'll say, but for my kids. They deserve the best. Or, for the kind of work I do, I've got to keep to a certain standard. Or, if I don't go along with the rest of them I'll lose my job and they'll take the house away from us and my family will be thrown out on the street. You wouldn't want that to happen, would you, Jesus?

And what I think Jesus is saying to us is, in effect, that while he's as concerned about the welfare of our families as we are, he also would prefer that we not go along with the rest of the crowd, with slippery business ethics and silence in the face of oppression and conspicuous spending and consuming in a world where 10,000 die each day of hunger.

You can say, as some commentators have, that Jesus was accustomed to the use of hyperbole, to setting impossible goals, so his words about hating our families need to be understood from that perspective.

But I think he meant it just the way he said it. If across the centuries there had not been those willing to take up their crosses for the sake of the kingdom, willing to abandon their own flesh and blood for the truth of the Gospel, not a one of us today would believe. It is a faith for people willing to give up everything they are and have, for people who see what it will cost and then accept that price, even if it means the loss of their deepest love.

If you're lucky it won't mean that for you. But there will be another cross anyway. There is no easy way to be a Christian, but there is no other way to really be alive.

CARL T. UEHLING
St. Matthew Lutheran Church
Moorestown, New Jersey

SEVENTEENTH SUNDAY AFTER PENTECOST

Rejoice with Me
Luke 15:1-10

Of Sheep and Coins

These two parables, of the lost sheep and the lost coin are two of the best-known of Jesus' many parables. The image of Christ as the shepherd returning after a long diligent search with the errant sheep carried lovingly on his shoulders has been one of the most popular motifs in Christian art down through the centuries.

Luke ties these two parables with a third and longer parable: that of the lost son. Many commentators go to great lengths to explain the ins and outs of sheepherding and the nature of sheep in dealing with the first parable. As a city boy, I must plead ignorance of the finer points of sheep psychology or of sheepherding, and yet, I feel this parable speaks clearly to me despite my lack of first-hand knowledge. As for the second parable, I don't need anyone to explain to me the reaction of the woman who has lost a substantial sum of money.

Others have made much of the differences between the two parables. For example, the fact that the sheep loses itself whereas the coin was lost, perhaps due to someone else's carelessness. But this seems to me to confuse the issue and detract from the plain and simple message in both stories: Jesus came to seek and to save the lost, and the finding and restoration of even one lost sinner is cause for joyous celebration.

Four Words

Like so many of the words of Jesus, these can speak to us in different ways depending on our situation or on how the Holy Spirit helps us to hear the words. I would like to talk about four words that speak to us from these parables: a word to the Pharisee in us, a word about individual worth, a word of grace and assurance, and a word of joy.

A Word to Us Pharisees

Luke presents these parables as coming right after the Pharisees have voiced their criticism of Jesus for associating with sinners. And Jesus may be speaking directly to the Pharisees, offering these parables as an explanation or a defense of his ministry.

When we read the Gospels we really don't like to think of ourselves as having much in common with the Pharisees. After all, their attitudes are so obviously wrong. We can hardly be put in the same category as them. But is their position really all that different for us to relate to? If we can get beyond the negative reaction we have whenever we so much as hear the word Pharisee we might see that, in their own way, they probably were very religious, upstanding people. They had a great concern that the distinctiveness of the Jewish way of life not be lost. And for them, to associate with those whose lifestyle showed no respect for the law probably seemed like the hole in the dike which could eventually lead to the collapse of the entire Jewish religion and way of life.

Put in contemporary language, they were only trying to guard the church from undesirables, who they feared would do damage to the church. Is it any wonder that they were critical of Jesus, who seemed willing to accept just anyone—who seemed ready to open the gates and let in all of the riffraff?

If we put it that way, don't we find these same thoughts creeping into our heads now and then. Perhaps we are not always as far removed from the Pharisees as we would like to think.

Let me tell you a story about my grandfather, Hans. It seems that on my father's confirmation day, Hans, who had not attended church much, agreed to go with his son to Holy Communion. Unfortunately, it seems the word got back to him that some of the members had criticized him for going to Communion, since he was obviously not a confessing Christian. You can bet it was a long time before Hans felt like attending church or receiving Communion again. Luckily, the pastor did not give up on him, and eventually he did become active in the church.

Of course, things are different now from the way they were back in that small Norwegian-American parish 50 years ago. But are they really so different? How do you or I feel about the Hans or the Zacchaeus in our lives? How do we feel about those who show up at church occasionally who so obviously don't belong there?

How do we feel about church programs aimed at the down-and-out, at drug addicts or juvenile delinquents. What about bar ministries or ministry to prostitutes. It's one thing if these people repent and come to church but must we seek them out? Isn't that going a bit too far? And yet . . . that's exactly what Jesus did, isn't it. To save sinners, he went to them. The shepherd doesn't wait for the sheep to repent and return on its own; he goes looking for it and brings it back. The woman doesn't wait for the coin to show up; she turns the house upside down and inside out until she finds it.

And that's what Jesus does. Indeed, isn't that the message of the incarnation? God came to earth to save sinners because that's where they were —and still are. How can we argue with that? As for guarding the church from undesirable elements that's not really our job, is it? The Holy Spirit has managed to preserve the church for all of these centuries without our help. Perhaps we can turn our attention to more important tasks, like taking part in the search and recovery of lost sheep.

A Word about Worth

A second word from these parables is a word about individual worth. It has been said so often that it is almost a cliché but it is nonetheless true that our society places an inordinate emphasis on numbers. Never mind quality, just give us quantity. It is only to be expected that this way of thinking has many adherents within the church as well. Don't worry about the one who is lost, let's concentrate on the ninety-nine. If we look at the situation in the first parable, the law of averages would tell us that the shepherd ought to keep an eye on the 99 sheep who are still with him. But the shepherd doesn't care about the law of averages. For him that one sheep must be found. And his rejoicing over that one sheep, like the woman's over her single coin is nothing compared to the party they throw in heaven when just one sinner repents, when just one lost one is found. God overturns our careful calculation of the odds. Every single sinner who is lost is worth the risk. This word has special meaning for me because I am working in Japan, where less than 1% of the population is Christian. There is great rejoicing here too over every single sinner who is found by the grace of God.

Besides our fixation on numbers, another attitude which tends to belittle the value of the individual is our replacement mentality. We live in an age where if some appliance is broken, or worse still, outmoded, we just throw it away and buy another. If we lose something that we can't do without, we simply buy a replacement. We may even apply this way of thinking to people. If a friend moves away we fill the empty space in our lives or hearts by finding a new friend. If my wife and I have drifted apart, why I'll just replace her with someone else, legally or otherwise.

To someone who has grown up with this replacement mentality these two parables might seem a bit odd. Why all this fuss over one lousy sheep? Why go to so much trouble to find a single coin? Can't they be replaced? The answer from the parables is, "no". They can't be replaced. And neither can even one lost sinner be replaced.

You could almost say that God has an obsession about each and every one of his children. He doesn't want to lose a one. Each one is irreplaceable and if one becomes lost, God will go to any lengths to find that child and bring him or her back. Despite our society's preoccupation with numbers, despite our own throw-away, replace-it way of thinking, these parables give us a different message loud and clear: each individual is priceless. Each individual has a value that cannot be measured in human terms.

This word about the worth of each individual is one that we always need to hear. It is a word we can never get enough of. Because no matter how many books we may read that tell us how to look out for number one, or how to be good to ourselves; despite the selfish me-ism which characterizes so many today, deep down, we may fear that we really don't matter to anybody. Deep down, we may need to hear the word from these parables that, yes, you *do* matter to someone. You matter to God. You are irreplaceable to him. And this brings us to a third word—a word of grace and assurance.

A Word of Grace and Assurance

These parables speak a word of grace and assurance to each of us, since we know that we too, like the sheep or the silver coin, can become lost. Of course our lostness can take many forms. One kind of lostness is suggested by the setting of these parables: we may become lost by falling into the self-righteous attitude of Jesus' critics. We may lose sight of the relationship of grace into which God has called us. We may fall into an empty religiosity where we try to justify ourselves before God and others, and we may take a perverse joy in thinking we are more holy than others around us.

Or, like sheep, we may "nibble ourselves lost", being seduced by the green pastures of this world, and find ourselves going to church less and less often, finally dropping out entirely. There are many different ways in which we might become lost. And we are as unable to do anything to become "unlost" as is the sheep or the coin.

And so the parables speak a word of grace and assurance to us. Just as the shepherd searched high and low for his lost sheep, so will our Savior search high and low for us, and, finding us, carry us back to the flock on his shoulders. Just as the woman turned her house upside down to find the lost coin, our God will turn his universe upside down to find us. God will not rest until he has brought us back and restored us to a right relationship to him. God gave up his own Son to make us his own, surely he will not give us up without a fight!

A Word of Joy

The final word, and perhaps the underlying word, is joy. In both parables we hear the invitation, "Rejoice with me". God invites us to share in his joy every time a lost one is found. We have all experienced the joy of finding something that had been lost. Perhaps we have also shared in someone else's joy at the recovery of some lost item. There is something poignant, albeit comical, about what happens at a basketball game when a player loses a contact lens on the floor. Play is stopped and all of the players and often even the referees join in the hunt, getting down on hands and knees. When the lens is found, there is almost always a spontaneous burst of applause from the fans. They are sharing in the joy of finding. (Of course they are also happy that the game can go on.)

Perhaps a better example would be the return of the hostages from Iran.

For that moment, politics were forgotten as all across America people joined in the celebration, sharing the joy of those who had family and loved ones, whom they had feared were lost, returned to them.

Just so, we can join God in celebration when one of our sisters or brothers in Christ, feared lost, is returned to his or her rightful place in the family.

Of course, we may be tempted to grumble and ask why such a fuss is made over one person. But when we remember that our shepherd would do no less for us, then we can not help but join in the celebration. We cannot help but respond with gladness when our Lord says, "Rejoice with me, for I have found my sheep which was lost."

SAUL STENSVAAG
Hakodate-Shi
Japan

EIGHTEENTH SUNDAY AFTER PENTECOST

Decision Under Fire
Luke 16:1-13

We've all seen the boarded-up storefronts on main street. We're all aware of the layoffs at the mill. We've all seen the unemployment statistics in the morning paper. We need not be reminded that times are tough.

Times are tough, and for those of us who are still hanging on to our jobs, we can't help but be a bit anxious. We worry about what the boss is going to think about our poor sales performance this quarter. We worry that when the funding crunch hits our office, which of us will be the first to get a pink slip. During these depressed times, our jobs too are under fire.

It's with an understanding of the thoughts and fears that go through an employee's mind when his or her job performance is under scrutiny that Jesus begins to tell the parable of the unjust steward, a story that comprises the first eight verses of today's Gospel. The parable speaks of what one employee did when he knew that his job was on the line, and as Jesus recounts the story for us, he seeks to tell us something about discipleship—the job, the vocation given us by virtue of our baptism into Christ. For often, as in the case of the steward in the parable, our job, our vocation as a Christian is under fire. Jesus develops the story in three scenes:

Scene I: Crisis

When the first scene opens we find that the steward has been called into the boss's office. "What is this I hear about you?", says the boss (Luke 16:2a). "What about these charges of mismanagement? Why are the receipts of olive oil and wheat down 50% and 20% respectively this quarter? You've either been lazy—not keeping after those tenant farmers with whom we contracted for oil and grain—or some of the produce has been ending up in your own pocket." And with these accusations from his boss's mouth, our steward knows that he's in trouble, deep trouble.

It may be that the crisis is of his own making. Maybe he has been pocketing part of the receipts intended for his boss. Yet maybe the crisis was brought about by factors out of his control. Weather, pests, blight— perhaps one or more of these has cut into oil and wheat production for the year. The steward may be thinking to himself that "what does my boss know about the problems I face on the job. He sits up there in his office unaware of the fact that I'm up against recalcitrant tenant farmers, hailstorms, irrigation problems, a mix-up in delivery of pesticides and fertilizer, and what have you. The low yield is not all my fault!"

The difficulties, the ambiguities experienced by the steward on the job, Jesus seems to imply, are not all that different from those faced by the disciple, by you and me as we seek to live out our Christian vocation. We too live and work under less than ideal conditions. None of us has all the resources, all the time and all the talent we'd like to have. As disciples, as parishioners, we sit in the pew while the pastor tells us about commitment. He calls us to tithe, to serve on this committee or that, to be on the church council, to work on the hunger campaign, to make evangelism calls. Like the steward we wonder with some indignation, "what does he know about all the other claims on my time—from family, from my job downtown? Maybe the time will come when I have evenings free for council meetings and will make enough so I can tithe. But I sure don't now."

It's precisely at this moment—the moment of rationalization, of excuse-making, of putting the blame on extenuating circumstances—when Jesus tells us that the boss says to the steward, "I'm of a mind to fire you . . . I want to see the books, the production figures for last quarter . . . I want them on my desk immediately!" "Turn in an account of your steward-ship, for you can no longer be steward" (Luke 16:2b). Here, in the language of parable or story, is the very same message that Jesus has said pointedly elsewhere, "The time is fulfilled and the kingdom of God is at hand; repent and believe in the Gospel" (Mark 1:15). The time is now, an accounting is required of us. There are no more opportunities to procrastinate, to rationalize, to fool around. And the steward, you and I stand paralyzed by this moment of crisis that none of us ever expected to happen. Sweaty of palm, knotted of stomach, with pulse racing we each ask, "What shall I do since my master is taking the stewardship away from me? I'm not strong enough to dig, and I'm ashamed to beg" (Luke 16:3).

Scene II: Decision

As we move into the second scene of the story, Jesus could have let the steward receive his just due. He could have surrendered the books to his boss, the mismanagement charge would have been substantiated, and our steward would have been given his pink slip and sent packing.

But Jesus does just the opposite in his portrayal of the steward. In this scene we don't find a man immobilized by the crisis he's in. Rather he's a person who quickly makes a shrewd assessment of his predicament, one that will enable him to use the crisis for his own benefit. He knows something has to be done—yet he has too much pride to go on welfare, and he's physically not able to go out into the field as a laborer—and so, he has an idea. "I have decided what to do," he says, "so that people may receive me into their houses when I am put out of the stewardship" (Luke 16:4).

Jesus' point here, it seems to me, is not to commend the steward's desire to save his own neck as somehow exemplary. After all, this is still the parable of the *unjust* steward. But what Jesus wants to stress is the steward's decisiveness. The man decided to do something, which is often far more than you or I ever do. We talk about discipleship; we philosophize, theologize about what our baptism means for daily life—but there we stop, short of any decision, short of any action.

The parable reminds us, however, that the mark of a good steward and a good disciple is his or her willingness to be decisive. And moreover to be decisive when the conditions under which we have to decide are less than ideal, and the consequences of our decisions are not neatly black and white. The disciples to whom Jesus first told this story, and you and I as Christians today, are asked to make our decision for the Gospel, express our commitment in situations that are less than perfect, situations permeated by selfishness and sin. It may be that we don't have all the time and talent and resources we'd like to have for the expression of our discipleship. It may be that the persons with whom we work and witness in the church are, like ourselves, irascible and cantankerous. Yet Jesus—by telling us of a steward who was not immobilized by the predicament and the problems in which he found himself—invites us to decide for him, to live out our

229

baptism, amidst all the ambiguities, uncertainties and little crises we meet each day.

Scene III: Action

Once our steward has made his decision, Jesus moves quickly to describe the actions that follow. Here, in the third scene, the steward summons the tenant farmers with whom his master had contracted for their crops of olive oil and wheat. "How much do you owe my master?", they are asked. One says, "a hundred measures of oil"—perhaps close to 800 gallons— while the other responds, "a hundred measures of wheat," which was probably the harvest off of 100 acres. Since the steward has been accused of mismanagement, such that the quantity bargained for had not reached his boss, he has the farmers—in their own handwriting—doctor the books. "Make the hundred measures of oil, fifty, and the hundred measures of wheat, eighty." In so doing the blame is lifted from the steward. "Look here," he can now tell his boss, "the reason you've received less than you expected isn't my fault. Rather, it's because we contracted with the farmers for less than we thought!" Our unjust steward, then, has coyly made the most of the embarrassing situation in which he found himself. The crisis, which only a moment ago had threatened to undo him, now— through his decision and action—has been turned completely around to his benefit. And so what can the boss say other than to acknowledge his steward for his chutzpah, his shrewdness: "The sons of this world are wiser in their own generation than the sons of light" (Luke 16:8b).

I suppose that we get a little uptight at this point in that Jesus seems to describe the steward's actions so positively. Perhaps it's because we often take the parables so seriously and fail to see the humor, the contrast, the irony, and the unexpected details that Jesus incorporates into his stories for their shock value. And maybe that's why Jesus depicts the steward's actions here as so blatantly dishonest. To be sure, we can't escape the fact that he altered the accounts, that what he did was against the law. The important point for Jesus, though, was that this man at least did something that made the most out of the circumstances in which he was caught. And that being the case, then, it would appear that Jesus is suggesting something for our lives as disciples. Our actions, which stem from our commitment to the Gospel, are certainly never free of mixed motives. We have to act while we are yet sinners. Our time, talent and resources are less than ideal. Yet all of these—as incomplete and ambiguous as they are —are the givens with which we live, and with which we respond to what God has done for us in Christ.

We may not have all the time we'd like to have in order to make calls for the evangelism committee or to serve on the church council; we may feel that we don't have the talent or the eloquence to be an effective witness for the Gospel; we may not be able to tithe at 10%. Yet Jesus, by commending the decisiveness of our steward in an embarrassing situation, seems to be saying to us that we ought not feel guilty about our shortcomings or paralyzed by our difficulties. If you can't tithe at 10%, well, then, 3% or 4% is better than none. While we may not be the most eloquent members of the evangelism committee, or the most talented members of the church council, or have all kinds of time on our hands, yet we each have some talent, some eloquence, some time to employ in the service of our Lord. Make the most of what you have been given is the word Jesus leaves with us as he draws this parable to its conclusion. Make the most of the time, the gifts, the grace he grants us in order that we may be received "into the eternal habitations" (Luke 16:9b).

We all know that times are tough, that our jobs are under fire. The boarded-up storefronts and the layoffs at the mill make us anxious, as worried as that steward was about whom Jesus spoke in today's Gospel. Yet under fire, he was not immobilized, but decisive. "I have decided what to do," he said. He decided, and then he did it.

And if he—as a "son of this world"—could act in such a way to save his own neck, can not we—as "children of the light"—be as decisive when it comes to living out our baptism, our vocation as Christians, amidst the challenges, uncertainties and crises that come our way with each new day?

THOMAS R. LEE
Lutheran Campus Ministry
University of Montana, Missoula

NINETEENTH SUNDAY AFTER PENTECOST

The Rich Man's Poverty
Luke 16:19-31

How many of you remember the story of "The Hare and the Tortoise"? It's a memorable little tale of two creatures who competed in a race. On any terms, the contest was a mismatch. The tortoise in particular appeared to be a fool for accepting the hare's challenge; there was no way for him to beat the self-assured speedster. But once the race began, you may recall, the hare got sidetracked. His lead was so great that he stopped to take a nap. In the meantime, the tortoise kept plodding along and passed up his rival slumbering under the tree. By the time the hare woke up and realized what had happened, he was too far behind to catch up. The tortoise had beaten him.

One of the reasons this story fascinates people is the irony of its outcome. "Irony" is a term used to describe any situation in which the opposite of what you expect, actually occurs. A firehouse burning to the ground is an ironic event. People never expect it to happen. Similarly, we find it ironic that an animal as quick as a hare would lose a race to one as slow as a tortoise.

An Ironic Story

By the same token, there is an ironic twist to the story of "The Rich Man and Poor Lazarus." As Luke depicts him for us, Lazarus was the poorest of beggars. In material terms, he had nothing. But when he entered the eternal realm, he stood alongside Abraham before the glorious throne of God. The rich man, on the other hand, had everything a person might desire in this life. The world's standard indicated he "had it made." But weighed out in God's eternal balance, he was dirt poor. The rich man's poverty is the irony of the story. It is also God's way of getting his message across to us today.

Lazarus and the Modern World

The story removes all doubt about Lazarus' plight. His needs were obvious to anyone who passed the rich man's gate. He was too weak to stand on his feet. His body was inflamed with sores from head to toe. He was hungry to the point that he would have settled gladly for the scraps that fell from the rich man's table. Even the dogs in the neighborhood seem to have recognized this man's helplessness. Nothing inhibited them from coming to lick his wounds.

In the world of today, Lazarus is still around. We see him in the form of the world's hungry and impoverished population. His number is legion. While the population of the United States is about two hundred twenty million, the list of the world's poor people adds up to about nine hundred million. That's a total approaching five times the population of our entire nation. Many of them are always sick. Most are hungry continually. Some will starve. The estimate is that 34,000 die every day from disease made fatal by malnutrition.

The Rich Man's Problem

Yet, Jesus' finger of condemnation falls not on Lazarus but on the rich man in the story. By itself, wealth is not a sin. God's blessing often rains down in material as well as spiritual ways. You and I do not need to be embarrassed about all that we have. Instead, we ought to recognize the Giver and look for ways to express our thanks for his grace toward us by sharing a portion of it with others. Similarly, the rich man's malady was not simply his great wealth. It was his belief that he had the right to do with it as he pleased. His sin lay in his choosing to ignore the impoverished man who was right at his door every day.

There is no way to rationalize the evidence. We in America are exceedingly rich. We are part of that 20% of the world's people who control 80% of its wealth, own 85% of its cars, possess 80% of its television sets, and use 93% of its telephones. In comparison to the rest of the world, we are the ones "clothed in purple and fine linen." We complain about the effects of inflation on our housing. Yet even the barest apartment or tract home located anywhere in America provides what the rest of mankind considers luxuries: electric lights, hot and cold running water, private bath or shower, indoor plumbing. On our tables every day there is more than enough to eat. We seldom have to delay our gratification for just about any treat our palate craves.

Our Ways of Ignoring the Needs of Mankind

Still, we have our ways of ignoring human deprivation in our world. One way is to claim that however severe the problem may be, it's not "our" problem. When I was in college, some of my friends and I liked to play a little game with anyone who dared to prick our consciences concerning world hunger. When such a person typically stated that two thirds or one half of the world's people "go to bed hungry," we would respond, "Name one!" Most often, this was enough to short-circuit further conversation. But we were in reality "copping out." We were insinuating that while hunger in the world is real, it's not "our" problem. Or is it?

Another way to ignore the Lazaruses around us is to take the position that poverty is somehow the fault of the poor. Some folks tried to say the same thing in Jesus' day. To them, poverty was a sure sign of God's judgment on a person. The fellow must have done something "wrong." On the other hand, they asserted that wealth identified the righteous. This brand of thinking continues to this day. You and I may even believe that people somehow deserve to be poor or rich. The story's conclusion serves to remind us that Jesus completely overturned such ideas with his whole life and ministry.

Nevertheless, the avoidance mechanism continues to operate within us all. We shy away from looking at the bloated bellies of hungry children on posters or in the magazines that deal with the problem. We stay away from nursing homes and hospitals in which the used-up bodies of humanity are often dumped because we cannot stand the smell. We find it hard to bear the anguished cry of a mother who has lost her child or the deep sobbing of a son who sees his father lowered into an open grave. Like the rich man, we would prefer to steer clear of such troubles. It's more than we can take. Or is it?

Still another way to ignore the Lazaruses around us is to turn poverty or hunger into an issue for debate. In most discussion of such problems, it doesn't take long for someone to start talking about all those poor people who are unwilling to work or the fraud in the welfare system or the sins of big labor. Participants in the conversation become animated, even agitated, and pretty soon it happens. The people who are hungry or poor are pushed into the background where we can safely ignore them. In the meantime we pontificate about our own philosophical or political persuasions.

But Lazarus was not a social issue. Nor was he a bill before Congress. Lazarus was a person! A human being! We are not told how he got the way he was. Maybe he was a ne'er-do-well, someone who had trouble holding a job, a bum. Perhaps he attended no church. Maybe his disease was so terrible that death would have been a blessing. Who knows? For his part, the rich man may have enjoyed the respect of many in his community. Perhaps he was very active in a local church. Maybe he sat out on his back patio with his friends discussing ways to improve the town's tennis courts and other recreational facilities. Perhaps he could tick off a whole list of causes to which he had contributed in the last year. But to the plight of his fellowman and neighbor, poor Lazarus, he was indifferent, even callous.

The More Basic Malady

The story may cut even deeper into our souls today. In its final chapter Jesus exposes a more basic flaw in the rich man's being. When he made his plea for someone to go and warn his five brothers about the great torment awaiting people such as he, Abraham replied, "They have Moses and the prophets; let them hear them." In other words, the rich man was ignoring not only Lazarus. His real problem was that he was ignoring God and the message of God's own Word. His excuses for leaving Lazarus at the gate may have been good. His philosophy of life may have been sound, sensible, and logical. Most of his cronies may have agreed wholeheartedly with his lack of sympathy for the poor. Nevertheless, these attitudes put him out of "sync" with God.

What God's Word Says to Us

In his Word, God has spoken very clearly to us. Today's First Lesson pulls no punches. Through the prophet Amos, God says to us:

Woe to those who lie upon beds of ivory,
  and stretch themselves upon their couches,
and eat lambs from the flock,
  and calves from the midst of the stall;
who sing idle songs to the sound of the harp;
  and like David invent for themselves instruments of music;
who drink wine in bowls,
  and anoint themselves with the finest oils,
but are not grieved over the ruin of Joseph. (Amos 6:4-6)

Better yet, God has spoken to us through his "Word made flesh." As God's Son, Jesus Christ was exceedingly rich. In heaven's court, he resided, far above this sinful and impoverished world of ours. Yet ironically, he chose not to remain there. Nor did he close his eyes to our helplessness. Jesus Christ came to earth and dwelt among us. He made his first home in Bethlehem, at the world's back door. He endured poverty, pain, and death on a cross. He gave up his life so that "we poor sinners" might have the whole inheritance of our heavenly Father. "You know the grace of our Lord Jesus Christ," writes the Apostle Paul, "that though he was rich, yet for your sake he became poor so that by his poverty you might become rich" (2 Cor. 8:9).

What God's Word Does to Us

When it is heard, this Word of God also does something to us. As our Second Lesson suggests, we "shun" selfishness. We "aim at righteousness, godliness, faith, love, steadfastness, gentleness" (1 Tim. 6:11). Several years ago, a group of farmers from the American Lutheran Church drafted a statement entitled "Farmers Speak on World Hunger." In it they called for some drastic revisions in America's patterns of consumption. We might learn to eat less, they suggested, as well as make use of leaner cuts of meat and refrain from processed foods that are often high in calories but low in nutrition. They also advocated the curbing of waste, especially in the packaging of food and the use of our energy resources. Perhaps these farmers recognized the irony in the huge amounts of time and money we Americans expend on weight-reducing programs. While much of the world struggles for enough food just to stay alive, we fight "the battle of the bulge."

At the present time, Congress is slashing the federal budget as never before. The President has told us that this is a painful but necessary remedy for the economic crisis of our time. He has called for deep cuts in those federal programs and services on which the poor and deprived in our country have come to depend. The reductions will not reduce the poor or their needs. The President knows this as well as we do. Hence he has asked that voluntary groups such as the church help pick up the slack. His idea is not new. Some Christians have been talking about it for years. A few have asserted that we have allowed the government to do the job that really belongs to the church. The difference is that the ball is now in the church's court. We can be sure that Lazarus will be lying at the church door. If anything, the bread line of people seeking assistance with medicine, food, and utility bills will be a little longer. Will we respond as the rich man did? Or will we, as the church, exercise (perhaps as never before) the love and compassion which God's own Word, Jesus Christ, stirs up in us?

John phrased the question this way: "If anyone has this world's goods and sees his brother in need, yet closes his heart against him, how does God's love abide in him?" (1 John 3:17). For several years now we as a congregation have tried to deliver our answer. On a fall afternoon, we have joined hands with other Christians from churches in our community on a five-mile walk for world hunger. Some of us have done the walking. Others of us have sponsored walkers at so much money for every mile walked. Some of us have done both. The effort we put forth is minimal. But it goes a long way toward raising the funds needed to supply seed, fertilizer, machinery, and know-how to millions of hungry and underprivileged people around the world. How will we respond this year on World Hunger Day?

There Still Is Time

In the story of "The Rich Man and Poor Lazarus" we find another irony. In Hades, the rich man came to his senses. Ironically, his ears were now open to what God had been saying to him through his Word. The rich man became concerned about other people. He cared about his five brothers on the other side of eternity. But it was too late. His eternal fate had been fixed. For you and for me, however, there is still time. We have the opportunities to exercise the love and compassion that Jesus Christ stirs up in us. Let's not waste them.

Jon Diefenthaler
Bethany-Trinity Lutheran Church
Waynesboro, Virginia

We Have Done No More Than Our Duty
Luke 17:1-10

Throughout history, society has recognized individuals from its midst who have generously given of themselves in the service of others. Public acknowledgments have ranged from local Citizen of the Year awards to the Nobel and People's Peace Prize. A woman rescues a child from a fire and is named the Good Neighbor of the Year. A man establishes a charitable foundation and receives the public's accolade. A scientist discovers a vaccination that will prevent the spread of a dread disease and is named the recipient of a large grant to enable further research. A diplomat gives of herself tirelessly in the pursuit of world peace and justice and her government rewards her with a promotion. A college professor's unusual dedication to his students results in him being named the Teacher of the Year. The awards seem endless in number and the impression they leave with us is this: If you perform good deeds, then you will receive your just reward.

In our Gospel for today, Jesus confronts those who hold this viewpoint and informs them that is not the way it is in the kingdom of God. In the kingdom of God, one cannot earn one's own place because there is no room for self-righteousness. Neither is it possible for one to lie back and do nothing, for the call of the Gospel does not allow for complacency. Rather, as Jesus informs his hearers in this text, there are certain responsibilities that we share as ones who follow Jesus.

No Room for Self-Righteousness

Yet, it seems that no matter how many times we are reminded that we cannot earn our own salvation, we often continue to operate as if we believe we can. We give money to the Seminary Appeal and to combat world hunger, and we tend to think that we have thereby cemented our position in the kingdom. We agree to serve on the church council or to teach Sunday school and we find ourselves tempted to believe that God is in our debt. We stand up and speak out against discrimination in our little corner of the global village and we wonder what our reward will be when we come into God's kingdom. We struggle against the power of death in our world as we seek to combat pollution, racial strife, persecution,

237

war, and disease and we are sorely tempted to believe that because we have spoken out on behalf of life, we have thereby earned for ourselves eternal life.

The temptation to believe that the kingdom of God operates in the same fashion as the kingdoms of this world is very real. We are tempted to believe that because society often rewards those who do good deeds, so also will God.

God, however, will not allow us to rest back on society's accolades. The kingdom of God is not God's Good Citizen of the Cosmos Award. It is neither something that we can earn for ourselves on the basis of the number of tears that we shed for the "little ones" in our world; nor is it something that we can gain for ourselves because of our toil on behalf of justice.

Rather, membership in God's kingdom is his free and gracious gift to those who have been baptized in his name. We neither earn it nor do we deserve it. It is a gift of a generous and compassionate creator to his erring and confused creation. There is, therefore, no room for self-righteousness in the kingdom of God.

No Room for Complacency

Neither is there any room for complacency. To say that we cannot earn our salvation by deeds of kindness does not excuse us from showing compassion to our brothers and sisters who are in need of our support. To acknowledge that it is God who is source and giver of all life does not exempt us from becoming advocates for those whose continued life is threatened in our world. To confess that it is God who is our Lord and Master does not release us from our responsibility to serve those whom Christ served—by his life and by his death. To concede that we cannot advance our position in the kingdom of God by our efforts to ensure that justice be established among us does not absolve us from our responsibility to do justice with one another.

For as Christians who live in this world, we are not only tempted to believe that we can earn our own salvation, we are also tempted to believe that if we cannot earn our own salvation, then we need do nothing at all. We can simply lie back, wrapped in the blankets of complacency, lulled into a hypnotic stupor, even while humanity continues to experience war, persecution, starvation, disease, and discrimination.

The disciples in our Gospel text for today experienced both of these temptations. On the one hand, they were tempted to believe that by their actions, they could earn favor in Gods' sight. By doing what Jesus requested of them, they felt that they deserved a pat on the back and perhaps

238

a word of thanks from their Lord and Master. On the other hand, they were also tempted to believe that they need do nothing at all. For the most part, they were tempted to operate on the assumption that they were the favored few. Whereas those outside the community of faith were subject to God's judgment, they considered themselves heirs of his grace.

The Challenge to End Self-Righteousness and Complacency

Jesus confronts both of these attitudes. To those who believe that they are the favored few he says, "Take heed to yourselves." And of those who look for rewards in the kingdom of God he asks, "Does the master thank the servant because he or she has done what was commanded?"

Jesus informs his disciples that there is no room for either complacency or self-righteousness in the kingdom of God. Rather, as people who have been called by name in the waters of Baptism, we are challenged to live out our faith. As the text reminds us, it is not a matter of increasing our faith, but of simply letting our faith inform the way we live our lives.

Thus, as people of God we are challenged to combat the power of death in our world. When the power of death in our air and water which we call pollution threatens to eliminate continued life on our planet, we are challenged to work to alleviate the sources of pollution. When the power of death in our international relationships which we call war threatens to destroy entire continents, we are challenged to work for peace. When the power of death in our human family which we call discrimination threatens the health and well-being of our brothers and sisters throughout the globe, we are challenged to strive for understanding. Whenever the power of death in our world threatens to overcome the power of life, we are challenged to let our faith inform the way we live our lives.

There is no room for complacency or self-righteousness in the kingdom of God. There is, however, room for service. For it is to service that we are called: service in God's name and for the sake of his creation. And when the time shall come that our period of service is at an end, may God enable us to say: "We are unworthy servants; we have only done what was our duty."

ADRIANNE HESKIN
Looney Valley and Cedar Valley Lutheran Churches
Houston, Minnesota

239

Twice Blessed
Luke 17:11-19

Why should we give thanks? Why, it is a matter of being gracious, isn't it? Yes, giving thanks for a gift is a common human courtesy. Few things embarrass parents more than their child receiving a gift without expressing thanks.

Why should we give thanks to God? I asked the confirmands this recently and they quite naturally answered, "Because it pleases God like it pleases our fathers and mothers." Of course, our words of thanksgiving have a sweet sound to the Lord. Giving thanks is a gracious and God pleasing thing to do.

There is yet another reason for giving thanks. God does something for us when we give thanks to God. This is the Lord's economy of grace. He gives us gifts and we in turn give thanks—that's usual. But God blesses us a second time in the very act of thanking him. We are twice blessed. God makes us wholly whole when we declare in thanks the presence of his grace in Christ in our life.

The way we receive something in our life is more important to us than what we receive. Luther makes this point in his explanation of the fourth petition in the Lord's Prayer, "Give us this day our daily bread." He stated, "God gives daily prayer, even without our prayer, to all people, though sinful, but we ask in this petition that he will help us to realize this and to receive our daily bread with thanksgiving." Luther echoes the biblical affirmation that God in generosity lets the rain fall both on the just and the unjust. God's generosity and the farmers' hard work will bring forth the harvest without our prayer. So why pray? Because the important thing for us is that we realize his generosity, and we receive our bread with thanksgiving. Then God blesses us twice. Once in the gift of bread and again in the declaring to each of us his gracious presence.

According to Luther we do not pray to God for daily bread, but we pray for God to be present in our sharing of bread in a human family. We grace our tables by saying, "Come, Lord Jesus, be our guest and your gifts to us be blessed"—doubly blessed.

The Gospel for today shows us how a man is doubly blessed in the giving of thanks. He was one of ten lepers living a life of social isolation and physical decay. Leprosy disfigures the body. It was so feared by the community that lepers were forced to live in their own colonies. These ten men in anguish see Jesus as he is going to Jerusalem and cry out, "Lord, have mercy upon us." They plead for mercy, which is undeserved love, the love given to those who cannot pay back, the love that can only come from a lover who loves for love's sake.

The Lord Jesus responds to their petition. He tells them to see the priest in accordance with the law. Somewhere en route to the priest the ten men discover their skin is cleared, their limbs are whole, they are healed. No doubt they rejoiced, sang, exuberantly told the world of their healing. All ten, Jew and Samaritan, wise and foolish, lawyer and laborer, just and unjust, were healed by the generosity of God. "God gave his healing indeed without our prayer."

All are healed, but only one received the healing with thanksgiving. A lonely Samaritan, the one least deserving in Jewish eyes anyway, returns to Jesus and we are told, "gave glory to God." He saw the light of God's grace in the healing and returned to thank the one through whom that undeserved love came.

Jesus responds to this act of thanksgiving with a double entendre, a statement with a double meaning. "Your faith has made you well." Were not all ten healed by God's generous mercy? Of course. But there is healing and there is healing. The word "heal" is the word for "save" or make whole. All then were made whole in their bodies, but only one was made wholly whole—the Samaritan who received his healing with thanksgiving.

When we consider the central message in Luke and Acts, the meaning of the story of the ten lepers comes into sharp focus. Luke's central message is that Jesus of Nazareth brought God's final and universal rule of grace into this world. The signs of that universal kingdom were found in his healing ministry, his liberation of oppressed, his care for the poor. But his own people would not see the meaning of his mission. Jesus would suffer and die in Jerusalem, but God would raise him and God's kingdom would spread throughout the world.

In this story, nine people are healed but do not see Jesus as the bearer of God's final salvation. The Samaritan, the foreigner, is healed and sees Jesus as the source of God's special healing in the world. He becomes the symbol of the church's outreach to the whole world. He is doubly blessed.

One of the ways human beings can be distinguished from brute beasts is the way they eat. In many ways we eat the same way hogs and dogs eat. The physical requirements for survival and mechanism for nourishment are similar. But in one important respect we can differ. The brute beasts simply attack the food set before them. With greedy and unreflecting taste they devour the food until satisfied. Some people, however, seem to bow their heads for a moment and, regardless of their hunger pains, pause to give thanks.

In giving thanks we express our freedom from the tyranny bread can exert on us and we live by the Word of God. In that moment we know their food is not simply survival material, but a gift from the Almighty. In calling for Jesus to be present we remember this food which is a gift, is also a sign of grace. It is a sign of God's salvation.

Receiving a gift with thanksgiving is more than saying, "Thanks." It is living the thankful life. The nine who were healed but gave no thanks were not fundamentally changed in their lives. They returned to the business life as usual. You remember the story of the merciful servant. He embezzled millions from his employer. When caught, he pleaded for mercy. His employer showed mercy and forgave him the whole debt. But lo and behold this same man goes out and encounters a man who owes him fifty dollars. He grabs the debtor by the throat and demands immediate payment or else. You see, nothing happened to that unjust man. He did not have to go to jail, and basically he remained the same as always. He was the same cheat, the same self-centered pusher. He is not twice blessed and is therefore a prisoner of a life in bondage to greed, fear, and death.

To be forgiven by God is a blessing. To know you are forgiven, to believe it, to rejoice in his grace, to be freed by it, is to be doubly blessed. And this knowing changes you when you meet those who owe you. The sign of the thankful life is that we begin to take the form of the gracious giver of grace.

We generally think of giving thanks for good things we receive. It is important that we learn to give thanks in the bad situations, for in the giving of thanks, God transforms that situation for us. Job was a prosperous man who lost his family and property. In the midst of adversity he said, "The Lord gave, the Lord has taken away, blessed be the name of the Lord." This is an astounding thanksgiving. "For my family and worldly possessions, I bless the Lord. In my personal loss, I still bless the Lord." How can anyone say this?

Frances and Ed are an inspiration to us all. Frances suffered a stroke that left her partially paralyzed, confined to a wheelchair. Yet they come every Sunday and praise God from whom all blessings flow. There is a loyal love that binds them together. There is a reason that spurs their will to live life to the fullest. They express a life of thanksgiving. How can this be?

There is a saying, "Seeing is believing." The reverse is more to the truth. "Believing is seeing." You may recall the little verse, "Two men looked out from prison bars. One saw mud, the other saw stars." The way we perceive a situation in faith does more to determine reality than the bare bones facts looked at from a neutral corner.

Job experienced the loss of family and possessions, but when he looked out his window with the eye of faith, he saw stars. They were not dream stars. They were as real as the mud on the ground. This is true of Frances and Ed and all the saints of God who see with the eyes of faith that God's gracious presence is in their own situation. The love of God in Christ is stronger than their sin and the power of the evils they experienced. They see forgiveness and not punishment. They see opportunity to grow in faith and not personal disintegration. They see God's future opening their futures and not shooting them down.

God seeks to bless us twice this day. First in the hearing and tasting his Word of grace in Christ our Lord. But we pray he would give us his spirit so we can sing from the heart, "Bless the Lord, O my soul and all that is within me, bless his holy name." In that song of praise he will bless us a second time. "Go in peace, your faith has made you whole."

ANDREW M. WEYERMANN
Holy Cross Lutheran Church
St. Louis, Missouri

TWENTY-SECOND SUNDAY AFTER PENTECOST

How Do We Know When Our Prayers Are Answered?
Luke 18:1-8

The most anguishing question a Christian can ask is, "Why didn't God answer my prayer?" There are times when we simply cannot understand why something happens, and it is particularly difficult when we have been praying for something else.

There are, of course, some standard answers. They are correct, even though in the midst of pain they do not take the hurt away. We can say, for instance, that God does not always answer prayers in the way we desire or hope for. We can say that perhaps the prayer is not yet answered. We can point to the fact that we know there is evil and sin in the world and we do not understand why God does not take it away, although he did not create the world that way. There are times when we go through a painful period, wondering why it has happened that way despite our prayers, and then with the passage of time look back and see that out of all that hurting something good did come after all. Or maybe some good came to somebody else because of what happened to us.

Yet somehow all our explanations do not take away our questions.

"How do we know when God answers prayer?" What more urgent question is there?

A man sat in my office hardly a month ago and said, "Pastor, I pray every day, but lately it's as if my words go up and hit a brick wall and don't get in at all. It's like God isn't listening."

Haven't we all thought that at one time or another?

The Gospel text for today is about prayer and the answers to prayer. Jesus is telling a parable, a story. It is one of Jesus' stories with a touch of humor, because he uses a scoundrel as the main character. A widow had come to this rascal judge for a favorable judgment. She knew this dishonorable fellow would probably not grant it to her, so she figured her only hope was to pester and bother him so much that she might just finally wear him down. And sure enough, it worked! The man was so exasperated that he finally gave in. Now, Jesus says, if persistence gives results with a fellow like that, how much more will a loving Father God be inclined to grant the petitions of his children?

The actual story ends there, and I used to wonder why that next sentence was tacked on after the story: "But will the Son of man find faith on earth when he comes?" It was not until I was older, and I hope wiser, that I realized that Jesus' little question at the end of the parable was the key to the whole story!

You see, the real answer to the question of prayer is faith. Without faith we probably would not recognize answers to prayer when they came. With faith, we simply trust that God will answer, *even though* we might not recognize his answer.

It is the only way to understand prayer.

We could try it without faith, that is, wait for a definite answer each time we pray, skeptically putting God to the test as it were, and if we did not see the answer, we could shrug our shoulders and conclude that he does not answer after all. Or maybe he does not even listen.

The only other way is to approach prayer in faith that God does listen and answer. We still wait for an answer. We may still wonder how he is answering. We may wish he would have answered another way. There will be times when we wonder indeed if he is answering. But we cling to the promise in faith, that he does answer, and it is that faith which makes sense of praying.

Does God answer prayer? That question is answered by asking about faith, so Jesus puts his finger on the heart of the matter when he concludes the story: "Will the Son of man find faith on earth when he returns?" The question, "Does God answer prayer?" is ultimately the question: "Do we have faith through it all that he does?"

Our natural human desire, of course, is for God to give us definite, visible signs as answer to prayer. How we wish for that! I have always liked the story of Gideon, the leader of the Israelites back in the times after they had returned to their promised land from Egypt. At one time they were being bullied about by the Midianites, another tribe in the area, and they prayed to God for help and deliverance. How they prayed! And he answered by telling Gideon to gather a force of men to drive the Midianites away. Gideon did this, but shortly before the battle he still was not too sure of himself. So he decided to check out God's answer and said to God, "I'm putting some wool on the ground tonight. If you really want me to battle the Midianites, make this wool wet during the night, but keep the ground around it dry."

Sure enough, when Gideon got up the next morning, the wool was soaking wet, and the ground around it was bone dry.

Good enough, you would think? That should convince anyone! Not Gideon. The next evening he said to God—rather apologetically this time —"Pardon me, Lord, and don't be angry with me, but tonight let's reverse it. Keep the wool dry and make the ground around it wet, and *then* I'll believe you for sure!" So that's exactly what happened. The next morning the ground was sopping wet with a heavy dew, but the wool was dry. That did it for Gideon, and he decided God really was behind it all, and he went out and did what God wanted him to.

There is something wonderfully human in that story, isn't there, because we all wish God would give us answers like that. (We tend to think of the Bible heroes as such superhuman people of faith, but we so often discover they have the same questions as the rest of us!) I suspect we all put our wool out at night once in awhile: "God, if you will only do this, then I will do so-and-so for sure!" Sometimes we wish God would just tell us.

There are times in our lives when we do receive a really clear direction in answer to prayer, or at least something that we take to be a clear direction.

I remember an interesting experience like that. It was in early 1969, when we were living in France, where I was working for the Lutheran World Federation at the Institute for Ecumenical Research in Strasbourg. I had been asked to stay on for another three-year term. We had been talking about it, thinking about it, and praying about it. One day in the spring we went to a movie. I forget now what it was, but the short feature before the main film was about Disney World in Florida. I have never been there, before or after, and it showed the figure of Abraham Lincoln, which is animated to move and speak. So there on the movie screen, I saw Mr. Lincoln stand and give part of his 1865 Inaugural Address, after he had been reelected to the presidency. The country was torn by civil war, and his words were a plea for all Americans to get together in this time of crisis. There I sat, thousands of miles away from home, with Abraham Lincoln telling us all to pull together! He had barely stood up and started talking before I was all choked up, and after only a minute or so I had tears streaming down my face. I thought to myself: What am I doing here in a foreign country, cut off from my family, friends, and church, far away from everybody and everything that was really important to me. The next morning I went into the institute director's office and told him I was going home that summer at the end of my term. I did, and I have never regretted it!

Was that film an answer to prayer? Maybe. I probably would have gone home anyway. But that little episode in the theater caused me to make up my mind.

How do we know when our prayers are answered?

Ultimately it is a matter of faith. We simply believe that God does answer prayers.

But there are ways God uses to answer prayer, and we should use them.

In the first place, God works through *our minds*. God gave us brains, and he wants us to use them. If we are faced with a decision, we do so in prayer, but we also use our minds to weigh what is the best course. When I was wondering whether or not I should stay in France in 1969, I believe God wanted me to pray about it, but he also wanted me to sift carefully through the good reasons for staying and the good reasons for going home. Mr. Lincoln's appearance on that movie screen probably just ratified what my mind had been telling me all along.

I once had a young man in my office who told me that he did not have enough time to study for a test, so he had prayed that God would give him some help toward the right answers, and he was discouraged when he ended up with a poor grade. I think it is all right to pray for help in an exam, but one of God's answers to prayer for that young man would certainly be for him to plan ahead better and allow more time for study!

Now God might surprise us, and something will happen in our lives that we would not have thought about in our own minds. But God does want us to use the intelligence he has given us to reason out what would be the course he wants us to take.

A second means God can use in answering prayer is *the Bible*. Some people have found answers almost by accident—like letting the Bible fall open at random—but it is far more effective if one steeps oneself in the Scriptures through regular study and develops a feel through one's whole being for the kind of person Jesus is and the kind of life he wants us to live. Sometimes it is indirect advice we get from the Bible, because our situations are not exactly like those in the Bible. But if we catch the spirit of the Scriptures, we will be in a much better position to evaluate our own course in life. Obviously God will answer prayer in a way consistent with his Word in the Bible, so it is important to know what is in there.

A third means God can use to answer our prayers is through *Christian family and friends*. I do not mean that we let others dictate our life, but it is helpful when we are facing decisions or looking for answers to share our thinking and feeling with those we are close to. We might not even follow their advice, but at least we will have opened ourselves to a more objective insight, and maybe it will help us to see the situation in a different light. God can send us other people as an answer to prayer, to help us find our own answers.

"How do we know when our prayers are answered?" There is no one answer for everybody and for all occasions. However much you use your mind, or search the Scriptures, or listen to good advice, something happens within you to lead you in a direction which you have come to believe is God's way for you. Or you go ahead with a prayer that it is the way God wants.

The key is faith. "But will the Son of man find faith on earth when he comes?" We live in the faith that God does listen to prayer and that God does answer. Behind all our other prayers is always the prayer for faith, that we might always trust him!

MICHAEL ROGNESS
First Lutheran Church
Duluth, Minnesota

TWENTY-THIRD SUNDAY AFTER PENTECOST

"We Are Beggars"
Luke 18:9-14

Two days before he died, Martin Luther wrote, "We are beggars, it is true."

What an odd way to sum up a life—especially his life! This is the man who stood up to kings and councils, burned Papal Bulls, challenged sixteen centuries of church tradition and more than survived. This is the man whose written work fills over 30 volumes, whose scholarly translation of the scriptures shaped the German language and whose courage reshaped the geography of Europe. Surely at the end of such a life there must be time for a bit of boasting—a few brief moments of crowing. Yet, like his soul mate, Paul, the boasting was in his weakness, and the power of the cross.

Martin stands in a long line of beggars. From St. Francis to Mother Teresa, there is a host of faithful people whose portraits could well be painted with their palms outstretched, awaiting a gift from God. The New Testament is filled with stories of these people with a humble spirit.

There was a mother who came begging Jesus to heal her little daughter. "It is not fair," he responded to this woman of Canaan, "to take the bread of the children of Israel and give it to gentile dogs."

"Ah," the woman said, wringing a yes out of Jesus' no, "even the dogs eat the crumbs that fall from the master's table." Crumbs indeed! This woman knew that the master's scraps were like Beef Wellington in the mouths of beggars.

A Roman soldier approached Jesus on behalf of his Jewish servant who lay paralyzed in his home. Jesus' response was customarily warm and brief, "I will come and heal him."

"Lord, I am not worthy to have you come under my roof; but only say the word, and my servant will be healed." Amazed at the humility and faith of a foreigner, Jesus granted his wish.

Not worthy. Those words are almost a liturgical refrain on the lips of the congregation of beggars who populate the pages of the New Testament. Zacchaeus, the quisling who sat in the sycamore tree, was content to merely get a glimpse of Christ as he passed by. The woman who suffered from massive hemorrhages did not dare to ask too much from Jesus. "If I only can touch the hem of his garment," she thought. Mary, who sat at the Master's feet soaking up every word he spoke, was also one of the humble. Bartimaeus, the blind panhandler who boldly cried for mercy, is another of this lowly cast of characters. At his death the thief on the cross chastised his cynical companion and humbly asked to be remembered. Unworthy. Beggars all.

Yet each of these humble supplicants ends up more wealthy than they could ever dare dream. They receive precious gifts of healing, forgiveness, and the presence of the Lord. They receive grace upon grace. As surely as the exalted are humbled, the unworthy who come to Christ are exalted.

In our text today two men come before the altar of the Lord. Each prayed. One, a just and sincere man, thanked God for making him a religious good ol' boy. His many accomplishments were laid out for God to see. Not only did he avoid dishonesty in his business and infidelity in his personal life, he exceeded the legal requirements in piety by fasting twice a week and figuring his tithe before taxes.

The second, a no-good cheating turncoat, could find nothing worthy of a boast. His only recourse was to beg for mercy.

Both men received what they asked for. The Pharisee asked for and received nothing. The publican received that for which he petitioned—mercy.

It is ironic that in the kingdom of God our normal expectations are constantly turned upside down. Power is exemplified in humility, the greatest among us is a servant, little children instruct their elders in faith, and penitent scalawags go home justified rather than the self-sufficient religious leaders.

In the "real world," where *Looking Out for Number One* and *Winning Through Intimidation* sit atop the best seller list, beggars remain beggars and kings remain kings. People are encouraged to think of themselves as self-sufficient, autonomous human beings. They can take care of themselves in all things, including religion. There is precious little in this kind of current literature about becoming servants and losing our lives in order to find them.

In a world that attempts to eliminate guilt and where most efforts, to use Edna Hong's phrase, are toward reconciling people to their sins rather than to their God, the publican seems unnecessarily brutal to himself. It is difficult, if not nearly impossible for folks who talk of "massaging our self-images" to understand either the publican's repentance or Dr. Luther describing himself as "poor stinking maggot fodder." This is beggar language, and in most circles that just doesn't wash.

Yet in the kingdom of God, the metaphor of the mendicant is a profound one. It is an eloquent description of our relationship to God.

We come to God with nothing, realizing that neither our morality nor our religion counts with God. We come vulnerable and poor or we don't come at all. "Nothing in my hands I bring," sings the hymnwriter. We enter the waters of baptism as strangers and aliens. We emerge washed, cleansed, named, and adopted; we are children of the king. Our new status is a gift that gladdens the heart of every beggar, large or small.

Actually we should want it no other way. If our being children of God depends on what we do, how much we have accomplished in the moral realm, how well we have performed or even how sincere our faith happens to be, we can never be certain we belong. We will never know whether we have done enough.

One can read all of the best-selling psychology tracts such as *Jonathan Livingston Seagull, The Little Engine That Could* or any of the books on the power of positive grunting and look in vain for anything that helps us deal with our great need for mercy. We seldom read a word of grace.

Rather the current literature preaches a gospel of success, a message of "can do."

What happens when our engines continue to sputter and the sea gulls never do soar? What happens when broken human beings find the gospel of self just one more impossible burden to bear? What happens when the great movers and shakers, the great kingdom builders falter? We who have tasted the bitter tears of failure and who have grown weary of trying to save our own lives know that there is little hope in positive thinking. It is in moments like this that we turn to a gospel for beggars, and read, in less than 150 words, a story of a God who understands wounded human beings, who lifts our burdens and who delights in giving mercy.

A Lifetime of Begging

Being a beggar is not a one-time experience. In the *Small Catechism,* Luther reminds us that through our daily plea for mercy our old self is drowned, and by God's forgiveness we live anew in Christ. Being born again is a daily occurrence.

Though we are always recipients of God's grace, always dependent on his mercy, and always beggars, we are commissioned to act in behalf of Christ. In so doing we learn with the sons of thunder that life in the kingdom has more to do with serving and suffering than with sitting.

We are commissioned to go with the gospel, to carry the marvelous good news that a broken spirit and a cry for mercy are requirements enough to live with God. This sharing is called evangelism, and contrary to popular opinion, it is not a matter of the superior providing information to the inferior. Rather, evangelism is, as D. T. Niles has reminded us, one beggar telling another beggar where to find food.

A Beggar's Meal

In a moment, after the singing, after the offering, we will change our focus from spoken word to visible word. We will gather around the Lord's table to receive the Lord's meal. Those who come will be graced with the mysterious but real presence of Christ. He is the host of this meal and he is present to all. His presence is not dependent on us, or our faith. He comes not because of our confession or the soundness of our doctrine. He comes on his own, as a gift. Thus relieved of our need to do something or believe something to receive Christ, we are able just to receive. It is truly a meal for beggars.

The Lord's Supper is a meal where we image the death and resurrection of our Lord. It is a meal filled with forgiveness and joy and hope. It is a feast of victory, a foretaste of the great and last banquet, where after a lifetime of panhandling we will gather to eat as kings and queens.

Until that day, lifted by his word, filled by his meal, we come to him with empty hands awaiting his gifts to make us right and sustain our very existence. In all of life, we are beggars, it is true.

WILLIAM R. WHITE
Immanuel Lutheran Church
Mount Pleasant, Michigan

TWENTY-FOURTH SUNDAY AFTER PENTECOST

Peak to Peek to Peak
Luke 19:1-10

When the gaze of God focuses on our lives, it can cause dramatic ramifications. Business as usual rarely results after an encounter with the Almighty. If you question this for a moment, just ask Zacchaeus when you enter into the realm of eternal timelessness and glory. For one day in the oasis of Jericho, the transforming gospel of God rocked Zacchaeus, and in the process it redeemed his past, changed his present, and redirected his future.

Until his Jesus encounter, Zacchaeus was a candidate for little more than contempt. He was a short man who was having a mid-life crisis. He had chosen the unpopular profession of tax collector. Not only was he a member of the Jericho branch of the IRS but was probably the supervisor of the region with the title of Chief Tax Collector. Small in stature but large in power, he was into some of the big bucks of his time. Much of the money he collected in the name of Rome stuck to his fingers before the rest made its way into the Roman treasury.

Tax collectors and robbers were spoken of in the same breath and considered one and the same. They were also considered to be collaborators with the despised Romans. Therefore, people avoided them, and we can surmise that they were very lonely people.

If you had to be a tax collector, Jericho was a good territory, for it was known as the City of Palms and was a veritable Eden. Mark Antony had presented it as a gift to Cleopatra. Herod the Great died there. With his last breath he ordered the slaughter of its foremost Jewish citizens, that there might be someone to mourn his passing. Jericho was the place through which great caravans moved from the north and the east. Pilgrims traveled through Jericho on their way to Jerusalem for the yearly festivals. Jesus was on such a journey.

Although Jericho was a nice place, Zacchaeus, like his fellow tax collectors, had all the popularity of terminal cancer. It is quite understandable why no one was willing to move over so the little fellow might be able to see. We can even imagine that he might have been pushed and shoved into the background. This only heightened his feelings of aloneness and made him feel miserable. But Zacchaeus was not going to be so easily denied.

Peak to Peek

Judging the route Jesus would take, Zacchaeus ran on ahead and climbed up a sycamore tree to a peak which would assure him a peek at the man who had a reputation of taking interest in his kind of people. Therefore, Zacchaeus ascended the heights to seek relief from the depths of his despair.

As the Son of God moved down the road, his gaze fell upon the little man with the big reputation. Jesus said to him, "Zacchaeus, make haste and come down; for I must stay at your house today." Quickly climbing down the tree, Zacchaeus received Jesus joyfully.

Do you hear it? All the murmuring which is always spoken against anyone who associates with the wrong kind of people.

"Oh, no, he is doing it again. Doesn't he have enough to do with his own congregation without bothering with all the trash?"

"We are going to be late for the festival if he tries to convert everybody, and this one is beyond hope."

Others joined in the murmuring, "He has gone in to be the guest of a man who is a sinner."

Throughout the Gospel of Luke we find the Lord rubbing elbows with the undesirables and the outcasts of the day. Prostitutes, lepers, and tax collectors were not outside his caring concern. How quickly the outwardly righteous Jews had forgotten that Moses was a murderer, that Jacob was a con man, that David was an adulterer, and that Isaiah was a streaker. Jesus had not gone out of the bounds of God's love, for the Lord was sent to save the lost, and Zacchaeus eminently qualified as an object for his attention.

As we read in the Psalms, "The Lord is good to all, and his compassion is over all that he had made. . . . He fulfills the desire of all who fear him, he also hears their cry and saves them."

When Zacchaeus had climbed to the peak to peek, nothing was probably further from his mind than that the prophet from Galilee would choose to stay at his home.

St. Francis of Assisi once wrote, "God is always courteous and does not invade the privacy of the human soul." Jesus knew that in Zacchaeus' heart a welcome awaited him. After he entered his house, we can surmise the Lord spoke the message of salvation, and through it the soul of Zacchaeus joined the community of saints.

So far we have seen Zacchaeus' resourcefulness in the presence of handicap, his religious hunger, and his decisiveness in opening his home and his heart to the Lord. Now we witness his power for radical repentance and restitution.

Putting his money where his confession was, Zacchaeus said he would give half of his riches to the poor and return fourfold to any he had defrauded. Zacchaeus' radical repentance and restitution was made possible by Jesus' radical love and redemptive power.

Peak to Peek to Peak

When we open ourselves up to God and allow the love of God in Jesus Christ to invade us, only then are we empowered by the Spirit to realign our lives with God's will. Only then can our way be transferred into his way. From the peak of the sycamore tree in order to peek at the Lord, Zacchaeus' eyes were opened, and his life was changed to the peak of becoming a disciple of Christ.

Coming to worship the Lord today, have we entered with eyes and hearts open to the possibility of a God encounter? Most of us have risen to the peak of this sanctuary to peek at the Lord to see what he might have to enhance our lives. Few of us came with the thought of the possibility of a dramatic change in our lives brought about by the peak experience of becoming a disciple of Christ.

Some of us may be up a tree with emotional or financial or family problems and have been in the process of slowly closing the Lord out of our lives. Jesus is saying to all of us, "Come down, I want to enter your hearts and bring joy and meaningful challenge to your lives."

There may be someone here today who has not accepted the Lord as their friend and Savior, or someone who has once accepted him only now to have doubt's insidious growth taking place in their heart. Jesus calls to you the same way he called to Zacchaeus. The cacophony of doubt needs to be silenced in our minds so that the clear, inward voice of God can once again speak its purposeful message in our lives.

To those of us with a flickering faith, we are reminded today that Jesus was the friend of sinners, and that if Zacchaeus qualified for his love, we do also. The love of God is ours for the taking.

It was not long after Zacchaeus climbed the sycamore tree that the Son of God ascended a tree of his own, the hardwood tree of the cross. And from that cross all humankind observed the unparalleled love of the Father.

From the peak of the cross, Jesus sees you and me standing below, having tied his hands to the crossbars by our offenses and having impaled his feet to the stump by our neglect. Not only does his body and blood communicate the Father's love, but his words assure us as he utters, "Father, forgive them, for they know not what they do." Only foolish people keep themselves away from the love of God in Christ.

There are others of us here today who have received Jesus as their Savior, but have failed to have the peak experience of having him as the Lord of their lives. We have not had the supernatural high that comes from the peak experience of having Jesus' will so intertwined with our own. To put it simply, we need to let go and to let God direct our lives. And when we do, we face the exciting risk of ascending the pleasurable peak of discipleship.

Today the Lord is challenging each of us to go for it . . . go for it all . . . to let God rule our hearts and lives not only from peak to peek but to the peak of the life of a disciple of Christ. In other words, to go from peak to peek to peak.

JOHN H. KRAHN
Trinity Lutheran Church
Hicksville, New York

TWENTY-FIFTH SUNDAY AFTER PENTECOST

Whose Wife Will She Be?
Luke 20:27-38

That was the thorny question some Sadducees put to the Lord Jesus one day. Listen: *(Verses 27-33 of the text should be read at this point.)*

The Correct Position

Now it should be noted that the Sadducees in our Lord's day represented the correct, traditional, and orthodox view on this controversial resurrection question which they were raising with the Savior. Doctrinally speaking, they were on firmer and surer ground than the modernist Pharisees who with little or no support from either the Hebrew Scriptures or ancient Jewish tradition nonetheless taught and proclaimed a bodily resurrection. In the rare instance of this controversy the Savior sided with his traditional foes, the Pharisees, and insisted that despite the lack of Scriptural evidence and the testimony of tradition the modernists were right and the guardians of orthodoxy and tradition wrong.

The Uncategorized Christ

Two points might be made of this. First, you can never categorize or stereotype Jesus Christ. He is always his own person. He is never the exclusive property or possession of any one group or party. He belongs to no race, ethnic group, nation, religion or denomination. He is God's *universal* Son and Savior. Which means that the views he holds, the words he speaks, and the deeds he does are never determined or dictated by party lines or ties, loyalties, obligations, or prejudices. He is a man for all seasons, times, and peoples.

The Unorthodox Jesus

Secondly, in the view of the religious establishment, Jesus was frequently unorthodox and heretical. For example, he proposed unorthodox teachings, suggesting that mercy means more than sacrifice. Today he would probably say: "If it's ever a question of sitting in a church pew on Sunday or helping a needy person, you must always choose the latter over the former." The Savior commanded love for Samaritans and other assorted enemies. Food and drink for persecutors? Cheek-turning compassion for hated foes and adversaries? Whoever heard of unpalatable, unacceptable, and unorthodox teachings like that? The Man also urged payment of taxes to despised, tyrannical, and oppressive Rome. Why he even taught that adultery is not limited to couches and beds. You can do it in your heart. How unorthodox can you get?

The Man's teachings were unorthodox and so were his actions. For one thing he spent far too much time with the wrong kind of people. He constantly ran the risk of soiling and defiling himself by his frequent association with social outcasts and gutter-dwellers. He was eternally touching both moral and physical lepers, the kind of people everybody in his or her right mind shuns and avoids. And understandably so. After all, lepers can contaminate you, make you sick, even kill you. And who wants to run that risk? I guess the Galilean Rabbi hasn't heard "cleanliness is next to godliness."

The Man also broke some time-honored religious laws. One time he condoned the scandalous action of his disciples when they had the nerve to pluck some corn from a field and eat it on the Sabbath day. And another time he shocked the daylights out of the religious leaders when he healed a sick man on the Sabbath. You can't let religious revolutionaries get by with such a blatant snubbing and disregard of our precious sacred laws and traditions.

Similar Questions Still Raised

"Whose wife will she be?" We still raise questions like that as we understandably speculate on the life of the world to come. Will infants be infants still, and the aged still aged? Will we know and recognize our loved ones and friends? What kind of relationships will we have with them? Will we miss and mourn the people who are not there? Where on earth—or in other imaginable places—will there be room for heaven, with some two billion candidates every thirty years or so, not to mention the constant arrivals since Adam? In any case, how do you suppose we shall spend eternity when so many of us don't know how to spend and manage time?

And so there is no end of questions about the after-life. Why? Is it mere curiosity that produces these questions? We simply have an unquenchable desire to know more about the unknown and in this case unknowable? Is that it? Or is it doubt that makes us wonder about it all? Do the questions we constantly raise about life after death only mask and veil the fact that we really don't believe or seriously doubt such a life actually exists? Or is it laziness that's behind our questions? If we can just while away the time asking questions about heaven we don't have to work and labor and love to improve conditions here on earth. Or do the questions we raise demonstrate that the only way our finite minds can ever conceive of heaven is in earthly terms?

Our persistent inclination is to reduce the timeless heavenly and eternal to the familiar conditions of our present existence. But when we do that we are as an unborn child, there in the warm and sheltering dark of mother's womb, dreaming and imagining what it might be like on the other side of that last convulsive shudder called birth: The glint of the sun on water, a forest ablaze with fall colors, the majesty and awesome beauty of the wild ocean, the grandeur of a fiery sunset, Niagara Falls, or Grand Canyon, snow flying crazily in the wind, a loved one's embrace, mouth-watering food, a cold drink on a sweltering summer day, the roar of a jet, blooming flowers in spring, the sound of words, rain dripping on a roof, music in the air. As far as heaven is concerned, just let your imagination go. Give it free rein. Let it run wild. Only God knows the joys, beauty, wonder, and surprises in store for us who cling for dear and eternal life to his crucified and risen Son.

The Answer of Jesus

"Whose wife will she be?" Well, what was Jesus' answer? Listen: (*Verses 34-38 should be read here.*) Now the Savior makes the following points.

"You Sadducees Are Wrong"

"You Sadducees are dead wrong. There is a resurrection. In fact," the Savior might have added, "it is scheduled to begin in a few days." You see, the Lord Jesus uttered these words during Holy Week. On the following Sunday he himself would begin and lead the resurrection parade, would burst the bonds of death and triumph over the tomb for us all. And you know what that means. It means that the cobra has lost his poison sac. One day when my two boys were young we visited our local zoo and went to the snake house. As we stood before the cage of a particularly deadly cobra one of the attendants came along and I asked him a rather foolish question. "Does this snake still have his poison sac?" "Of course," he responded, "If we remove his poison sac he begins to die." Well, that is precisely what happened to the cobra called death at the crack of that first Easter dawn when the Lord Jesus emerged raised and alive from the gloomy garden grotto. The cobra lost his poison sac. His deadly bite and sting are gone. Hurrah and halleluiah!

Our Lord's Easter triumph also means that our own resurrection is assured and certain. The New Testament author calls the risen Christ "the first-born from the dead." That means he is simply the first one out of the womb of the tomb. Mother earth still has many more "babies to bear." How we hunger and long for the "multiple-birth" of the resurrection.

"Your Own Scriptures Prove and Proclaim a Resurrection"

"Whose wife will she be?" asked the Sadducees of the Savior. How impossible and absurd the belief in a resurrection becomes in the light of their clever example. Surely she won't be wed to all seven of those brothers in the new life and world of the resurrection. You can't even envision such nonsense. Perhaps! And yet the very Scriptures, in fact, the *only* Scriptures accepted as authentic and canonical by the Sadducees, namely, The Pentateuch, proves and proclaims a resurrection. Listen: (*Read verses 37-38*).

And so there it stands, as clear and bright as day, right in the heart of the Sadducees' own Scriptures—the doctrine of the resurrection. God is addressing Moses at the burning bush, centuries after Abraham, Isaac, and Jacob are dead. And yet the Lord says he is still their God. "How can that be," reasons Jesus, "if there is no resurrection and those beloved patriarchs are dead and buried in their graves?" For God is the Lord not of the dead, but of the living.

Things Will Be Different

Yet how different things will be. As Jesus points out: *(Verses 34-36 should be read here.)*

And so marriage with all its joys and blessings is for this world only. In the resurrection life, death itself will have died and departed and there will be no mourners. With the death of death, the need of marriage and the preservation of the race disappears, and we shall be like angels. Now angels according to Jewish belief in those days are both sexless and eternal.

How angelic our resurrection bodies will be! Which means of course that they will be the same and yet gloriously different. In First Corinthians 15, Paul uses the familiar analogy of the seed and the mature plant. Plant a seed in the soil and to all examining eyes it looks totally dead and lifeless. Into the ground it goes, there to await the miracle of germination. Down come the gentle rains and the soft rays of the sun and that "dead" seed suddenly and miraculously springs to life. Up it pushes through the soil as a new plant and at last when it is ripe and mature is picked and stored in the granary.

So it will be with our bodies. One day some loving hands will tenderly deposit the dormant seed of our lifeless bodies into the soil of the grave, there to await the miracle of germinaiton, the wonder of the resurrection. And up we will spring as God's new plants, the same and yet different, glorified, deathless and immortal, ripe, mature and ready to be harvested into God's heavenly granary, there to enjoy his presence forever.

That's how it has to be. For there he is, Jesus Christ crucified and risen, called by Paul, "the first fruit of those who sleep." Well, if the first fruit has already sprung up from the soil of the grave, it won't be long until the entire field is ripe and ready for the harvest. The harvest is at hand, resurrection just around the corner. Prepare for joy unspeakable!

HERBERT E. HOHENSTEIN
Unity Evangelical Lutheran Church
Bel Nor, Missouri

The End Is at Hand!
Luke 21:5-19

How typical! Jesus and his disciples have finally arrived in Jerusalem, and are standing in the Temple. A widow has come in, and deposited a couple of copper coins in the Temple treasury, and Jesus marvels to his disciples about how she has given all she had—far more, proportionately, than what is being given by those of far greater means than she. The disciples obligingly nod their heads, but they are taken up with much bigger things. Widows and copper coins they had by the cartful back in Nazareth—but would you look at this marvelous architecture? Herod may have been generally obnoxious, but he had certainly spared no expense in reconstructing the Temple for his Jewish subjects. Why, look at those stones! To think that mere mortals could cut such massive blocks to such exact tolerances—and then move them—and then assemble them into such a majestic structure!

"You see these beautiful stones? One day soon they will all be dashed to the ground! Not one will be left standing!" What was that? Why . . . it was Jesus speaking again. And his startling words brought the disciples back to earth very quickly. These stones—this Temple—destroyed? Why, yes, there were those prophets who spoke in terms of a Day of Yahweh when such things would happen. But when? Soon? How will we know?

What follows in Luke 21, as well as in Matthew 24 and Mark 13, is Jesus' answer to his disciples' question. And, mixed in with all the wars and tumults and signs in the heavens, we can hear three admonitions: Be wary; be ready; and be confident.

Be Wary!

First of all, be wary. Be wary! Don't let anyone deceive you or lead you astray! Isn't it interesting that this would be the first bit of advice Jesus would give his disciples when they asked for some signs of the end of the age? When will the end of the world occur? "Be wary! Be careful! Be on your guard when this subject is brought up! For there are many who would like to lead you astray!" And we know how true that is even today. We don't need to turn any farther than the religion section of our Saturday morning newspaper to see the astonishing number of groups offering lectures on prophecy—or what they understand to be prophecy:

signs of the end; roadmaps of the future; seminars which will give you "the" key to unlock both the book of Daniel and the book of Revelation. It seems we don't go a year without some group riding to infamy in the media with their predictions of an end to history on a certain date—sometimes selling all of their earthly possessions and traveling to a remote location to wait.

"Be wary!" Jesus tells us. "For many will come in my name saying, 'I am he.'" And we think of thinly veiled would-be-messiahs such as the Rev. Sun Young Moon of the Unification Church, and his "Moonie" followers. Or perhaps David "Moses" Berg of the Children of God. Yes, there are many self-proclaimed expects out there who would like to ride to fame, and especially fortune, on the crest of a wave of scriptural "crystal ball gazing." And who isn't interested in the future? Why, just imagine what you could do if you even knew what the prime rate was going to be this time next year?

"Be wary," Jesus tells us. For the future is not ours to know—at least not in detail. Why, according to Jesus, even he himself didn't know what the day of his return was going to be (Mark 13:32).

The year was 1818, and the people of Low Hampton, New York, were excited as they listened to the man. "I believe," he said, that "the time can be known by all who desire to understand and to be ready for his coming. And I am fully convinced that some time between March 21, 1843, and March 21, 1844, according to the Jewish mode of computation of time, Christ will come and bring all His saints with Him; and that then he will reward every man as his work shall be" (Walter Martin, *The Kingdom of the Cults,* Minneapolis: Bethany, 1974, p. 361). The man was William Miller, and for the next quarter century the nation waited in excitement and agitation to see if his prophetic words would prove true. One has to feel compassion for Miller, who was a very honest and sincere man, and who later wrote

Were I to live my life over again, with the same evidence that I then had, to be honest with God and man I should have to do as I have done. Although opposers said it would not come, they produced no weighty arguments. It was evidently guess-work with them; and then I thought, and do now, that their denial was based more on an unwillingness for the Lord to come than on any arguments leading to such conclusion. I confess my error, and acknowledge my disappointment; yet I still believe that the Day of the Lord is near, even at the door; and I exhort you, my brethren, to be watchful and not let that day come upon you unawares.

(*Kingdom of the Cults,* p. 362)

"Be wary!" Jesus warned. For there are many people—even many well-intentioned people—who will lead you astray if you are not careful.

Be Ready!

But there is another theme which again and again jumps out at us whenever Jesus talks about his expectations concerning the end. "Be ready!" In spite of William Miller's complete failure to predict the date of Christ's return, one does have to give him this: he was waiting. He was looking eagerly for that day when his Lord would return.

Martin Luther once said that we're all like a bunch of drunken peasants: we either fall off one side of the horse or the other. And I suppose that's true of the way we deal with passages such as the one we have before us this morning. On the one hand, there are those who do get all wrapped up in dates and signs, and are forever saying "this generation." On the other hand—the hand that may hold many of us—it is all too easy to place it all in the realm of the *mañana* which never comes. We are told that we are to be pilgrims in this world. We are told that we should consider our present dwellings to be like tents, temporary in nature. But soon we are found to be building some rather permanent foundations under our tents. And eventually, perhaps one wall at a time, we begin to replace the tents themselves with rather substantial fixed structures, with no thought for the day when we will be called upon to strike camp.

"Be ready!" Jesus counsels us. And he speaks of prisons and kings and governors, and the possibility that we may be called upon to give an account of ourselves—not before God, in this case, but before fellow human beings.

What is the proper "holding pattern" for the follower of Jesus who lives between the ages? How are we to pilot our fragile craft between the Scylla of end-times fanaticism and the Charybdis of careless lethargy? Several places, Jesus gives the picture of watchful servants, going about their appointed tasks, but always with one eye on the door for that moment when the master returns. Watchful activity. And the watching does not hinder the activity so much as give it meaning and purpose and direction. The essential differences between the activities of people of faith and those of people of this world are differences of focus and perspective. We are to be a waiting people, and all that we say or do should be informed by that ultimate end for which we wait.

But, then, we do have to be honest. It's impossible to constantly live in a state of high-pitched expectation. For the disciples, who after the Resurrection expected to see Jesus return within a matter of months at the most, it was one thing. But even they began to question and reassess as the years went by—until we finally encounter the sober observation in 2 Peter (3:8) that "with the Lord one day is as a thousand years, and a thousand years as one day." What about today? Even if we are utterly convinced that, yes, the day is coming when this present age will be rent asunder, how do we—in light of the 2000 years which have passed—how do we maintain a sense of the imminence of such an event? A hundred generations have passed. Are we anything short of presumptuous to think that our generation will be the final one? Perhaps William Barclay has answered best:

> The simple fact is that behind this there is one inescapable and most personal truth. *For every one of us the time is near.* For every one of us the hour is hastening on. The one thing which can be said of every (person)—and the only thing which can be said of every (person)—is that we will die. For every one of us the Lord is at hand. We cannot tell the day and the hour when we shall go to meet our God; and, therefore, all life must be lived in the shadow of eternity.

> (William Barclay, *Daily Study Bible Series: The Letters of James and Peter;* Philadelphia: Westminster, 1960, p. 297)

"Be ready!" Jesus tells us. For you don't know the time or the hour. And therefore all of life should be lived with a sense of expectation.

Be Confident!

But there is now a third word—a very important word—that comes to us. "Be confident!" Yes, we must be wary. And, yes, we are to be ready. But we are also to be confident. We are not to be overcome or frightened by all of the speculation and scare-stories that are sometimes associated with discussions of the close of the age.

When I was at the Lutheran Bible Institute, I well remember a chapel speaker who went after this issue. "There are certainly many theories and ideas floating around about how history is going to end, aren't there?" he asked. "You've probably heard of pre-millenialists, post-millenialists, a-millenialists, and so on. Well, I'm here to take a firm stance as a pan-millenialist! I believe it's all going to pan out in the end!" And as humorous as that may sound, there is far more truth than whimsy in the statement. "Be confident," Jesus would tell us. Know that God is for you, that the future is his, and that he has made you his own. It *is* all going to "pan out" in the end. Jesus mentions prisons and kings and governors. But then, just when the disciples might have begun to tremble, thinking, "What will we ever say before kings and governors?" Jesus adds, "Don't worry about what you are going to say. I will be with you and tell you what you need to know."

"Be confident." Know that in Christ, all the battles that need to be won have been won. That's what Calvary and the empty tomb are all about. All the talk about signs and wars and tumults is meant not to scare, but to assure. To assure us that no matter what happens, there will be no surprises for God in our future, for he holds it all in his hands.

That, after all, is the basic message found throughout the Bible, isn't it? God is one who hovers over his creation not as a master waiting to lash out at a faltering slave, but rather as a mother seeking to comfort a hurting child, a father seeking to bring back a wayward son. Again and again, God is the one who seeks out before it is too late. The one who speaks judgment not that he might destroy, but that he might warn and call back. The one who sends his son in human flesh into our midst to bear scorn and abuse and death in order that we might be healed and forgiven and made new.

"Be confident," Jesus tells us. I am for you. I am with you. At present, we may see through a glass darkly, but we trust in one who sees clearly, and who cares more about our future than even we ourselves do. When the "end" comes, whether it be the end of the age or our own personal end in this age, we have the assurance that he will be there waiting for us. Other details, while perhaps interesting, are non-essential. There are many things we simply don't need to understand, because we know—and are known by—the one who understands all.

Be wary! Be ready! Be confident! Amen.

JAMES C. BANGSUND
Holy Redeemer Lutheran Church
San Jose, California

TWENTY-SEVENTH SUNDAY AFTER PENTECOST

Occupy Till I Come
Luke 19:11-27

Antonio Stradivari is considered to have been the world's greatest violin maker. He lived in Cremona, Italy, until his death in 1737. Today only the finest musicians own a Stradivarius because they can draw from that instrument its finest music and also, because only the famous can afford such a prized violin.

263

One day a critic told Stradivari that if God had really wanted violins he would have made them himself. "No," said Stradivari, "not even God could make my violins without me." He was wrong of course. God can do anything he wants with or without human beings. However, it happens to be the truth that God has chosen to use human beings to do his will. He chose Stradivari to make violins in the 18th century and today he has chosen you and me to be a part of his plan.

The Freedom of the Christian

In his parable of the pounds, Jesus tells a story to help us understand the importance he attaches to our human efforts in the kingdom of God. Since he is the "nobleman," since he is the King of kings and the Lord of lords, he could extend his kingdom without us. He could force every human being to bend his knees and bow down before him. He could turn you and me to jelly by the slightest thought. But that is not his plan. He doesn't want human beings to be spineless peons or pawns manipulated by some outside force. He could have made us automatons or puppets always conforming to his perfect will.

Instead, he chose to make us human beings with freedom to decide our own course in life. He has set us free to think, to speak and to do whatever we want. In the parable, the nobleman left a sum of money called a pound with each of ten servants before leaving on a long journey to a country far away. He left the money in trust to each of them without oversight or compulsion. He gave them complete freedom to do whatever they willed. His only instruction was to "trade with these pounds until I return" or, as the Authorized version puts it: "Occupy till I come!"

Equal Grace

It is interesting to note that each of the ten servants received the same amount—exactly one pound, and the same instruction. The nobleman decided to give an equal amount to each but he left it up to the servants to use it in the best way they could.

In the same manner, God has given each of us the same gift. That gift is the gospel of Christ which is the power of God to salvation. The forgiveness of sins, the promise of life in him now and through eternity is given equally to you and me. I have no greater spiritual gift of grace than any other Christian. Each one of us has equal access to God. Not only that. For God also has given to each and every one who believes in him the same instructions: "Go into all the world and make disciples, baptizing and teaching. . . ." "Occupy till I come!"

Unequal Response

But notice how the servants in the parable differed from one another. One man put his pound to work in the market place with such diligence that with his one pound he gained ten more. He did his best and was able to return eleven pounds to the nobleman. So also the second servant. He took seriously the king's command and was able to gain five pounds. Apparently he did his best and, with the first servant, was commended for his loyalty and faithfulness. They were rewarded by the king who placed them over ten and five cities respectively. Each received the reward for which he had fitted himself.

So God has dealt with us. He has given us the treasure of his grace and mercy equally. He expects us to proclaim the message of his love and forgiveness until his return. He has been gone a long time but, at a time known only to God, he will return to claim his bride, the church. He will return in judgment to demand an accounting. And the rewards of grace and favor to those who have been faithful are beyond our comprehension. We can only leave this to him who will come, not as he first came (to a lowly manger bed) but in great power and splendor. Then, and only then, every knee shall bow.

But now the Lord directs our attention to a third servant. He is a pathetic figure who was honest, well meaning and careful. Indeed he was careful, too careful, too conservative. Though he was given the same amount of money as the other nine, he wrapped it in a napkin and hid it until the king's return. Of course the money earned no interest. He heard the instructions: "Occupy till I come—Trade with these till I come!" He knew the money was valuable. But he was lazy, fearful and disobedient. He ignored the king. He had ears but chose not to hear.

The King's Judgment

This is the course chosen by so many who regard themselves as Christians. They have ears but do not hear. They have been given the same treasure but they choose to hide it, taking it out of hiding on special occasions such as Christmas Eve or Easter morning. The saving Gospel of Christ is so hidden that no one would guess that they belonged to the King. What good to the kingdom of Christ is such timidity and fear? No wonder Jesus puts such harsh words in the mouth of the nobleman upon his return. No wonder that whatever comfort the Gospel may have given is taken away and given instead to faithful witnesses.

The treasure of the Gospel is lost when we fail to give it away to others. To keep it is to lose it. To neglect our neighbor's need means a loss both to him and to the Christian. Our daily and consistent witness is crucial to our faith.

Artur Rubenstein, the great piano virtuoso, played a recital in the White House when he was 90 years old. He said that if he missed a single day's practice at the keyboard he could tell that he had lost some of his technique. If he missed two consecutive days' rehearsal, his audience could tell it!

Hope for the Day

How important for us to lend out the Gospel daily so our witness may not be lost. You know how it is. If we miss worship two consecutive Sundays, how easy it is to miss another and another. So also our witness to the world: if we neglect it we lose the courage, lose the excitement, lose the desire to proclaim Christ to others. But how good it is, how lovely, how beautiful it is to speak the peace and joy in Christ to others. When we do that, we know that we are obedient to the King and that we are faithful servants, investing the pound he has given so we can return it to him with interest!

It is time for us to wake from our slumber. Christ has come. He has won the victory over sin and death. He has announced the kingdom and has given each of us an equal share. With that gift he has given us the responsibility to proclaim Christ to the world. Soon he will come again to judge the living and the dead. And he wants you and me to bear him faithful witness. "Occupy till I come!"

Only Stradivari could make a Stradivarius, with the help of God. Only you can make your particular witness, with the help of God. You are unique. God wants you. God has chosen you (not me) to make your kind of witness. He has chosen me (not you) to make my kind of witness.

ERLING C. THOMPSON
Trinity Lutheran Church
Parkland, Washington

Cruciform Kingship
Luke 23:35-43

Irony is the discrepancy between the reality of a situation and the words used to describe the situation. In a moment of national crisis, a confused and perspiring government official asserts, "I am in control," and the irony of his words (and the reality from which they are far removed) is not lost on the nation, for everything about the man and the situation seems to cry out, "Help! Things are out of control." There is, I believe, more that a hint of irony in the advocacy of abortion "rights" under the banner of "freedom of choice." Surely the rights, freedom, and choice pertain only to one of the parties in question, while for the other the words are heavy with a lethal reversal of their ordinary meaning. Irony may appear in arenas as complex as sociopolitical policymaking or in situations as ordinary as conversations around the dinner table. In every case, things are not what they are said to be, or, they are so, but only in a perverse sense.

The Irony of Christ's Kingship

Pilate certainly thought he had an eye for irony. Above the cross he had inscribed the words, "This is the King of the Jews" (Luke 23:38). (The Evangelist John tells us Pilate wrote the inscription; Luke says only that it was there). What a huge joke! The one who proclaimed the gracious rule of God, who had coolly "reflected" Pilate's question about royalty, had been dressed out in royal garments, mock-worshiped, and finally nailed to a cross beneath the explanation, "This is the King of the Jews." In Pilate's eyes the joke revolved around the discrepancy between the regal bearing of Jesus and the dismal reality of his impending crucifixion.

Later Christians have appreciated the double irony of the situation in which Pilate's huge joke is but a tool of a deeper and more unexpected irony: the one who was mocked as a make-believe king and crucified on the cross *is* indeed a king, Christ the King. Pilate, along with all those who mocked and crucified Jesus, is caught in his own net. Those indulging in ironic acclamation of the king are not aware of the deeper significance of their words.

At the beginning of his ministry Jesus was confronted by a Tempter who doubted his messianic authority ("If you are the son of God . . ."). When the final purpose of his ministry brought him to Jerusalem, he entered to the strains of "Blessed is the King who comes in the name of the Lord!" (Luke 19:38). And now, as he hangs on the cross, his kingship remains open to debate. In the wilderness, the royal son's vulnerability had brought him to the brink of defeat; on the cross his royalty has once again failed to protect him from suffering. The temptations return like demons multiplied sevenfold: the soldiers taunt, "If you are the King of the Jews, save yourself!" (Luke 23:37) One of the criminals rails at him, "Are you not the Christ? [the anointed king] Save yourself and us!" (Luke 23:39). The nub of Satan's question in the Temptation account was not "Are

267

you the Messiah?" but rather, "What kind of Messiah will you be?" Not "Are you a king?" but "What kind of king?" At Golgotha we hear the answer.

Only the "good" thief gets it right, and even he gets it wrong. He knows that Jesus saves others only by refusing to save himself. He knows that the mockery and temptations of Christ are unjust. He knows that things are not what they are said to be. In some measure, his prayer puts it all right. What he does not see, however, is that the crucified one has already entered into his kingly power, that the fulness of Jesus' royalty is revealed in a promise that is made from the midst of suffering to one in desperate need. The suffering and the promise—that is what makes him king.

The Irony of the Cross

The reversal of all our expectations occurs in the crucifixion of the king. By means of crucifixion Jesus exercises his kingly power. Here is the irony. What was so obviously a huge joke—is true. But there is more. For out of this dismal ending God will produce a new beginning. Friday's lullaby of death will become Easter's trumpet solo. Friday's fool will become Sunday's victor. In words laden with ironical double significance, the disappointed travelers on the Emmaus Road tell the stranger, "But we had hoped that he was the one to redeem Israel" (Luke 24:21). We require a resurrection in order to see the vastness of this reversal and the hugeness of this joke. Without our fellowship in the risen one we surely would not perceive the kingly lineaments of the crucified one. Cruciform kingship is not easily detected.

Thus the reading of this traditional Good Friday text in November seems as odd to us as Christmas in July. Our ideas of Christ the King Sunday will gravitate toward the imagery of the triumphant, terrible, and universal events portrayed by Michelangelo in the Sistine Chapel. While we realize that all the final glory is made possible by Jesus' death on the cross, we do not truly see the cruciform character of his kingship. We do not linger at the cross long enough to hear the promise.

If we are at the cross at all, it is not likely that we are there as repentant thieves. Perhaps we are among those people Luke tells us who stood by watching (Luke 23:35). If we are to hear the promise at all, we will need to *over*hear it as it is spoken to criminals, outsiders, and desperate people. As Luke's Gospel shows throughout, it is possible for us to hear the message of salvation only if we do not claim that salvation as our privileged possession. Blessed are the poor, says the Jesus of Luke's Gospel, as well as the criminals, the tax collectors, the women, and the powerless in society. To whom is God making promises today? Listen in on this promise. By God's grace it can be ours also.

If we dwell on this story of Jesus and the repentant thief, we may perhaps see it as a kind of typology of responses to Christ. Some people, unlike us, make fun of the Christ. Others, like us, trust in his kingly power. Augustine somewhere raises the ante in this contrast by saying, "Do not despair; one thief was saved. Do not presume; one thief was lost." While the contrasting responses are important, they should not dominate our thinking. What is important is that the king is there on the cross, willing to promise salvation to a dying criminal. That is what makes him king.

So important is this event of the cross that it sums up and completes our pilgrimage through what Pius Parsch calls "the church's year of grace." On the first Sunday of Advent we heard Luke's story of the royal welcome afforded Jesus when he entered the city. On this, the last Sunday of the church year, this same man's death unfolds the meaning of his kingship.

"You Will Be with Me"

We have difficulty imagining the end of all things which the final Sunday of the church year has traditionally symbolized. Nuclear weaponry has made it easier for us by providing an image—that of the explosion—but for most of us the words of the poet are truer to life:

Not with a bang but a whimper.

If we cannot imagine a general resurrection and return of Christ on clouds of glory, we can relate to a personal ending, death. We can encapsulate the end of history in our own personal history. And our own ending is a sorry affair. Life's tempo slows to such a pace that the more frustrated and impatient among us would welcome an explosion. In this winding down each of us stands for the whole human race on his terminal course. But God has also individualized the human story and encapsulated a different ending in his son. Why is his life and death so significant?

In the death and resurrection of this one man God reveals another goal for the human race's pilgrimage. Life does not have to slip away, as the poet Stephen Crane pictures the good ship Earth slipping away from its Builder before he has attached the rudder. Human existence finds completion, a true sense of ending, in Christ the King. When all doors close and the last shovelful of sod has filled the grave, God is not defeated.

"You will be with me." "It is the loneliness of death that bothers me," said my friend. Even that loneliness God reverses. It is the cosmic joke that Donne alludes to:

Death, thou shalt die.

For into the ultimate desolation come the words, "You will be with me." That is what paradise means. It is not a cloying vision of pearly gates and angelic choirs but the promise that invades ("Today"!) every hopeless situation, every terminal case, and every bad ending. "You will be with me."

RICHARD LISCHER
Duke University
Durham, North Carolina